The Isle of Wight Central Railway

by
R.J. Maycock
and
R. Silsbury

THE OAKWOOD PRESS

British Library Cataloguing in Publication Data
A Record for this book is available from the British Library
ISBN 0 85361 573 X

Typeset by Oakwood Graphics.
Repro by Ford Graphics, Ringwood, Hants.
Printed by Cambrian Printers Ltd, Aberystwyth, Ceredigion.

Railway Travelling Facilities in the Isle of Wight

Simple Simon met a pieman
Going to the fair;
It is not of Simon
That my muse it now declares,
But one would raise dividends
By raising of the fares.

We used to go to Newport
For 9*d*., there and back;
Solemn the race and slow the pace
On Cowes and Newport track.

And this was on the Saturday,
But now 'tis told to me -
That in future for the crawl,
We'll pay eleven D.

Then in the evening we could go
For 6*d*., up and down,
And always biggish was the crowd
That went from West Cowes town.

But now the Powers That Be declare
If we are going hence
The double fare, just mark my word,
It shall be now eight pence.

Now surely, surely it is time
Such baby work should cease;
All o'er the country fares are down,
Why should our line increase?

'Tis nothing but extortionate
Such prices for such ride;
Are the directors made aware
Of how these tricks are tried?

We know the dividends are small,
That do they all confess
But with this rise absurdum
That divvy will be less!

Isle of Wight Herald, 7th July, 1894

Published by The Oakwood Press (Usk), P.O. Box 13, Usk, Mon., NP15 1YS.
E-mail: oakwood-press@dial.pipex.com
Website: www.oakwood-press.dial.pipex.com

Contents

Abbreviations

Whenever possible, the quotations and wording in Minute books, Parliamentary Bills, Acts of Parliament and press reports are exactly as written. Promoters repeatedly used the titles 'Isle of Wight Railway' and 'Isle of Wight Central Railway' to describe early railway schemes that had little or no connection with later companies of the same name. The following abbreviations have been used in this book:

BHIR	Brading Harbour Improvement & Railway
CNR	Cowes and Newport Railway
FYN	Freshwater, Yarmouth and Newport Railway
GWR	Great Western Railway
IWC	Isle of Wight Central Railway
IWES	Isle of Wight (Eastern Section) Railway
IWNJ	Isle of Wight (Newport Junction) Railway
IWR	Isle of Wight Railway
LBSCR	London, Brighton & South Coast Railway
LCDR	London, Chatham & Dover Railway
LD&EC	Lancashire, Derbyshire & East Coast Railway
LNWR	London & North Western Railway
LSWR	London & South Western Railway
MSWJ	Midland & South Western Junction Railway
NGStL	Newport, Godshill and St Lawrence Railway
NLR	North London Railway
REC	Railway Executive Committee
RNR	Ryde & Newport Railway
RPC	Ryde Pier Company
SECR	South Eastern & Chatham Railway
SMJ	Stratford-upon-Avon & Midland Junction Railway
SR	Southern Railway

Although many of the plans and drawings are to scale they are for illustrative purposes and should not be relied upon as accurate in all respects. No attempt has been made to update imperial measurements or pre-decimal currency. A number of the drawings are reproduced with permission of Railtrack Plc and remain their copyright. The illustrations have been selected for their historical interest and as a result a few photographs may not be to the standard we would wish.

Foreword

At 28 miles, the Isle of Wight Central Railway was the longest of all the railways in the Isle of Wight but was never as prosperous as its smaller neighbour, the Isle of Wight Railway. It was created by an amalgamation of three disparate and poor railways, each born after lengthy battles in Parliament but with high hopes dashed by the inevitable financial problems that accompanied the construction of their lines from Newport to Cowes, Ryde and Sandown.

Weighed down by the burden inherited from its predecessors, improvements were slow in coming and in the meantime minor accidents and complaints were legion. An intensely secretive company, it managed to antagonise the local population who dubbed the railway the 'dustbin on wheels' and warned of the need to carry umbrellas when travelling in the badly lit and leaky carriages. Visitors complained at the high fares, whilst the railway was an easy target for the local politicians and the Board of Trade in London, whose Inspectors' patience was sorely tested by the company's dilatoriness. The company avoided bankruptcy and by the turn of the century had addressed its more obvious deficiencies. After a change of regime in the Boardroom in 1911 the railway could reasonably be regarded as the equal of its contemporaries.

Acknowledgements

When delving into the history of the IWC, we have been conscious how our work has been similar to the way in which Victorian ladies would reveal no more than a tiny ankle to prying eyes. Much of the company's activities have passed by without record but we hope enough has survived to permit something of its character to emerge in this book. Much information has been gleaned from the Minute books and other documents of the Island railway companies, now in the care of the Public Record Office. Where there have been gaps we have used extracts from contemporary newspapers and other documents. Records of proceedings in Parliament and the activities of the Railway Department of the Board of Trade also provided useful material.

In a reflection of the company's spartan image, this account concentrates on management in preference to staff simply because of a lack of detailed records. Equally few early photographs or drawings of stations have survived.

For anyone who is unfamiliar with the Isle of Wight railways, there is a brief introduction and summary of the dates of opening and closure. This book is one of a series of histories of the railways of the Isle of Wight and complements our published account of the Isle of Wight Railway (Oakwood Press, OL109). Further books are in preparation.

A number of organisations have helped in the preparation of this book including the Public Record Office, House of Lords Record Office, National Railway Museum, the Museum of Science and Industry of Manchester and Railtrack Plc. Some information has come from the archives of the Isle of Wight Steam Railway for which we must thank the archivists, Paddy Jardine and Norman Thearle. Many anecdotes from the Willmott era were supplied by the late R.W. Kemp who joined the IWC in 1911 and is thought to have been the last living employee of the IWC at the time of his death in 1996 at the age of 98. Thanks are also due to several members of the Isle of the Wight Steam Railway particularly Tim Cooper whose local knowledge has greatly added to the accuracy of the book, to Dr John Mackett and Roy Brinton for the loan of photographs and to Mark Brinton and Gordon Weddell for the carriage drawings.

A shabby locomotive No. 3 stands in Newport up platform with two of the IWNJ Market carriages in about 1905. The island platform waiting room has yet to be built. Note the two tone paint finish on the platform covering and the litter on the track - clearly not a new phenomenon.

G.W. Tripp, NRM Collection

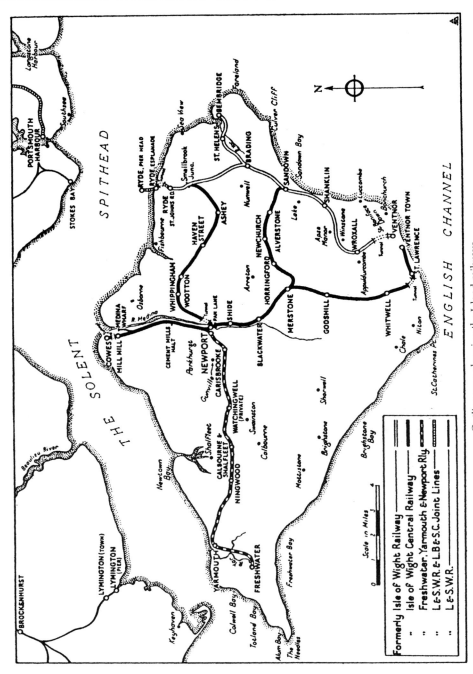

Outline map showing the Island railways

1841. The Deputy Chairman was Henry Tootal, a man with involvement in a number of railway schemes on the mainland. An impressive list of names included several northern investors, Southampton merchants and at least two Directors of the London & South Western Railway. Those who gave Island addresses included Charles Popham Hill, Lord of the Manor of Bonchurch. That month a letter in the Hampshire newspapers announced the formation of the company and completion of a preliminary survey of the route by Charles Vignoles, the first of a succession of Engineers who pronounced upon the need for railways within the Isle of Wight.

The 20 miles of standard gauge railways were designed to provide a comprehensive network by connecting the main points of entry to the Island with Ventnor. One line would have begun close to the foreshore at Ryde and skirted the town before heading west to the bank of the River Medina about ¾ mile north of Newport. There, a line from Cowes crossed the river to trail into the Ryde line before it headed for Newport. Beyond Newport, the railway continued to head south passing east of Godshill and through a tunnel to end in The Quarries at Ventnor (later to become the terminus of the Isle of Wight Railway opened in 1866).

Punch dismissed the idea as a hoax:

We read in a newspaper that a Company is in course of formation for the purpose of constructing a railway through and across the Isle of Wight. Now the Isle of Wight is just 21 miles long and 13 broad, so that with a railway through and across it, it would be like a good sized hot cross bun. Its traffic consists in the transference of pigs, sheep, cattle, and sacks of grain from farm to farm, and from market to market; between which, the communication about as much requires to be facilitated as that between Leicester Square and the House of Commons . . . The notion of an Isle of Wight Railway is too outrageous for any sublunary Bedlam. It is, in fact, inconceivably maniacal and the advertisement must be a joke. The wag who wrote it might have added, as part of the scheme, a proposal for a tunnel to Cowes, under Southampton Water.

In June a petition was presented to the deputy sheriff, Robert B. Sewell, asking that he convene a meeting of the principal landowners and ratepayers to express their opinion of the scheme. Signed by about 140 landowners, the petition was really a device so that their opposition could be vented. The meeting took place at 3.0 pm on 26th June, 1845 at the Guildhall in Newport; so many attended that it had to be moved outside into the street. Mr Pring, a local coal merchant and described as one of the town's radicals, spoke in favour of the railway but was outnumbered by the landed gentry who claimed the railway would be prejudicial to local interests, would not pay and investors faced losing their money. Given the tone of the meeting it was hardly surprising that a resolution in opposition was passed by a large majority. Similar meetings were held in Cowes, Ryde and Ventnor.

The main opponents to the scheme were several influential landowners in the Island: the Earl of Yarborough who lived at Appuldurcombe near Wroxall, his son Lord Worsley, Lord Ashburton, Sir William Oglander of Brading and Sir Richard Simeon of Swainston near Calbourne. They wrote to the *Hampshire Telegraph* on 1st July stating that '. . . possessors of property to the amount of 76,000 acres' opposed the projected line but its supporters were only '. . . possessors of about 8,000 acres.' On that basis the proposal should be dropped: 'Our answer is we don't want your plan. It is not a question of which direction your line may take; we say, and we have declared publicly that we don't require and we won't have *any railways* on the Island.'

The local population was more evenly divided; there were those who hired out horses, carriages and river barges that opposed development, others feared that the railway would take away their business to other towns not thinking that it might do the reverse. It was left to the 'common people' to voice the view that they, too, wanted to see what Ventnor was like and visitors would be more inclined to come to the Island if transport links were improved. The press followed the saga with much interest:

Map of the Isle of Wight Railway of 1845.

The following notice has been posted up on the walls of Newport, Isle of Wight:

CAUTION: Any person found trespassing on the Estate of the Earl of Yarborough, under the pretence of making surveys, or for any other purpose connected with the proposed formation of railways, will be proceeded against according to the law.

This means honesty is the best policy, and so it is. So if you go to the Appulducombe Estate 'under pretence of making surveys' you will be kicked off. Right and proper! Go with a truthful tongue - throw pretences to the wind - say bang and bold, 'Come, Sir, to make a survey for the railway', and the answer will be, 'Glad of it, Sir, happy to see you - pray make yourself at home.' Such is the purport of this ingenious and encouraging poster. [*Hampshire Independent*]

We think our contemporary treats his Lordship more leniently than he deserves. By the bye, at the meeting held last week against the railway, we perceive Sir R. Simeon stated that a railway would be of no use, because he could proceed from place to place sufficiently expeditious by his carriage. Sapient Sir Richard, do the whole Islanders possess carriages? - or will he and his brother opponents furnish them with that luxury? [*Herapath's Journal* 5th July, 1845]

On 18th July, 1845 the Promoters issued a Prospectus that extolled the virtues of their scheme. (A prospectus was the first stage in a process to gain support for the railway.) Potential investors were invited to add their names to a subscription list and make an initial payment for shares in the undertaking. Such was the level of interest that the list closed in August because all the £300,000 of capital had been applied for.

Not all meetings were hostile to the railway. At Newport a resolution was passed that 'Railways were Generally Desirable' whilst members at a Newport town council meeting on 17th November voted to support the proposals. In the press, the railway's opponents held sway:

RAILROADS IN THE ISLE OF WIGHT

That the public may not be misled by the various statements that have appeared in the public papers, and in the Prospectus of the Isle of Wight Railways, I am desired to state, that a general meeting of the landowners and ratepayers of the Island, held at Newport on the 26th of June last, resolutions were carried declaring the opinion of the meeting to be adverse to the introduction of railways into the Island, and that a Committee of gentlemen was at the same time appointed to watch the proceedings of the railway projectors. And I am further directed by the Committee to state, that not only will the scheme be opposed by the most influential landed proprietors through whose estates the railways would pass, but that it is also intended to offer a vigorous public opposition to the project in Parliament should a Bill be sought for.

C. W. ESTCOURT*

Hon. Secretary to the Committee.

PS. - Another scheme having been preliminarily announced as the Direct Ryde and Ventnor Railway, I am instructed by the Committee to state, that this latter will meet with the same decided opposition as the former project. [*The Railway Times* 8th November, 1845]

On 8th November, 1845 the Promoters gave notice of their intention to place a Bill before the next session of Parliament but later that month the *Hampshire Independent* reported that

. . . it is at such a time the more mortifying to the prospectors to be forced to postpone it for the present, owing to the difficulties thrown in the way of the surveyors by some of the landowners on the line. The people of the Island will know who to thank for this unnecessary and unwonton delay in the accomplishment of their wishes. As it was, the promoters had no choice. In justice to their Shareholders they were compelled to pause rather than risk an expensive trial and a probable defeat on the Standing Orders of Parliament.

A similar fate faced the Direct Ryde to Ventnor Railway scheme mentioned by Mr Estcourt in his letter. Within months the fevered speculation in railways within Britain peaked and numerous schemes failed including some that had already obtained an Act of Parliament. The income from shares declined and investors shied away from risking their money in railway companies.

* Charles W. Estcourt served briefly as Secretary to the Cowes & Newport Railway.

Whilst several years elapsed before fresh proposals appeared in the Island, mainland railways continued to bring visitors to the area. On 1st September, 1849 three South Western Company steamers brought 1,800 excursionists to Cowes. No doubt the visitors hoped for a glimpse of Queen Victoria or some other personality who had purchased property in the Island.

Confidence in railways took time to return, especially in the Island where in 1852 a discussion class concluded the 'moral evils of a railway in the Isle of Wight would outweigh any pecuniary advantage' because there would be 'an increase in Sabbath desecration, unwholesome speculation, many bankruptcies, levelling tendencies of the times would be fostered and the utilitarian spirit of the age would be encouraged'. Fortunately, not everyone felt this way and during 1852 three competing schemes emerged:

1. The Isle of Wight Railway Company resurrected the 1845 scheme with railways from Cowes and Ryde to Newport and then via Godshill to Niton, a distance of 22 miles.
2. The Isle of Wight Central Railway proposed to build a main line from Ryde to Ventnor via Newport and a branch from Newport to West Cowes.
3. J. Woodman and T. Hellyer of Ryde put forward a repeat of the 1845 Direct Ryde & Ventnor Railway from Ryde along the east coast to a terminus near St Catherine's lighthouse with branch lines from Brading to St Helens and from Sandown to East Cowes.

The Isle of Wight Railway was the most active; it issued a Prospectus inviting subscriptions for £240,000 in £10 shares. The original six Directors included three that were either Directors of the LSWR or LBSCR; none was resident in the Island. The Engineer was Hamilton H. Fulton, the Secretary Frederick Marshall and the solicitor John Bethell of London. It was claimed that Fox, Henderson & Co. had agreed to construct and equip the railway for £230,000, work it for seven years and pay investors at least 5 per cent dividend on their shares. By January 1853 the promoters included George Young, Francis Fitzroy, Edward Crowley, Charles S. Mortimer and Stephen Gazelee, a LSWR Director.

At a meeting held at Newport on 7th December, 1852 opponents sought to whip up opposition to the Isle of Wight Railway. In a rerun of events in 1845, a notice convening the meeting read:

Being convinced that it is of essential importance to the interests of the Isle of Wight, that immediate steps should be adopted to prevent the formation of Railways in the Island, we earnestly request you to attend a meeting, to consider and adopt measures by which the further progress of the scheme may be at once effectively checked. The Earl of Yarborough and other influential gentlemen have signified their intention of attending.

The booked premises at the Bugle Hotel proved too small and a second meeting had to be held in the street. Again the landed gentry opposed the railway and consequently the meeting passed a resolution to oppose it by a large majority. A week later the Isle of Wight Railway called a meeting at Newport under its Chairman George Young to canvass support. The *Hampshire Advertiser* carried a full report of what became a very noisy and rowdy meeting. Some townspeople voiced their opposition to the promoters' attempts to force a railway on Newport; the promoters virtually slandered the landowning classes leading the paper to report: '(We) have only space to express our disgust at the unfavourable language used in speaking of the landed gentry in the Island. It would be a perversion of terms to allow the proceedings of such a meeting to go forth as the voice of the town'. Despite this, the meeting appointed a local committee to help the promoters obtain an Act of Parliament. The *Advertiser* commented '. . . thus concluded one of the most successful and disreputable attempts to gag free discussion, and to put down local opinion'.

Whilst residents of Newport seem to have opposed the railway, this was not the view elsewhere. At a meeting in Cowes there was great support; the 1845 scheme had been opposed because the Earl of Yarborough, who was Commodore of the Royal Yacht Squadron, swayed

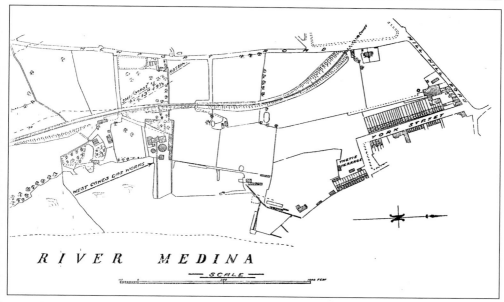

The Mill Hill area of Cowes as drawn by the Ordnance Survey in about 1862 after the arrival of the railway to the town.

Track plan of Newport pre-1875.

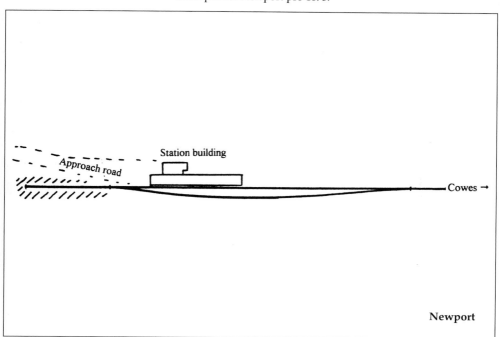

The *Isle of Wight Observer* for 2nd November, 1861 followed up with a description of the railway:

> This railway commences at Cowes, and its station is situated in Carvel Lane; and being several feet above the level of the street is reached by a flight of about twenty stairs. The station is as yet incomplete, but it has a general waiting room, apartments for the Station Master, etc., and for about fifty yards up, the line is covered in. There is but one line of rails laid down, and on leaving the station it forms a gently curve until Mill Hill Road is reached under which there is a tunnel. As soon as the southern extremity is reached, a view opens up of the River Medina, and the line pursues its course by its side until Newport is reached; passing in succession the Cowes Gasworks, brickyard, through another brickyard, past the cement mills, and then across a wooden viaduct about 100 yards in length, supported on wooden piles, over a small arm of the river. There are several bridges over the line, and the most conspicuous objects visible from the line are the tower and spire of St Thomas's Church, the keep of Carisbrooke Castle, Parkhurst Barracks and prison, the Poor House, and the downs above Newport, and the green and shrubberied banks of the River Medina. The rails are laid down nearly the whole length of the line except for about half a mile near Newport. A large number of navvies is employed on the works. The Newport termination of the line is close to Woodwar Wharf, Sea Street, but no station or accommodation is yet erected there. The engines have arrived at Cowes, and have already run up and down the completed part of the line for test, etc., and the carriages are on the road; so the opening of the line may be expected very shortly to take place.

The writer omitted to mention the unusual arrangements at Cowes. Immediately beyond the 100 ft-long platform, Cross Street bisected the line by means of a level crossing. Legally the track in the platform was a tramway as the railway did not commence until the other side of the level crossing where there was a run-round loop; the existence of the tramway was a legacy of the intended extension to Fountain Quay. This oddity seems not to have been remarked on, despite the fact that the company's Act specifically forbade the use of steam locomotives, 'atmospheric agency' or ropes in connection with a stationary steam engine on the tramway and hence in and out of the platform. The locomotive had to be dropped off short of Cross Street and haulage taken over by horse; more likely the train free-wheeled into the station whilst, when the Board of Trade was not looking, the locomotive sneaked across the crossing to collect the train! The matter was not regularised until 1877 when Parliamentary powers were obtained to rebuild the station.

The terminus at Newport was situated in an area known as Little London reached from the north end of Holyrood Street by a narrow wooden bridge spanning Lukely Brook. The wooden platform and station building was aptly described as a '. . . shed with a very short platform'. It must have been a great disappointment to the burghers of the town but they accepted that the station was temporary and expected that extensions beyond Newport would soon be opened. The lack of facilities was emphasised by the existence of just a loop road and neither terminus had any accommodation for goods traffic. The CNR Board deferred a decision to construct an intermediate station at Dodnor to serve Parkhurst - it was never built.

At a Board meeting on 12th December, 1861 it was announced that the contractor had given up the contract after battling with earth slips for months. Henry Martin took charge and employed the workmen until a replacement could be found - Messrs Jackson and White subsequently agreed to complete the railway in exchange for £3,000 in debentures. The financial position was not good as investors had subscribed for only half the £30,000 share capital; 10 shareholders who failed to pay for their shares faced having them forfeited and the Board decided to chase others for their calls. A month later the Secretary was asked to approach the National Provincial Bank for a loan of £1,000 but evidently the pressures were becoming too much as Mr Estcourt resigned and Edward Lincoln was appointed in his place. In a progress report given to shareholders at a meeting on 4th February, 1862 Henry Martin claimed the line would already have been opened but for trouble with landslips. It was confidently forecast that trains would run from Cowes to Newport in 11 minutes - the coach journey by road took ¾ hour.

On 8th March, 1862 the *Isle of Wight Observer* reported an incident on the line. It seems a carriage stored at Cowes had been hauled by a horse to the tunnel but ran back down the gradient, smashed through the level crossing gates at Cross Street, jumped a pile of sleepers and ended up against the station house. This was followed on Saturday 3rd May, 1862 by the running of the first experimental train. The locomotive *Pioneer* hauled a 'tender' and a carriage filled with workmen or, according to one correspondent, with employees of the railway and their families: '. . . to the surprise and astonishment of all the old women who domicile on or near the banks of the Medina, and who, for the first time in their existence, heard the screeching of a railway whistle'.

Capt. Tyler, a Board of Trade Inspector, visited the line in May 1862. His report highlighted the problems that had dogged construction:

The permanent way is laid with a single-headed rail of the [flat bottom] section, weighing 60 lb. to the linear yard, and in lengths of 18 and 21 feet. It rests upon transverse sleepers stated to be 9 feet by 10 in. by 5 in., and 3 feet apart. One through bolt has been inserted through the rails and sleepers on each side of each joint, and the rails have been secured to the sleepers elsewhere by means of dog spikes.

I should be glad to see a greater number of through bolts employed and particularly on the curves; and a little more ballasting is required in places.

Most of the banks have given trouble in construction in consequence of the slipping nature of the soil, and they will require careful maintenance. In one place a diversion has been made, and the gradients have been altered, to avoid the employment of a bank which was found to let the ground on which it rested in motion towards the river below.

There are 4 bridges under and 2 over the Railway of moderate spans, constructed with timber tops upon brick piers and abutments; and there is a timber viaduct 94 yards long and 40 feet high. I have recommended that the permanent way should be better packed up at the ends of this viaduct, that horizontal struts should be added between the bearing piles, that the longitudinal timbers which carry the rails should be connected by tie-rods and transoms to secure the gauge and that the handrails should be improved.

There is a tunnel near Cowes about 200 yards long which has been completed about 18 months and is in good shape, though there is part of it, near the centre, which it will be desirable to watch.

The temporary station at Cowes [this should have read Newport] is not yet complete as regards the passenger platform and the fencing on the approach.

Pending the completion of these different details; I am obliged to report my opinion that the Cowes and Newport Railway cannot by reason of the completeness of the works be opened without danger to the public using it.

It took three weeks to complete the works to the Inspecting Officer's satisfaction; he returned to the Island on 14th June and sanctioned the opening of the line. The *Hampshire Independent* described the event:

- Long Looked For, Come at Last! -

The Cowes & Newport Railway opened for traffic and transit on Monday morning 16th June, when the Precursor locomotive hauling three laurel and bunting bedecked carriages, reached Newport Station in about ten minutes. There, crowds had assembled to hail its arrival, and similar scenes were witnessed throughout the day. However, as the public had only been notified of the hours of departure by the distribution of a few handbills late on Saturday evening, a considerable number of the inhabitants were unaware of the opening and missed the opportunity of travelling to Cowes and back within half an hour. Despite this, business was by no means slack, and many visits were made to friends during the sixteen return journeys.

Other newspapers were less positive in their praise. The *Isle of Wight Observer* sniffily commented that '. . . very few persons were made acquainted with the opening, so that scarcely half a dozen persons [of substance] were among the number of those who took the

The earliest known photograph of the railway at Cowes shows the state of the locomotive and carriage sheds following damage by a freak whirlwind on 29th September, 1876.

T. Cooper Collection

CNR 2-2-2T locomotive *Pioneer* is seen painted in workshop grey in this maker's photograph taken at Bristol before delivery in 1861.   *R. Silsbury Collection*

In June 1871 the firm proposed to build a tramroad across the railway to connect the mills with clay pits on their upper land. The CNR Board refused to grant permission but learned in August 1874 that rails had been laid across the line; they ordered that they be taken up at once. Later plans showed the existence of a tramway passing below the railway; a formal agreement concerning the tramway bridge was not signed until it was renewed in 1895.

Apart from the opening of the station at Mill Hill and the purchase of a third locomotive, the railway remained largely in the state in which the contractors left it. William R. Galbraith, a civil engineer, was disparaging about the condition of the permanent way when he travelled over the line in 1872 to inspect a railway to Sandown. It was said that the train ran '. . . so slowly you can catch it'; Henry Pinnock was asked whether the CNR was worked '. . . with a very small engine and generally not more than one carriage?' to which he answered 'Sometimes four - yesterday [18th April, 1872] there were six because it was Steeplechase Day.' This met with a second question: 'That I believe is the whole rolling stock of the Company?' He responded 'yes' - how six carriages could be accommodated in the platforms was not explained.

The service was so unreliable that the Board received claims for compensation from travellers who had missed connections because of the late arrival of trains; typical was a payment of £3 5s. to three passengers who had missed the Southampton boat on 14th June, 1873. Derailments occurred regularly and even the local press no longer bothered to mention them! There was also the ever present risk of fire because buildings and other structures had been built in wood. Perhaps fortuitously, it was 2nd December, 1874 before a conflagration struck when the station at Newport burnt to the ground.

Soon after the RNR opened in 1875, a Joint Committee of the two companies took on the operation of the railways. As far as the CNR Board was concerned, fewer meetings were necessary and they inevitably centred on finance, or the lack of it. The financial position was so poor that as early as 1872 Henry Martin's 'Advance Account' had risen to over £35,000. Such was the size of the debt that the auditors insisted that legal advice be obtained and the outcome was the issue of a Lloyds Bond to him for £35,692 7s. 7d. The bond was exchanged in 1877 for £30,000 in preference shares authorised in the 1863 Act at £75 per £100 and £9,800 in debentures, all paying interest at 5 per cent per annum. By February 1880 Martin was owed a further £24,283 5s. 11d. and received the preference shares and debentures authorised in the 1877 RNR Act, giving him possession of virtually all the preference and debenture capital with a face value of £90,000. From this he received 5 per cent debenture interest per year and in the years 1881 to 1886, ½ per cent on £20,000 of the preference stock. This equated to an annual income of £1,500 to £1,600 from these investments alone, quite a sum in the 1880s.

Despite the way he carried the company financially, Henry Martin never became a Director of the CNR, probably because of the obvious conflicts of interest. By the 1870s none of the Directors was resident in the Isle of Wight. The Secretary's office was in London whilst the Manager had his office at the station in Cowes. Joseph Bourne, Manager of the IWR and IWNJ, was appointed to the Board in 1876 but he ceased to have any involvement in Island railway matters after leaving the IWR in 1884. The last recruit to the Board was Joseph Groves, a local doctor, appointed in 1886.

In 1887 the CNR became part of the newly-formed IWC. Henry Martin was the only individual connected with the old company to join the IWC Board. Of Mr Petre, he married a second time in 1886 and upon the formation of the new company retired from the scene; he died in 1889. Of the two, it is Henry Martin who has been remembered as the 'father' of the Isle of Wight railways - certainly he was the only person to make money out of the CNR!

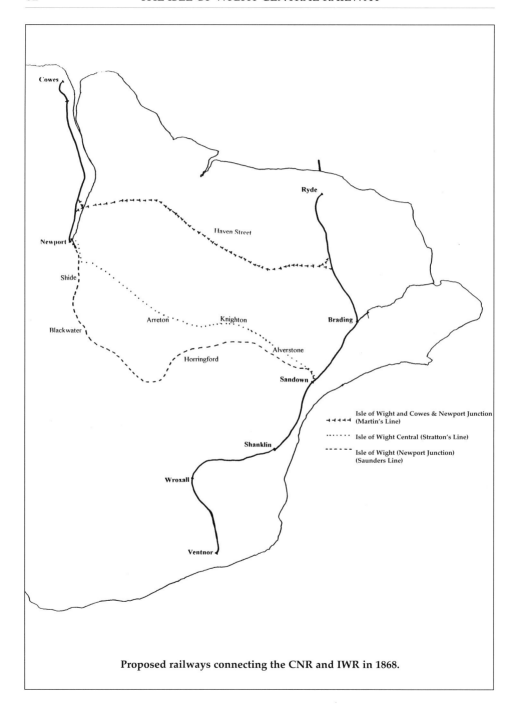

Cowes

Ryde

Haven Street

Newport

Shide

Arreton   Knighton   Brading

Blackwater

                                    Alverstone
                    Horringford
                                        Sandown

⊣⊣⊣⊣⊣ Isle of Wight and Cowes & Newport Junction
        (Martin's Line)

······· Isle of Wight Central (Stratton's Line)

‑ ‑ ‑ ‑ Isle of Wight (Newport Junction)
        (Saunders Line)

        Shanklin

Wroxall

Ventnor

Proposed railways connecting the CNR and IWR in 1868.

Chapter Three

A Network of Railways

In Chapter One we saw how three Isle of Wight railway Bills went before Parliament in 1859 but only that for the CNR became law. In the years 1860 to 1872 there followed a veritable flood of schemes for railways linking the eastern part of the Island with Newport and the CNR; we have summarised them in Appendix Three.

The Isle of Wight Railway (the Birkenshaw scheme) promoters decided that it would assist their objectives if they could link up with an existing railway company - the CNR. On their part, the CNR Directors recognised their railway had to be extended beyond Newport if it was to be a financial success. The two parties agreed that Bills would be promoted in the CNR name; this was on condition that capital be separated so that the CNR would be liable for neither Parliamentary nor construction costs - given the likely risks this might seem to have been a sensible decision. In the autumn of 1859 a Cowes & Newport Railway Extensions Bill was placed before Parliament. The provisional Directors were named as Francis Pittis, George Young, Sir John Simeon, John Bonham Carter and Henry Pinnock - all men with strong local connections.

In opposition was the Isle of Wight (Eastern Section) Railway Bill for a line from Ryde to Ventnor and a branch from Ryde to the CNR at Newport. The Engineer Hamilton H. Fulton incorporated elements of the Livesay and Saunders scheme in his plans. Much to the consternation of its promoters, Parliament threw out the CNR Extensions Bill in February 1860 and allowed the IWES Bill to continue its progress through Parliament. Objectors (who also happened to be supporters of the CNR scheme) succeeded in having the IWES Ryde to Newport branch deleted but could not prevent the Bill from becoming law. To appease Parliament, the competing promoters tried to reach some agreement on a common network of railways within the Island; a committee met frequently during 1860 but broke up after its members tried to get the Eastern Section promoters to withdraw parts of their scheme just when the Bill was about to become law!

Parliament's decisions in 1859 and 1860 left the Isle of Wight with two railway companies serving separate parts of the Island. A railway was needed between them but it was a matter of opinion whether it should run from Newport to Ryde, Brading, Sandown or even Wroxall. The general consensus was that there was insufficient traffic to justify more than one line but again, this was not a view held by everyone. With this in mind, it is best to divide the Bills presented to Parliament in the sessions from 1861 onwards into two broad categories (those that became law are shown in bold type):

	Newport to Sandown (and/or Brading or Wroxall)	Newport to Ryde
1861	Cowes & Newport Extensions	Cowes & Newport Extensions
1862	Isle of Wight Railway	Newport & Ryde Direct Railway
1863	**Isle of Wight Railway* - Central Lines**	**Isle of Wight Railway - Central Lines**
	Isle of Wight Valley Junction Railway	
1865	Brading, Newport & Yarmouth Railway	
1866	Sandown & Newport (Isle of Wight) Railway	
1867	Isle of Wight (Newport Junction) Railway	
1868	Isle of Wight Central Railway	Isle of Wight and Cowes & Newport Junction Railway
	Isle of Wight (Newport Junction) Railway	
1871		Isle of Wight and Cowes & Newport Junction Railway
1872		**Ryde & Newport Railway**

* The Isle of Wight (Eastern Section) Railway was renamed the Isle of Wight Railway in January 1864.

Thomas Webster was the principal advocate of a Newport to Sandown railway. A London QC, he owned Beachfield estate at Sandown and invested heavily in the Isle of Wight Waterworks Company whose works near Alverstone supplied the neighbourhood. In 1868 he boasted that, except for the CNR, since 1854 he had been involved as promoter, opponent or counsel in every Isle of Wight railway Bill.

George Young equally strongly supported a Newport to Ryde railway. He was a rather colourful Scot who made money as a London corn merchant and in 1868 was '. . . largely concerned in commercial matters in the City of London'. A widower with two adult daughters, he married a second time during the 1850s and at different dates resided at Appley Towers and Brigstocke Terrace, two of the most desirable properties in the town of Ryde. In 1857 Mr Young bought a large farm at West Ashey and used the latest techniques to revolutionise its productivity - it was a Model Farm in the style of Prince Albert's farm on Osborne Estate. There were dreams of building on land at Ashey and a railway was a prerequisite for such a development. An active supporter of the CNR Extensions, George Young gave evidence in Parliament against the IWES Bill in 1860 but eight years later spoke of how he subsequently became embroiled in the management that railway:

> I am not a speculator in Railways at all - I have not had a Railway Share except those I hold now . . . Since 1845 and 1846 I have been a Director in the Direct Portsmouth to facilitate the traffic between London and the Isle of Wight - my time at that time was valuable and I joined it for that purpose . . . In 1863 I was a member and Director of the Isle of Wight Railway - I was not an original Director, but they were in difficulties and they came to me to ask me to assist them. I said I would do so if they got rid of one Gentleman from the Board - They did get rid of that Gentleman, and I joined them, telling them that I would take no shares beyond £500. However, I got into it through helping them out of their difficulties and I am now a holder of 12,000 in Shares of that Railway.

The 'Gentleman' concerned was Thomas Webster with whom he had crossed swords whilst serving as a Director of the RPC. We encounter this antipathy between these two worthies time and time again during the 1860s.

Mr Young was one of the promoters of the Cowes & Newport Extensions Bill that went before Parliament in the 1861 session. It progressed as far as a committee of the House of Commons but encountered opposition and on 22nd April it was announced that the promoters had decided not to proceed with the Bill. An IWES proposal for a Sandown to Newport line was abandoned even before it reached Parliament due to 'unexpected opposition'.

In November 1861 the newspapers announced there would be three Bills in the next session: a revival of the Cowes & Newport extensions (although no Bill appeared), the Isle of Wight Railway and the Newport & Ryde Direct Railway. The title Isle of Wight Railway was resurrected for a line from the IWES between Brading and Sandown to South Street, Newport. Wrongly described by the press as an IWES scheme, the Bill was promoted by 'friends of Thomas Webster'. It seems that he put up some of the money because the IWES Board refused to reimburse him when he agreed in June 1862 to withdraw the Bill.

The other Bill to come before Parliament in 1862 was for the Newport & Ryde Direct Railway. The CNR and IWES lodged petitions in opposition and then followed a hearing before a committee of the House of Commons. Evidence was given that the two Island companies were at loggerheads and repeatedly opposed their opponent's attempts to promote lines to connect them. As regards this railway, counsel for the IWES gained the admission that the plans had been obtained from Mr Burke, joint Engineer of the CNR, and none of the Promoters had any Island connections. Mr Carnsew, solicitor and principal promoter, had already sold a previous undertaking (the West Sussex Railway) to the LBSCR, whilst Thomas Brassey was prepared to build and equip the line in exchange for shares. This was a 'contractors line' promoted for sale at a profit, a not uncommon practice on the mainland.

In July 1874 the Board authorised the sale of unwanted materials at Coppins Bridge. Joseph Bourne, General Manager of the IWR, was asked to supply the furniture and fittings for Horringford station. Richard Saunders was asked to give up lamps and other articles in his possession. On 29th July, 1874 the Secretary wrote to the Board of Trade giving notice that the line would soon be opened and on 6th August enclosed drawings of the track - Vignoles pattern flat bottom rail fixed to half round sleepers measuring 9 ft by 10 in. by 5 in. using fang bolts. Col Rich visited the line, when he noted that a shelter for passengers at Sandown was incomplete as was a footbridge between the platforms and the interlocking of points and signals. Gates to the level crossing at Horringford required stops to prevent them opening outwards, whilst fencing was very light, missing or insufficient in some places. Mr Sheward asked if the Board of Trade would sanction opening of the railway on receipt of an undertaking to build the footbridge but when Col Rich refused, the IWNJ Secretary complained that his company had no powers either to build or compel the IWR to provide the footbridge. Col Rich was unrepentant and wrote to his staff:

The Company have had ample notice of this work being required . . . The excuse of contemplated alteration of Station, is in my opinion merely an excuse . . . the Company would hardly have gone to the expense of the present signal arrangements if they contemplated altering them all, which they would be required with station alterations . . . they must provide an approach to the terminal station of their line which shall not oblige the passengers to cross the rails of the Isle of Wight Railway on the level. The Bridge might easily have been built since I inspected the line and they had better commence it at once if they wish to open the railway.

And complete the footbridge they did! The carriages were taken out of storage and prepared for use. A locomotive *Newport* was purchased by George Sheward from the London & North Western Railway and hired by the credit company to the IWNJ; the LSWR locomotive *Comet* had gone back to its owners.

Meanwhile, work was continuing on the Horringford to Pan Lane section and on 25th November, 1874 the locomotive *Newport* ventured over the line. A local newspaper wrote:

On Wednesday in last week another important step toward the long looked for opening of this railway took place by the running of an engine through the whole completed portion of the line, from a few yards distant to Pan Lane to the station at Sandown. The engine - *Newport* by name - was driven by Mr A.J. Parsons, the resident Engineer, representing the firm of Sir Charles Fox & Sons,* and there were also on the locomotive in addition to its usual attendants, Mr B. Pollard, the contractor, Mr H.J. Orchard, and the writer of this paragraph. Starting from Shide, where the station is all but completed, the *Newport* steamed in the direction of Pan Lane, and aroused the echoes with a whistle - a sort of shriek of triumph - which must have reached the very heart of the Metropolis. Thence back again through Shide, where some people had assembled in spite of pouring rain and a chill wind to see the start; on past Standen and Marvel, through the lovely vale of Blackwater, the first station from Shide; on and on, by Birchmore and Merston, Redway and Stickworth, rushing into Horringford with a whistle and passing thence by the fine range of Arreton Downs framing the view to the left; on by Heasley Farm towards Newchurch, with Godshill church visible in the distance and a charming intervening landscape: through Newchurch, speeding along the straight line there at almost 40 miles an hour; past Alverstone, opening up everywhere fresh fields and pastures new, and with another whistle, heralding its approach, the *Newport* steams into Sandown, the terminal point of one of the prettiest little lines in the Kingdom. After a short stay at Sandown, the return to Newport was rapidly accomplished, and so was completed a journey which proved that, after many difficulties and delays, this important undertaking is on the verge of consummation. We may add as a few details of interest, that a bridge to connect the Newport Junction Station at Sandown with that of the Isle of Wight Railway is in course of construction; that the stations on the line are admirably built, with a view to consult, in the best possible manner, the comfort and convenience of passengers; and that the line from Sandown to Shide is expected to be opened early in the ensuing year.

* The firm's change of name followed the death of Sir Francis Fox on June 1873, Charles Douglas Fox then became senior partner.

CORONATION DAY.
23TH JUNE, 1872.

Isle of Wight (Newport Junction) Railway.

FREE PASS BY ALL TRAINS
FOR BEARER AND FRIENDS.

J. T. DARKE,
Secretary.
SHAREHOLDER'S Signature.

Invitation to celebrations upon the opening of the IWNJ in 1872.

Drawing of the locomotive *Newport*.

In January 1875 the IWNJ was able to notify the Board of Trade that the whole of the line between Sandown and Shide was ready for use. Col Rich carried out an inspection on Saturday 30th January and sanctioned opening of the Sandown to Horringford and Horringford to Shide sections. The *Hampshire Independent* published an account of the inspection on 1st February, 1875:

A long-looked-for day has at last arrived, and Newport has the benefits of railway communication with Sandown and the east of the Island. Colonel Rich, the Government Inspector, arrived at Sandown shortly before 11 o'clock on Saturday morning, and was received by Mr Sheward, the Chairman of the Company, Mr Charles Douglas Fox, C. E., Mr J. Bourne C. E., the Contractor, the Resident Engineer, and others connected with the line. Having glanced at the new platform roof and the footbridge, the Inspector started at once to examine the signal arrangements for Sandown Station. This, which was considered the critical part of the day's work, having stood the test of a very severe examination, the whole party started out at a slow pace for Newport, the engine carrying the Inspector, the engineers and the contractor, a carriage behind being attached for the use of the others concerned. Each bridge and level crossing underwent an examination in its turn; also the signals at Horringford, Merstone and Blackwater. After a very pleasant ride, the day being beautifully fine, the party arrived at Shide station, where after an examination of the signals, etc., the Inspector received the usual certificate under the seal of the Company, and the line was declared open. The return journey was performed in 18 minutes, the Inspector regretting that his time did not permit of his availing himself of a visit to Carisbrooke Castle.

Regular traffic began on Monday morning, 1st February, the first train arriving at Shide at twenty-six minutes past nine. Newport has evidently been taken by surprise. So much has been said about the Sandown Railway - so many hopes raised only to be crushed - that now these hopes have been realized, many can hardly believe the news. The bells indeed rang out a merry peal on Saturday evening, but of the crowd collected to see the first train or travel by it, no one could raise a cheer - mute astonishment seems to have been the order of the day, and it was only on arriving at Sandown that we saw the least signs of enthusiasm. There, indeed one gentleman had displayed a few flags at the station, but, although he had many more ready for use, there was no-one to lend a hand in getting them up. However, if the weather is an omen, the Sandown Railway certainly has luck in store; its most ardent supporter could not have wished for a finer day than Monday, and we hear that a very credible amount of money was taken for fares. A few mistakes - we could not expect otherwise - but no accident; thus opened the Sandown Railway.

The first train departed from Sandown at 9.0 am and consisted of an IWR locomotive hauling six carriages (presumably the company's locomotive *Newport* was *hors de combat*). Under brilliant summer skies the return journey arrived back in Sandown at 10.0 '. . . literally crammed with passengers'. At the Newport end an omnibus was run by 'Messrs Mew of the Bugle' to connect with each train. The *Southampton Times* reported how William B. Mew, the Mayor of Newport, had promised three years earlier to send the value of 10 shares to the Directors when the line opened to Shide. He duly dispatched a cheque for £100 and on the evening of 24th February the Borough hosted a banquet for the Directors and company officials at the Bugle Hotel - no doubt Mr Mew and his brewery did well out of the festivities! Tickets costing half a guinea were available to others who wished to partake of the elaborate meal.

The initial passenger service was as follows (the title Newport rather than Shide was used in advertisements):

		am	am	pm	pm	pm
Sandown	dep.	9.00	10.00	12.30	3.50	6.35
Horringford	dep.	9.12	10.12	12.42	4.02	6.47
Newport	arr.	9.26	10.26	12.56	4.16	7.01
Newport	dep.	9.27	11.55	2.45	4.50	7.35
Horringford	dep.	9.41	12.09	2.59	5.04	7.49
Sandown	arr.	9.53	12.21	3.11	5.16	8.01

Sunday services began on 6th June with four trips from Sandown and three in the reverse direction. The first trains each way carried third class passengers but otherwise only first and second class were catered for. The fares were:

		Single			Return	
Between	First	Second	Third	First	Second	Third
Newport and Horringford	11d.	9d.	4d.	1s. 4d.	1s. 1d.	not issued
Newport and Sandown	1s. 9d.	1s. 5d.	8d.	2s. 7d.	2s. 1d.	ditto
Horringford and Sandown	10d.	8d.	3½d.	1s. 3d.	1s. 3d.	ditto

Return Market tickets at second class single rates were issued on Wednesdays and Saturdays for use by trains leaving Ventnor at 9.35 am, Ryde at 9.40 and Sandown at 10.0; the return tickets issued on Saturdays were available for return on Monday. The company also issued season and workmen's tickets. Examples of tickets headed *Isle of Wight [Newport Junc.] Ry* have survived; returns were printed with the two halves side by side rather than vertically, as issued by the Joint Committee.

Comment was made of the inconvenience of Shide station to the town of Newport and one local newspaper expressed the hope that no time would be lost in extending the railway to Pan Lane - trains began running there on 11th August, 1875. This followed a curious resolution by the IWNJ Board that the manager 'Mr Bourne be authorized to run the trains to Pan Lane but to avoid coming into collision with the Board of Trade'. Collide they did as on 21st August the *Newport Times* reported, 'The trains are now running to Pan Lane, but the Board of Trade have ordered this to stop in the next few days, the line not having passed the inspection beyond Shide'.

David S. Derry, Secretary of the finance company replaced John Darke as IWNJ Secretary earlier in 1875; he wrote to the Board of Trade explaining there was no space at Shide for a goods siding and they had extended the line '3 or 400 yards' (given that the distance was nearer half a mile he was being somewhat economical with the truth!); the work was '. . . of so trifling a nature and only intended as a temporary measure' he hoped that no inspection would be necessary. The letter fell on deaf ears and Col C.S. Hutchinson duly made his way to the Island; his report dated 31st August was almost kind in listing the deficiencies:

1. *Pan Station*. A shelter shed, water closets and clock visible from the platform should be provided and the platform should end in a ramp at the Shide end.
   The incoming home signal should be moved to the goods line facing points and these points, the engine loop points and the blind siding points should be interlocked with it. The blind siding points should also be interlocked with the outgoing signal. The normal position of the Engine loop points which lead to the siding should be reversed. The inside rails of a curve require bending.
2. *Shide Station*. The siding should be provided with Catch points and these and the facing points should be interlocked with the home signal at Pan and the catch points with the home signal from Pan. The points at the Pan end of this siding are to be removed.
3. Additional transoms and ties are required at the wooden Viaduct, also additional fencing and some ballast on the planks.
4. At the cattle creep the bedding of the wall plates should be improved.
5. There is a deficiency of fang bolts in some of the Rails which should be made good.

Having committed themselves to extending the line to Pan Lane the company had to comply. Col Hutchinson's report of 6th October, found fault with the interlocking of points and signals but he sanctioned opening when Joseph Bourne promised to have the deficiencies dealt with 'at once'. Unfortunately, the railway suffered its first interruption to services on 8th November when the track was flooded! Pan Lane, or rather Newport (Pan Mill) as its official name seems to have been, remained the Newport terminus of the IWNJ for a further four years, but it is best to look at that in a later chapter.

Clerk wrote that the Corporation favoured a fixed bridge, as proposed by the RNR, but this was at variance with the Corporation's own agreements with the companies and the IWNJ 1872 Act which specified an opening bridge. Attempts by the Corporation to get some agreement between the RNR and IWNJ failed, whilst the Board of Trade refused to intervene as it was unsure of its powers. After weeks of delay, Mr Stileman admitted defeat by the IWNJ, 'Wharfowners and Wharfingers' and put forward revised plans for a bridge with an opening span. The Board of Trade was confused by the need for three lines crossing the river but in January 1875 finally sanctioned construction of the bridge. By then it was said 'The line is completed to the river bank and the bridge is only wanted to finish it'.

Having resolved one problem, another cause for delay surfaced. Shepard Bros, who operated their carriers' business from a wharf near the Town Quay, wrote to the Board of Trade in February 1875 complaining that they had only just been given notice that land was needed for the incline and low-level bridge to the quay; they wanted to sell the whole wharf and neighbouring cottages for £3,000, a sum that the railway considered exorbitant. An exchange of correspondence lasted until 7th April when £845 was paid to the Court of Chancery to gain possession of the land; the wharf was eventually bought for £1,350.

Meanwhile, work was progressing at the Ryde end of the line. In February 1875 the IWR let a contract for the second line of rails between Ryde and Smallbrook to Mr Pritchard and John Langdon started on the station at Ashey. Completion of the remaining half a mile of cutting near Newport had been delayed by wet weather that had predictable effects on the clay subsoil; a locomotive was being employed with some side-tipping wagons hauling spoil from the cutting at Fairlee to an embankment about ¾ mile to the north. Five miles of track had been laid and ballasted with chalk supplied from the quarry at Ashey. A collection of Roman coins discovered at Haven Street was secured by the Mayor of Ryde for display by the Ryde Literary and Philosphical Society in their museum.

During June 1875 the vessel *Ino* delivered wrought-iron girders weighing 65 tons for the river bridge; a month later, the brick bridge supports were being constructed by the contractors Campbell Johnstone & Co. By 28th August the brickwork was almost complete and fitters were installing the opening span. Stevens & Co. had installed the signals whilst Mr Langdon was working on Osborne, the name initially given to Whippingham station, and constructing the platform wall and station building at Newport.

In exchange for paying numerous bills, George Young received the capital authorised in the 1875 Act. This amounted to £30,000 in £10 Preference shares at a discounted price of £7 a share, '. . . being the best price they can obtain' and £10,000 debentures at £90 per cent for a term of three years. Both the Preference shares and debentures paid interest at 5 per cent per annum but Preference shareholders received their interest only if the Directors declared a dividend - they never did!

Prompted by a forthcoming shareholders' meeting on 27th August, 1875, the Board decided to give notice that they intended to open the line for traffic in a month. The shareholders heard that a working agreement had '. . . not been confirmed' by the IWR and the Directors had been compelled to make other arrangements. The Board of Trade received a letter from John Darke, Secretary of the IWNJ, insisting that the opening of the RNR be delayed until it had completed the works for both companies; the Board of Trade responded that it had no powers to do this.

After months of delay, on 22nd October Messrs Young and Stileman made a trial trip over the railway. The journey was successfully accomplished in 20 minutes but that same day a contractor's locomotive ran into a flock of sheep killing 18 of them; the RNR also received a bill for a cow allegedly killed on the line. Lt Col Hutchinson carried out an inspection and on 8th November, 1875 wrote a report of what he found:

The permanent way consists, for the most part, of wrought iron flat bottomed rails in lengths of 24 feet weighing 72 lb. per yard, these are fished at the joints and secured to Baltic sleepers (9 ft x 10 inches x 5 inches) laid at an average distance of 3 feet from centre to centre by fang bolts.

The Ballast is of chalk and stone and has an average depth of 12 inches below the under surface of the sleepers.

The steepest gradient on the line has an inclination of 1 in 61, and the sharpest curve (except down to Newport Station, where there are curves of 7 and 6½ chains radius, round which steel double headed rails and check rails have been laid) has a radius of 20 chains.

There are 9 bridges over the line all constructed of brickwork: one of them for a double line of rails: under the line there is one wrought iron girder bridge of 34 ft span with brick abutments 5 constructed entirely of brickwork: largest span 23 ft, two with brick abutments and timber tops, span 8 feet; there is also a Viaduct over the Medina river consisting of 4 wrought iron spans 26⅓ feet each (one of which opens) resting on brick abutments 12 spans of 23½ ft each and 1 of 16 feet consisting entirely of brickwork - there are also several large culverts - these bridges appear to have been substantially constructed and to be standing well. The girders have sufficient theoretical and practical strength and gave moderate deflections: the rolling bridge works well and quickly.

There are no public road level crossings or tunnels.

The fencing consists partly of wire and straining posts and partly of post and rail.

There have been a great many slips on the line, both in cuttings and banks and owing to the late heavy rains these are still giving trouble and will be likely to do so for some time to come.

At Newport Joint Station the arrangements are incomplete and were more or less so at Ashey and Whippingham.

Some additions to the fencing were required at places as pointed out.

I must now report that by reason of the incompleteness of the works the Ryde and Newport Railway cannot be opened for passenger traffic without danger to the public using the same.

As on previous occasions, the Inspector got some of his facts wrong. He repeatedly referred to Cowes rather than Newport station whilst the 73 yard Newport tunnel was described as an overbridge. The *Isle of Wight Times* commented:

We have repeatedly heard during many months past that this line was to be opened in two or three weeks. Once more the Inspector - Colonel Hutchinson - has been down, and refused to pass the line. Over and over again there have been serious landslips, and in one the rails were carried away. However, we presume the line will be opened some day, and then we might possibly have a cheap run to Newport. Now one can take a ticket from St Johns Road to Newport and back by the Sandown Junction Railway for 1s. 6d. - the same as is charged for a return ticket from St Johns Road to the Pier Head by tram. If passengers are to be carried 30 miles at the same rate for three, and Mr Young charges a like scale, we should get to Newport and back for 10d.!

On 17th December the Board of Trade Inspector wrote another report following a further inspection of the line. He ordered that trains between Round House Bank and the Newport end of Fairlee cutting be restricted to a maximum of 10 mph while earth slips remained a problem. They also had to stop at the Newport down distant signal until the block signalling system was operational. Several other matters remained incomplete but none were sufficiently serious to delay opening of the railway between Ryde and the joint station at Newport.

On Monday 20th December, 1875 the railway opened to the public without ceremony worked by Henry Martin as an extension of his CNR contract. The *Isle of Wight Observer* commented: 'The weather which was most disagreeable prevented a wider interest being taken in this auspicious event'. The *Hampshire Independent* covered the event in more detail:

The Ryde & Newport Railway was opened for traffic on Monday morning, and, in spite of the very unfavourable weather, considerable numbers of people assembled at the new joint station to witness the departure of the several trains. The engine was gaily decked with flags and evergreens, and hearty cheers were given as it steamed off for Ryde, which is now so closely linked with the old Metropolis of the Island, The writer of this paragraph then left Newport on Monday by the 'Ryde Direct' at ten minutes past twelve. Whippingham was reached in 6 minutes, Ashey in 16, and Ryde in 25 minutes. We congratulate the promoters of the Ryde & Newport Railway on completion of their project, and cordially wish success to the undertaking.

The *Isle of Wight Times* took a different line:

After many shipwrecks a port! The Ryde and Newport Direct line has at last been passed by the Government Inspector, and was opened for traffic on Monday. As yet we have not seen any chalk trucks. How ever we may care to disapprove of many of Mr George Young's schemes, we cannot but admire his zeal and determination, and his surmounting of great difficulties. Though old, he's not worn out yet!

At Newport the railway from Cowes was diverted to enter a new through station about 75 yards east of the original terminus. Trains could cross at up and down platforms (at that time up trains ran to Ryde and down to Cowes) and there was a short bay road at the north end of the down platform. The tracks in the CNR station remained in use as two sidings albeit cut back by a new approach road. North of the up platform was a fan of four sidings; the pair closest to the main line served a 130 ft by 30 ft carriage shed that had come into use by September 1876; a kickback road from the most easterly siding descended steeply to Newport Quay. The Board of Trade Inspector took exception to the lack of facilities on the up platform and asked for the construction of a waiting shed, a name board and a ramp at the south end (the latter was never provided). The station building was a rather plain two-storey brick structure on the down platform containing a booking office for passengers at ground level and living accommodation for the station master on the upper floor; it was reached by an approach road curving from the bridge across Lukely Brook. The station was fully equipped with interlocked points and signals and controlled by a 20-lever signal box adjacent to the opening span of the bridge. The line to Ryde left the station at the south end over a hand operated drawbridge and viaduct spanning the river. The drawbridge had brick piers supporting wrought-iron girders and timber decking; the viaduct was entirely in brick and had two 16 ft spans and eleven 23 ft 6 in. span arches. The opening bridge was one of the most complicated pieces of equipment to grace the Island railways; John Mackett wrote an excellent description of the bridge in the *Railway Magazine*:

Each of the three bridge spans is approximately 26 ft 6 in. long and two of the spans are fixed. the third span can be tilted up and then drawn back into a cavity under the track bed. This span was originally in two parts, one for each track, and each section could be opened and closed independently. These moveable sections were each supported on a pair of rollers at the shore end and were prolonged on to the embankment for a further 36 ft. The outer ends were each supported on a pair of cams which could lower the bridges on to the two other pairs of rollers. A chain was attached to the underside of the outer end of each bridge and ran over a driving sprocket to a 10 cwt. counterweight housed in a pit. The drive from a windless was transferred to either pair of cans or to either driving sprocket by a four-position clutch. At least three men were needed for the windlass and four was the optimum number for very speedy operation . . .

Preparing to open the bridge was quite a complicated procedure. The first job is the disconnection of the signal wires and the unbolting of the fishplates. Meanwhile, the signalman withdraws a token, inserts it into the bridge bolt release lever and pulls it. This enables the bridge to be unbolted and allows the cams to be rotated, tilting the far end of the span upwards. The drive is then transferred to the sprocket and the counterweight is raised. The bridge runs back beneath the track by gravity.

The appearance of the railway contrasted sharply with the CNR and IWNJ. The RNR had well-built red-brick bridges of a strength and solidity similar to those on the Isle of Wight Railway, albeit to a tighter loading gauge. The intermediate stations at Whippingham and Ashey were far too lavish for the small populations they served and there is a persistent rumour that Ashey was built for the convenience of George Young whilst Whippingham was for Henry Pinnock. The romantic notion that Whippingham was for the exclusive use of Queen Victoria and members of her court is sadly untrue - it was never a private station. Whippingham consisted of a single platform on the up side, a roomy two-storey station building and a short siding facing Newport. Ashey had a crossing loop served by two platforms, the one on the up side having a station building that was a mirror image of the building at Whippingham. A siding from the down loop led to George Young's quarry which apparently came into use in May 1875. During his inspection in December 1875, the Board of Trade Inspector asked for the provision of a waiting shed and name board on the down platform and the

RNR locomotive No. 4 was photographed by the maker's, Beyer, Peacock & Co. in its works yard at Gorton shortly before delivery to the RNR in May 1876. Although the locomotive carries a number on the chimney, it lacks the nameplate *Cowes* with which it ran for several years.

The Museum of Science and Industry of Manchester

disconnection of a siding at the up (Ryde) end of the station; he could not authorise the crossing of trains at Ashey because the signalling arrangements on the line were incomplete.

On 11th March, 1876 Col Yolland reported that he had inspected 'the new road side stations' at Wootton and Haven Street, neither of which existed when the line opened. Built of wood, they were noticeably inferior to the other stations on the line. Col Yolland wrote: 'There are no sidings, points or signals at these stations and there is no necessity for passengers to cross the rails, but the platforms require to be covered with a fine gravel, conveniences should be provided and the stations should have name boards and clocks and the Engineer (Mr Stileman) has stated that these requirements shall be complied with' - the conveniences were still absent in April 1879.

The passenger service consisted of seven trains each way on weekdays and four on Sundays, each running to and from Cowes, calling at Ashey and Whippingham by request only. Initially the line was worked under the same, one engine in steam, system operated to Cowes and to Sandown; this arrangement was temporary because on 1st June, 1876 the staff and ticket system was introduced working with Preece's electric block instruments. At the same time the crossing loop at Ashey came into use along with signals at Wootton and Haven Street, a Board of Trade requirement. The bridge mechanism at Newport was interlocked with the block instruments so that the line had to be clear as far as Wootton, where there was a block post, before the drawbridge could be opened.

Construction of the quay for Newport Corporation began in March 1875 but little had been done because of negotiations to substitute an inclined siding for a wagon hoist. To reach the quay the siding needed to pass over the low level road bridge; whilst the RNR offered to build an alternative road bridge between the old and new quays, attempts to get the Corporation to pay the additional £200 met with no success and the whole matter dragged on without conclusion.

The RNR had largely exhausted the resources of George Young but was still in debt to numerous suppliers. As a first step, £3,000 in debentures were sold at discounted price of 90 per cent on 6th October, 1875 and the proceeds used to repay Mr Young - they brought borrowings up to the £31,000 authorised by Parliament. In January 1876 the company borrowed £5,000 from the National Provincial Bank of England to pay immediate bills, guaranteed by Mr Young on the understanding that the company would substitute its own sureties.

The Ryde, Newport & Cowes Joint Committee took on the operation and management of the railways during 1876 leaving the RNR Board to pay outstanding bills and fund capital expenditure. The Board of Trade authorised additional capital which brought the total up to £95,000 in ordinary and Preference shares plus £41,600 in debentures - it was not enough. In May 1877 brokers H.D. Anderson & Co. agreed to take 600 Second Preference shares and within months Anderson & Co. loaned another £1,500 to pay off P.W. Martin and T.C. Clarke, landowners who had been pressing for their compensation. Naturally there was a price to be paid for this generosity and in 1877 Henry Anderson joined the Board. Numerous plots of land and several cottages near Newport were put up for auction in January 1878 - more sales took place in April, May and June. Roderick MacKay, an accountant of Moorgate Street, London joined the Board in June 1878 and in 1882 J. P. Benwell took the seat vacated by the resignation of Mr Anderson.

George Young was finally released from his guarantee to the bank in June 1880 after a client of H. D. Anderson & Co. loaned £3,000 for two years. This, together with the proceeds from the sale of some debentures, permitted repayment of the bank loan and various other debts. The lender, a Mr W.S. Steel, received £5,000 in First Preference shares as security and Anderson's 2½ per cent commission. In October 1883 Mr Steel refused to renew the loan and when payment was not forthcoming issued a writ. To safeguard his investment, Henry Martin took proceedings for £8,003 16s. owed to him and the resulting court hearings led to the appointment of Francis Beard as Receiver. The Receiver remained in place until after the company amalgamated with the CNR and IWNJ to form the Isle of Wight Central Railway in 1887.

Mr Young did not live to see the end of the company as he died early in 1887 - Henry Pinnock took his place as Chairman. This was, perhaps, a sad end as George Young had achieved what he had set out to do. In doing so he lost his money leaving the company to fall into bankruptcy when it tried to do what the CNR had not!

ISLE OF WIGHT (NEWPORT JUNCTION) RAILWAY COMPANY.

Particulars and Conditions

OF SALE OF

100 FULLY PAID UP SHARES

OF

TEN POUNDS EACH

IN THE ABOVE COMPANY,

To be Sold by Auction, by

MR. C. H. WADHAM,

AT WARBURTON'S HOTEL,

NEWPORT, ISLE OF WIGHT,

ON TUESDAY, 14th SEPTEMBER, 1875,

AT SIX O'CLOCK PRECISELY, IN LOTS.

Particulars and Conditions of Sale may be obtained at the principal Hotels in the Island; of MR. T. C. SUMMERHAYS, Solicitor, 166, Gresham House, Old Broad Street, London; and at the Offices of the Auctioneer, St. James's Square, Newport, and Sandown, Isle of Wight.

W. BLAKE, MACHINE PRINTER, ST. THOMAS'S SQUARE, NEWPORT.

Poster announcing a sale of IWNJ shares.

Chapter Six

From Sandown to Newport 1875 onwards

The story continues from where we left the IWNJ history in Chapter Four.

Following an interview with the IWNJ Board on 9th February, 1875 Joseph Bourne was appointed traffic manager and a handful of other IWR employees were encouraged to join the Sandown & Newport Railway, at a slightly higher wage, of course. Mr Bourne proved to be just as much an asset to the IWNJ as to his principal employers the IWR, and in order to retain his services was granted a pay rise in January 1876 from £75 to £200 a year; he also received a percentage of any increased receipts. Despite statements by the IWR Directors that their company had no responsibility for working the IWNJ, George Sheward later told a meeting of shareholders that he was '. . . pleased to record the liberal assistance they had received from the Directors of the Isle of Wight Railway Company'.

Timetables were issued jointly with the IWR and contemporary maps referred to the line as the Isle of Wight and Newport Junction Railway. Even the 1878 edition of the IWR rule book treated the IWNJ as a branch of the IWR. The 1875 timetable was maintained by a shuttle service of passenger trains starting at Sandown. No separate goods workings were timetabled but at certain times of the day a return working was possible between the passenger services; alternatively, trains could be 'mixed' by attaching goods wagons to the rear, an undesirable habit from the passengers' point of view because they frequently caused delays and the occasional derailment.

Income was initially poor and in the week commencing 6th March, 1875 the railway earned just £67 3s. 8d. As the spring turned into summer there was a healthy increase in income and it was with some truth that George Sheward told a shareholders' meeting on 27th August '. . . he was very much astonished at the result'. There was a reverse in fortunes during the following winter; week ending 30th October, 1875 brought in £106 2s. 1d. but receipts were sufficiently encouraging for George Sheward to say at the next shareholders' meeting on 11th April, 1876 'The traffic for the half year was certainly extraordinary, seeing that it stopped at Pan Lane'. The *Isle of Wight Observer* reported that on Coronation day, 28th June, 1876, traffic over the line was the heaviest yet with trains of 13 or 14 coaches running between Sandown and Newport - trains were timed to allow walking time between the two Newport stations. Working expenses were increased by the need to pay the IWR for the loan of additional motive power and rolling stock, the costs of which they deducted from the traffic receipts; according to the IWR accounts, the IWNJ was being charged over £300 a year in hire charges at this time.

Mr Bourne was particularly adept at encouraging travellers between Ryde and Newport to take the longer route via Sandown by some astute publicity, through booking arrangements, fare discounts and good connections between trains at Sandown. Although the majority of traffic was between Sandown and Newport, he encouraged local traffic by the provision of short wooden platforms and goods sidings next to the level crossings at Alverstone, Newchurch, Merstone and Blackwater; their dates of opening to passengers have gone unrecorded but all were in use by 1878. The stations were undoubtedly a boon to the locality but, as one writer put it, 'That the people of Horringford might wish to visit the people of Blackwater was reasonable and proper to suppose, but the railway company could not really expect them to do it often enough to make the line pay'. The provision of sidings did not go smoothly; one to a quarry at Shide authorised in the 1868 Act had not been built and a request for a second to Messrs Roach's mill was deferred. Richard Webster offered to advance £400 for a siding at Alverstone but the matter dragged on for months after the Board refused to authorise construction without a written agreement; the siding was inspected and passed by Major General Hutchinson in October 1878. Joseph Bourne was more concerned about the state of the bridges; in February 1877 he reported the collapse of a wooden bridge and added 'Something must be done about the wooden bridges, they keep getting worse.' Repairs were instituted but to no long-term effect.

We last mentioned the company's finances in 1874 when Lloyds Bonds were issued in payment for the rails; they had to be redeemed within 12 months by which time the company hoped to have sold more shares. The opening of the railway did not generate the expected interest and on 14th September, 1875 100 shares were put up for auction. Buoyed up by good traffic receipts, Mr Sheward announced to shareholders in April 1876 that '. . . the sale of Preference shares would give £16,500 with which to complete the line . . . He was rather surprised the inhabitants of Newport had not given more support to the Company' - given the company's history, Mr Sheward should have been thankful for any support! In 1876 preference shareholders surprisingly received a dividend of 3 per cent and in 1877 2¾₁₂. Presumably it was paid in the hope of making the shares more marketable rather than a reflection of the railway's true profitability - it was the last dividend IWNJ shareholders got. A considerable amount of capital was raised in just 12 months:

Year ending 31 Dec.	Ordinary shares £	Preference shares £	Debentures £	£
1875	56,490	3,300 @ 6%	18,370 @ 5%	9,625 @ 6%
1876	56,700	50,000 @ 6%	{ 1,400 @ 4½%	28,845 @ 5%
			{ 10,100 @ 6%	*3,810 @ 5%

* in lieu of rent for land

The increased capital was not matched by activity on the ground; although the necessary land for the line between Pan Lane and the joint station had been bought and the contractor had erected the ironwork for the railway bridge across the road at Coppins Bridge, work ground to a halt and the bridge stood isolated from any connecting works for years. The delay was partly attributable to the company's dispute with the RNR. When the arbitrator decided the RNR should construct the bridges and viaduct across the river for the joint use of the two companies, he used plans that differed from those in the Acts. Eager to avoid expense, the IWNJ claimed that the joint works extended 75 yards further to the east than the RNR believed and in December 1875 took the company before the Railway Commissioners. The RNR had not completed the IWNJ portion of the viaduct because the IWNJ had paid virtually none of its one-third share of the costs; eight spans at the Newport end of the viaduct were shared by the two companies so it is likely that just the footings were in place. The RNR contended it had expended £4,500 on the joint line and £1,200 on the station, had no remaining funds and was unable to incur more expenditure without receiving financial guarantees. The Commissioners ruled that the RNR should construct the disputed 75 feet of viaduct as part of the joint works but added that the IWNJ had to give security that payment would be forthcoming before construction commenced. Even though the securities were said to have been inadequate, some work was done because by May 1877 the IWNJ's share of the works had risen to £8,790 0**s.** 6*d*. Progress was not swift enough for the IWNJ and in August the Directors threatened to take the RNR back to the Railway Commissioners. Early in 1878 the shareholders were told:

> The connections with the Cowes and Newport Railway, they hoped would have been completed before the close of 1877, and to accomplish this your Directors personally advanced the money necessary to complete the works under the terms of the Award, the sum which the Railway Commissioners decided they were entitled to. The works not being quite finished within the time limited by the Act, certain Landowners obtained an interim injunction on the ground of an alleged obstruction of the River Medina, thus stopping the progress of the works, and compelling your Directors to apply to Parliament for a revival of the powers to complete the 66 feet of line remaining unfinished.

The Bill became law on 16th April, 1878; it authorised additional capital, extended the time limits by a year and gave the IWNJ powers to complete the joint works if the RNR failed to do so. The Directors vented their frustration at a half-yearly meeting on 27th August, 1878; Mr Sheward '. . . expressed his opinion that what remained to be done could be completed in a week'.

Soon afterwards the steel for the second drawbridge identical to but quite separate from that of the Ryde line arrived from Messrs Vospers of Gosport. It was in place by 15th October, 1878 when Major General Hutchinson inspected the IWNJ. Whilst he was reasonably satisfied with the IWNJ's efforts it was evident that the RNR had done nothing to complete the junction and signalling:

The permanent way consists partly of flat bottomed rails and partly of double headed steel rails. The sharpest curve (provided with a check rail) has a radius of 6.14 chains and the sharpest gradient an inclination of 1 in 201. There is no station on this portion of the line but so soon as the junction has been completed with the Ryde and Newport Railway, the trains on the Newport Junction Railway are to use the Newport Joint Station.

For 9 out of the 23 chains there is a viaduct having 19 openings. Three of these openings are spanned with wrought iron girders of lengths varying between 68 ft and 37 ft resting in one case on cast iron columns and in the other on brick abutments. The other 16 openings of the viaduct which are from 15 to 23½ ft wide are composed entirely of brickwork. There is also a barrel culvert of 3 ft in diameter. The brick work appears to have been substantially constructed and to be standing well. The girders yielded moderate deflections under a load of engines but their theoretical strength is barely sufficient even for the comparatively light engines used on the Isle of Wight and the question of the sufficiency of these girders has to be further considered by the Engineers and myself.

The following require to be attended to

1. *Pan Station.* The facing points next Shide should be moved nearer to the frame, reversed in position and these and another set of facing points bolt locked with rods instead of with wire. The signal post next Shide should be brought nearer to the station.

The distant signal towards Newport should be repeated. A set of facing points at the Newport end of the station should be removed and the siding should end with buffer stops.

The level crossing gates should be prevented from opening outwards across the road.

2. The footing of one of the piers of the viaduct requires repair.

The uneasy partnership of the IWNJ and IWR began to fall apart in December 1878 when the IWR refused to allow a £400 debt for locomotive and rolling stock maintenance to stand over and gave notice that the £150 per annum rent for the use of Sandown station was no longer adequate. The IWNJ asked Mr Simmons, the Joint Committee's manager, if he would '. . . add the Superintendence of the Newport Junction Line to his other duties'. Before this could take effect the two companies patched up their quarrel and Joseph Bourne had his contract renewed on 1st January, 1879 for three months. The retention of Joseph Bourne as manager was no real concession as delays in opening the line at Newport meant that the IWNJ was still dependent on the beneficence of the IWR.

The Board of Trade Inspector made a return visit to Newport in March 1879 when he expressed his satisfaction with the IWNJ works and the drawbridge but refused to pass the connections into the station. Even so, Herbert Simmons took over as manager of the IWNJ on 1st April, the ties with the IWR were broken and Joseph Bourne's employment was ended. On 21st May, 1879 the Directors reported to shareholders: 'The connections with the Cowes and Newport Railway, to which the Directors have always attached the greatest importance, has recently been completed for Goods Traffic and several experimental trains have been run through from the Medina Siding to Sandown, Shanklin and Ventnor'. At their next meeting the news was that the junction '. . . was opened to traffic on the 1st of June, notwithstanding the unfavourable weather'. The IWNJ retained a signalman at Pan Lane until December 1886 when the signal box was closed and the block instruments moved to Shide.

In July 1879 the IWNJ's share of the joint works at Newport was settled at £12,500 after deducting £765 16s. 4d. spent on land and £1,000 handed over in 1877; payment was by means of a rent charge which the RNR promptly sold to a Mr Charles Morrison. This permitted repayment of £7,700 borrowed from Mr and Mrs Martin - they were given £1,250 in RNR

Third Preference shares 'as a bonus'. In September the IWNJ and RNR agreed to abandon competition for the Ryde to Newport traffic. Fares via Sandown were raised to their normal rates and the IWNJ undertook to pay its share of any through fares to the Joint Committee in return for compensation of £400 a year. This had the desired effect as in November the IWR Board expressed concern that traffic from Blackwater and Merstone was being sent to Ryde via Newport instead of Sandown. For the IWNJ, the loss of traffic proved to be more than they expected and in June 1881 the Directors were trying to reverse their decision. A formal working agreement between the IWNJ and Ryde, Newport & Cowes Joint Committee came into force in January 1880.

Completion of the junction with the CNR and RNR led to a few changes; in July 1879 Herbert Simmons was instructed not to start trains from Sandown station before the arrival of the boat trains from Ryde. This was with good reason as the IWR continued to encourage travel from Ryde to Newport via Sandown. Within a few years, however, the public learned not to rely on connections at Sandown and made alternative arrangements. At the opposite end of the IWNJ the *Isle of Wight Times* for 14th August reported that some Sandown trains were running through to Cowes.

Whilst there was no great increase in the numbers of passengers carried, the amount of goods traffic rose significantly, particularly from Medina Jetty to the east coast towns of Sandown, Shanklin and Ventnor. (From 1882 the figures were included in those submitted by the Ryde, Newport & Cowes Joint Committee.)

Year ending 31 Dec.	Passenger traffic Numbers carried			Goods traffic		Gross receipts		Working expenses	% of expenditure in
	First	Second	Third	Minerals Tons	General Tons	Pass. £	Goods £	£	relation to receipts
1875	17,754	108,902	25,741	536	2,083	5,710	348	3,647	60
1876	19,436	120,810	52,838	244	7,856	6,564	990	5,910	78
1878	18,499	114,157	57,618	777	14,623	6,353	1,550	5,838	74
1880	13,875	83,546	56,223	11,531	17,171	6,097	2,691	4,914	64

The financial position had gone from bad to worse. IWNJ debenture holders had not received their interest and a Mr Houghton took the company to court. David Derry, the Secretary, was appointed Receiver by the Court of Chancery on 23rd May, 1879. On 25th June, 1879 Richard E. Webster accepted an offer to become a Director for a limited period but actually remained on the Board until 1887. During a lengthy Parliamentary career, Richard Webster served as Attorney General and Lord Chief Justice; he was knighted in the 1880s, created Baron Alverstone in 1900 and Viscount Alverstone in 1913 two years before his death in 1915. Mr Webster took on the task of agreeing terms with those landowners whose claims for compensation had not been settled; being the largest landowner in the neighbourhood and a lawyer, he was a natural choice.

In March 1880 the Board went through a list of the remaining debts. The LSWR, who had supplied the defective rails and loaned a locomotive eight years earlier, were owed £777 9s. 5d. The English & Foreign Credit Company claimed hire charges since 1872 of £1,118 9s. for a locomotive and £1,967 7s. 4d. for six carriages - clearly it would have been cheaper to have bought them outright but the company never possessed the money. Almost £8,000 was owed in compensation to various landowners. On 15th December, 1880 the IWNJ lodged a 'Scheme of Arrangement' with the Court of Chancery to permit a reorganisation of borrowings to clear outstanding debts and regularise payments to debenture holders. In addition to the arrears of interest, many debentures had fallen due for repayment but the company had been unable to repay the capital.

The break from the IWR resulted in an increase in the Sandown station rent. Right from the start the IWNJ Directors thought the charges were excessive but since the IWR deducted them from traffic receipts it always managed to keep the whip-hand, despite the bitterness engendered. In June 1879 the IWR refused to accept £150 per annum and on 18th September it was reported that £450 a year was being taken from the traffic receipts.

The increasing goods traffic was viewed with some anxiety by the IWR as it was taking business from their railway. As IWNJ goods were carried a shorter distance over the IWR Joseph Bourne imposed a terminal charge for station accommodation and related matters. This provoked a catalogue of complaints from traders '. . . the consequence being that goods are now largely conveyed by road'. The matter surfaced at a half-yearly meeting on 21st May, 1879 when:

> A shareholder called attention to the great increase in the goods rates since Mr Bourne had quitted the Company's service, it was explained that such increase was entirely due to the increased rates demanded by the Isle of Wight Company for the transit of goods between Sandown and Ventnor, but this Company were advised that these rates were illegal and that the Isle of Wight Company's accounts only entitled them to charge 3d. per ton per mile for the highest class . . . including carting and unloading.

In October 1879 three Directors attended a meeting with Joseph Bravo, the IWR Chairman, in an attempt to gain some resolution to the disputes. The meeting went rather badly and the resulting venom as recorded in the IWNJ minutes virtually jumped off the page! The IWNJ Board asked the Receiver to apply for a court summons compelling the IWR to refund the excess rent charged for the use of Sandown station. The matter went to an arbitrator who decided on a payment of £210 per annum for four years from 1st January, 1881. This prompted more arguments as the IWR refused to light the distant signal at Sandown without an additional payment; the accounts show a slightly higher payment so there may have been some adjustment. After the IWR allegedly erected a fence on IWNJ property, the managers marked out the exact boundaries at the station - there was later a complaint that slot machines were trespassing! The dispute over mileage rates went before the Railway Commissioners who ruled on 19th July, 1882 that the IWR was entitled to charge only a mileage rate of 3d. per mile per ton. Much to the disgust of the IWR, rates for sand, gravel, cement, etc. had to be reduced. However, there were other subtle ways by which the IWR could discourage traffic passing off the IWNJ.

The great snow during the winter of 1880-1881 resulted in a suspension of services. Mr Sheward told shareholders that troops in garrison at Sandown had helped to clear the line.

The condition of the railway had not improved. Newport Corporation complained in September 1880 about rain water flooding from the railway structure at Coppins Bridge onto the roadway; the Secretary was instructed to write that the matter would be dealt with and if necessary galvanised sheeting provided. The fencing had been thought by the Board of Trade Inspector to be rather weak when he inspected the line in 1875 because fence posts had been made out of old sleepers of Isle of Wight fir, a most unsuitable timber that rotted quickly - in July 1881 a landowner took the company to court in an attempt to gain some improvement. The iron rails were also wearing out quicker than they could be replaced. Relaying seems to have begun in 1880, but a shortage of money meant that it was a slow and lengthy task. In June 1881 the Secretary reported he had ordered 20 tons of slightly defective steel rails at £5 10s. a ton from Messrs Green and Burleigh who agreed to take old rails in exchange at £2 15s. a ton. An additional 20 tons ordered in November coincided with a letter from Revd J.D. Dicker to the Board of Trade complaining that the Sandown to Newchurch section was in a dangerous condition. Col Rich visited the Island and on 14th November 1882 wrote:

> The permanent way consists partly of a double headed rail, which is fixed in cast iron chairs on cross sleepers and partly of a Vignoles pattern Rail, which is fixed by dog spikes and fang bolts to cross sleepers. These timbers are mostly 10 in. x 5 in. (rectangular) but there are some particularly under the Vignoles Rail that are half round.
>
> About one out of every 6 or 7 sleepers is very much decayed, but the fastenings generally are still firm, and the rails are fairly true to gauge and in good line particularly when it is considered that the Railway has lately been flooded in many places. The line is well ballasted.
>
> The inside edge of the Vignoles pattern rail that has been down ever since the Line was opened for traffic is jagged and the greater portion of these rails are worn out and should be renewed as soon as possible, as the rough edge will assist an Engine or some other portion of running trains in mounting and getting off the rails.

Above: Advert in *Shanklin Weekly News* 10th
June, 1882 for IWNJ Newport Market tickets.

Right: *Shanklin Weekly News* Season 1882,
advert for excursion tickets.

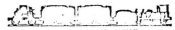

4. Compulsorily purchase property to widen the approach road to Newport station and build a low level bridge across the river for the Corporation.
5. Replace the 96 yard wooden viaduct at Cement Mills by a solid culverted embankment.
6. Build a siding at Shamblers Copse terminating '. . . at or near the end of the old pier or landing place from the brickyard' where a jetty was proposed.

The proposals met a barrage of opposition. Within weeks the IWR and Ryde Commissioners forced the two companies to abandon the amalgamation proposals, the railways at Ryde and the use of locomotives on the tramway. The other provisions fared no better and had to be withdrawn leaving the Bill to become law solely as a money raising measure.

The first recorded meeting of the Joint Committee took place on 1st September, 1875 when Messrs Petre, Young and Castle attended, Mr Petre was elected Chairman. Edward Lincoln, Secretary of the two companies, was appointed Secretary and meetings henceforth took place at his premises at 14 Queen Victoria Street, London. Henry Martin was designated 'Consulting Manager for Traffic' and Herbert Simmons assistant manager 'under Mr Martin's direction'.

A month later, the local press mentioned that the RNR was contemplating the construction of a branch from Haven Street to Fish House (the old name for Fishbourne), presumably with the intention of building a jetty at that point. Such thoughts evaporated and a Bill published soon afterwards listed proposals for works at Cowes, Newport and Shamblers where there would be a branch and jetty; in fact no Bill appeared before Parliament probably because it stood no greater chance of success than that 12 months earlier.

Meanwhile the RNR opened on 20th December, 1875 worked by Henry Martin and six months later, on 1st July, 1876, the Joint Committee took on the operation of the two companies' lines. Goods traffic began soon afterwards but was handicapped by the lack of a jetty for landing coal, minerals, etc. After payment of running costs, income was divided between the companies on a mileage basis. Frank Stileman wrote on 8th July, 1876 that he considered the distances to be 4¼ miles for the CNR and 7¾ for the RNR. Some Directors, however, were not satisfied and at the next meeting it was decided that the lengths were '. . . only to be used by the Secretary for making up accounts to 30th June last and without prejudice to the rights of either Company'. The mileage was later amended to: CNR - 4 miles 20 chains, RNR - 7 miles 56.6 chains and the joint station at Newport - 17 chains 20 links (roughly 378 yards).

At the beginning of 1877 the CNR Directors refused to attend meetings of the Joint Committee and gave notice that the agreement was terminated. The cause of the friction was the wording of the agreement that obliged the Joint Committee to pay only working expenses. The CNR Board were aggrieved that they were expected to pay the whole of the maintenance costs of their line, costs that were inflated by additional traffic the RNR brought to its railway. The rift proved short lived and on 19th March, 1877 a fresh agreement was concluded. It reconstituted the Joint Committee so that no meeting had a quorum unless at least one Director from each company was present. The CNR was obliged to execute any works required by the Joint Committee to put its line in a satisfactory order, but the cost of doing so was divided between the companies on a mileage basis. When it came to sharing out income, the CNR had prior claim to £2,000 per annum '. . . for the use of their railway and works'. All staff and running costs were then paid before the RNR could receive a sum of £2,600 and whatever remained was divided according to mileage.

The first meeting under the 1877 agreement took place on 11th April attended by Mr Petre, as Chairman, Messrs Young and Pinnock on behalf of the RNR with Petre and Bourne from the CNR - the CNR was firmly in the driving seat. The chief officers were re-appointed: Mr Lincoln as Secretary and Mr Stileman Engineer '. . . to carry out the Provisions of the New Agreement of the 19th March, 1877 as to reconstruction and New Works authorised by the new Act of the Ryde and Newport Railway Company'. Mr Martin was 'Consulting Manager with an allowance of £150 per annum for expenses' and Mr Simmons 'Assistant Traffic Manager under the Joint Committee'.

Meanwhile, a resurrection of the 1875 Bill had been under consideration. In October 1876 the press reported that the RNR was again contemplating a branch to Wootton Creek but this proved to be another red herring. A Bill was placed before the next Parliamentary session applying for powers to construct a siding and jetty near Shamblers Copse, alter and enlarge the station at Cowes, replace the viaduct at Cement Mills by a solid embankment and compulsorily purchase land for a widening of the approach road and bridge across Lukely Brook to Newport station.

After passing through the preliminary stages in the House of Lords, a committee met on 12th March, 1877 to look at the Bill in detail. Mr Porter, solicitor for the Bill, was called to give evidence of the negotiations between the company and Messrs Francis who objected to the proposed embankment at Cement Mills. Apparently the permanent way was laid direct on the timbers and there had been great difficulties in maintaining the bridge. He indicated that the relevant clauses were not essential and could be struck out - they were.

Evidence was given of the need for the jetty at Shamblers. George Garnett, Engineer, Secretary and manager of the Ryde Gas Company stated that his works used 8,000 tons of coal a year and supplies were being landed on the beach at Ryde at considerable cost. The CNR's 1864 Act had authorised construction of a siding and a jetty at Shamblers Copse on the site of an old jetty serving a nearby brick works and this plan had been resurrected in 1875. Frederick Stileman explained that the 1875 site was far from satisfactory as a zig-zag siding on 1 in 50 gradient would have been necessary in order to reach the jetty. He had selected a different location a few yards to the south and considered it to be the best possible spot, bearing in mind the depth of water and ease of access from the main line; his siding descended at 1 in 80. He and Henry Pinnock were questioned at length about the effect of the jetty on the activities of the Medina Oyster Fishery Company. Although the two companies could have built the jetty north of the fishery Mr Pinnock admitted it was cheaper to compensate the fishery than the brick yard: '. . . it is a financial question - the bed of the river is let on a lease to the Oyster Fishery Company at £125 a year and if we go further to the northward, we get into a brick makers business . . .' As a concession, the committee insisted on the insertion of clauses that obliged the railway to interfere as little as possible with the oyster fishery and navigation of the river. Newport Corporation was placated by a RNR undertaking to pay £40 a month for loss of tolls and complete Newport Quay and siding to the Corporation's satisfaction before bringing the jetty at Shamblers into use. There was also a clause stating that the jetty could not be used for passengers without the written consent of the owner of Fountain Quay.

The Bill sought powers to extend the station at Cowes across Carvel Lane in a north-easterly direction to the west side of High Street. Mr Stileman gave evidence that there would be three tracks across Cross Street but since road traffic was very small the tracks would not create any additional dangers to the public. The local authority had opposed attempts to close Cross Street since the 1860s but, after negotiation, Cowes Local Board finally gave way. When the Bill became law it contained the long looked for words 'The Ryde Company shall stop up and discontinue for public traffic so much of Cross Street, Cowes as is or will be within Cowes station'. This was on condition that no streets would be affected by the works apart from Cross Street and Carvel Lane. The companies were obliged to build the bridge across Carvel Lane with a 25 ft span and a headway of not less than 14 ft and a footbridge at Cross Street. If within 10 years the local authority resolved to build a road in place of Cross Street the CNR and RNR undertook to contribute £200 towards its cost - when they did finally make such a decision, the RNR was bankrupt and unable to pay its share!

On 12th July, 1877 the Bill received Royal Assent. The Act enshrined the 1872 and 1877 working agreements in law and authorised each company to raise more capital. The financial arrangements between them were, to say the least, unusual: two-thirds of the cost of the works detailed in the Act came from the RNR and one-third from the CNR. The RNR was required to carry them out to the satisfaction of the CNR and, with the exception of the approach road at Newport, they became part of the CNR upon completion.

Capital expenditure was financed principally by the issue of RNR Preference shares from which an investor could expect a dividend of up to 5 per cent per annum, payments taking precedence over any dividend to holders of ordinary shares. RNR preferential share capital rose steadily between 1875 and 1883 from nothing to £105,460 - an enormous sum for such a small company. This was in addition to the ordinary shares and debentures that by 1883 had grown to £51,800. Predictably the RNR Board never declared a dividend on its shares and even the debenture interest fell into arrears.

Although the Joint Committee had decided on 19th April, 1876 to put the CNR in '. . . good working order and condition for carrying the heavy traffic in Chalk, Coal, etc.', nothing had been done because of a predictable lack of capital. On 9th May, 1877 Mr Stileman reported that it was necessary '. . . to relay the Cowes and Newport line'. Henry Martin found the necessary cash in exchange for shares and on 4th July, 1877 the Joint Committee approved the granting of a contract. The CNR had to find two-thirds of the cost less two-thirds of the value of old materials disposed of - old iron was fetching quite a good price. F. Durnford & Son completed the task in December 1878. Rebuilding the wooden bridges, the weakest of which was Cement Mills viaduct, took rather longer. A £1,800 tender from John Cochrane & Co. was accepted on 16th June, 1880 and on 3rd November, Mr Simmons reported that the viaduct and other bridges had been renewed.

In October 1877 a £6,500 contract was let to G. Smith for the construction of a siding at Shamblers leading onto a wooden jetty parallel with the river bank. J. Taylor supplied a steam crane and Messrs Easterbrook installed a small signal cabin controlling a full complement of stop and distant signals in either direction. Major General Hutchinson of the Board of Trade, who was visiting the Island to inspect a new siding at Alverstone, carried out an inspection and sanctioned its opening on 23rd October, 1878. Unfortunately, Newport Quay was incomplete and it was prudently decided to delay bringing the jetty into use until November. By then the Joint Committee was discussing the construction of a 170 ft extension of the jetty with a 50 ft covered portion costing £1,600; such was its importance that Henry Martin agreed to find the necessary funds on receipt of guarantees (i.e. shares) from the RNR. Mr Smith initially refused to carry out the work until offered Lloyds Bonds for his existing debt; in May 1880 Mr Stileman informed the Joint Committee that the extension had been completed.

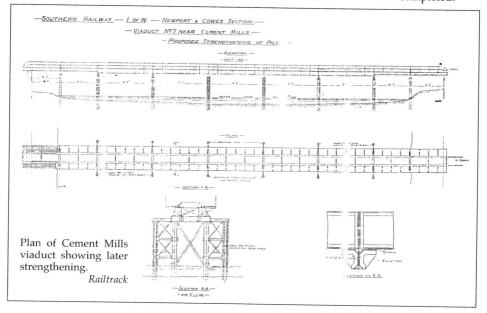

Plan of Cement Mills viaduct showing later strengthening.
Railtrack

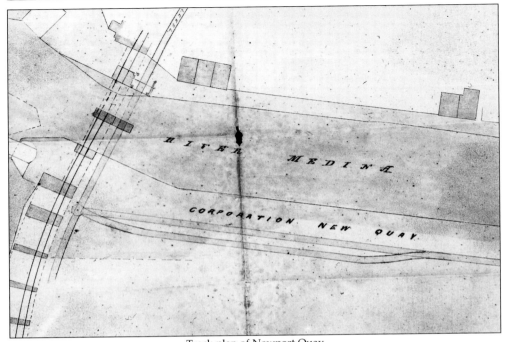

Track plan of Newport Quay.

Track plan of Newport *circa* 1879 to 1889.

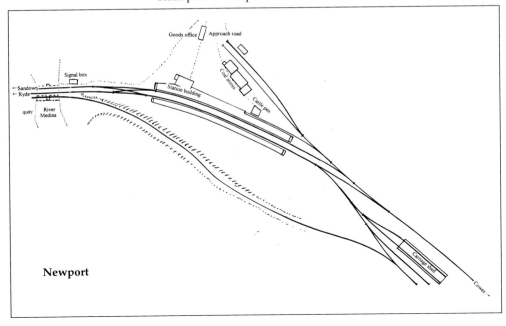

As regards Newport Quay, on 26th September, 1877 Mr Stileman was asked to report the cost of the provision of the low level bridge '. . . without which the Medina Siding cannot be opened for traffic'. On 3rd April, 1878 the Joint Committee authorised the expenditure of £282 on the bridge and a turntable; the latter supplied by Messrs Taylor of Birkenhead. The spur to the quay descended at 1 in 35 from a siding in the station through a cutting to emerge at river level and cross the river on a lifting bridge to reach Newport Quay; the turntable gave access to lines running the length of the quay. In November 1878 the Corporation was notified that the siding was complete although teething problems in opening the bridge persisted for several months.

The poor financial position of the RNR was the cause of another dispute that came to a head in May 1878. At a meeting of the RNR Board on 30th May, 1878 the Secretary stated he had been forced to take proceedings for payment of his salary. To be fair Mr Lincoln had raised the matter on numerous occasions but without response. Shocked by the disloyalty displayed by their Secretary the Board gave him £1,000 in third preference stock and three months' notice. When he refused to accept his dismissal the Directors at the next meeting on 14th June, formally terminated his services after 29th September and called on him to give up the books and papers of the company. Francis Beard assumed the position of Secretary on 7th August, 1878 and meetings of the Board moved to his offices at No. 3 Lothbury, London - Board meetings of the CNR, RNR and Joint Committee had usually been held at Mr Lincoln's offices. Mr Beard also took over as Secretary of the Joint Committee but the CNR Board appointed John Crick and met at his address at 8 Union Court, Old Broad Street, London.

The enlargement of Cowes station was delayed by the need to fund the purchase of additional property in the vicinity. A July 1877 decision that the 'Siding at Mill Hill be made fit for use in crossing trains' was rescinded after Frank Stileman suggested '. . . an alternative arrangement for passing of trains leaving Cowes Station' using the run-round loop. At the same meeting, construction was authorised of a 'carriage dock' at Cowes (apparently the siding opposite the locomotive shed). Later still, a kickback siding was added to another building probably built by Henry Martin in 1880 for painting rolling stock. On 17th April, 1878 it was ordered that the footbridge be constructed and in August tenders were sought for the closing of Cross Street and a widening of the station. In 1876 Henry Martin had spent £4,330 on land in the vicinity and two years later he added 'Ward's Cottage' in Cross Street to his portfolio for a further £250. Mr Stileman reported it was still '. . . necessary to pull down two more cottages before the bridge at Cross Street can be proceeded with'. In January 1879 the *Isle of Wight Chronicle* mentioned the demolition of houses at the top of Cross Street and added that the level crossing would shortly be abolished. This was evidently regarded as an improvement as several children had narrowly escaped being run over by the train.

Events elsewhere then called for some unlooked-for expenditure. The station at Mill Hill was completely destroyed by fire in April 1879. In May 1880 plans were approved for an extension of the platform northwards up to the tunnel mouth and a brick building at a cost of £363 - it was completed a few months later. Sited slightly to the north of the original, it was an attractive yellow brick single-storey station building with red brick trimmings. A stone plaque built into the wall of the building bore the initials 'C&NR 1880'. The cutting was never widened so the rear roof ended virtually at ground level and the access path to Newport Road became considerably steeper than previously. In later years a brick and glass screen was erected at the end of the building sheltering the booking office grille which had previously faced into the waiting room.

The IWNJ had largely completed its viaduct and bridge at Newport by October 1878 but the permanent way, connections and signalling into the station were incomplete - they were the RNR's responsibility. Unfortunately, there was a distinct lack of capital and many contractors had not been paid. Easterbrook & Hannaford were owed £303 11s. 6d. for signalling, mainly at Shamblers, and wrote in January 1879 refusing to send men to complete the work at Newport without payment of their bill. After the firm refused Lloyds Bonds, some cash was found but when Major General Hutchinson, the Board of Trade Inspector, carried out an inspection in March the signalling was still unfinished; he took exception to the number of facing connections and insisted on the provision of a scissors crossover. This delayed completion until June. By then Easterbrook & Co. was owed £259 11s. 6d. plus an additional £150 for alterations made at the insistence of the Board of Trade. To avoid increasing the number of levers in the signal cabin, certain connections at the Cowes end of the station were transferred to a ground frame locked from the cabin.

On 1st April, 1879 the Ryde, Newport & Cowes Joint Committee took over the operation of the IWNJ. By then goods trains were running over the viaduct to Pan Lane but passenger traffic had yet to begin. On 25th June next a single meeting was held at No. 3 Lothbury, London of '. . . the Delegates of the Isle of Wight Newport Junction Ry; the Ryde and Newport Ry and the Cowes & Newport Ry for the working of Newport Joint Station'. Messrs Petre, MacKay and Batten sensibly decided that the existing Joint Committee would manage the station on behalf of the three companies. Yet another Minute book was begun with a meeting on 1st April, 1880 '. . . of Delegates to the Committee of Management of the Ryde & Newport and Cowes & Newport and Newport Junction Railway Companies' and, as on previous occasions, each company sent a Director to every meeting. This led to the existence of *two* Joint Committees as the Directors of the CNR and RNR continued to meet separately for a further two years! The Joint Committee of the three companies went through a fresh round of appointments. Francis Beard was appointed Secretary on a salary of £100 per annum plus £250 expenses for managing the audit work, Herbert Simmons was made Manager of the whole system at £350 a year but Henry Martin's appointment as consulting manager was put off for a month as clearly some Directors felt his services were unnecessary.

Despite the lengthy delays in completing the IWNJ the CNR never did receive the £50 penalty payments mentioned in the IWNJ Act. In 1871 the CNR delayed petitioning in favour of a Bill for the Isle of Wight and Cowes & Newport Junction Railway because that might have jeopardised its rights. Thereafter the IWNJ's financial state precluded any attempts to enforce payment for fear that the IWNJ would never complete the junction!

Whilst the completion of the IWNJ undoubtedly benefited all three companies, the CNR Directors were acutely aware that it took them only part of the way to their main objective - Ventnor. At their insistence the Ryde, Newport and Cowes Joint Committee presented a Bill to the 1882 Parliamentary session applying for running powers over the IWR from Sandown to Ventnor. The promoters hoped for support from residents who complained about the existing monopoly, but it is unclear why the Joint Committee thought it could succeed because the IWR petitioned Parliament in opposition claiming that its railway could not cope with any additional traffic. It would be many years before the successors to the CNR got an independent line to Ventnor.

At Cowes, a lack of money threatened the rebuilding of the station. By March 1880 a footbridge had been built a few yards south of Cross Street to maintain the right of way but precisely when the level crossing was closed is uncertain. There ensued a delay until March 1882 when a decision was made to buy three houses and outbuildings in Carvel Lane for £400. Henry Martin was asked to employ Mr Pease to make '. . . the cheapest possible platform across the street at Cowes station' - by 1891 the wooden platform had been extended to about 220 ft long. A proposal to extend the station across Carvel Lane led to a letter in June from a Mr J. Atkey complaining that the proposed bridge '. . . will spoil his adjoining property and requesting compensation'. The Secretary was instructed to refuse and add '. . . that the requirements of the Act of Parliament will be carried out with as little detriment to the adjoining property as possible'. Even so, it is doubtful whether any further significant work was carried out before a Receiver was appointed to manage the financial affairs of the RNR in 1883. Mr Stileman's plans for a large three-platform station extending to High Street were destined never to come to fruition.

Chapter Eight

Operating the Joint Committee

Henry Martin worked the RNR for a few months as an extension of his contract with the CNR. Unfortunately, Mr Martin's grip on CNR matters soon brought him into conflict with the Joint Committee. Immediately the RNR opened, the Secretary was instructed to travel to Newport and make the necessary arrangements for keeping accounts, etc. This did not go smoothly as on 1st March, 1876 it was minuted:

The Secretary begged to report that in compliance with the Committee's instructions he had proceeded to Newport, where he learnt from the Assistant Manager, Mr Simmons, that since the opening of the Ryde and Newport Railway the whole of the Accounts papers and collected tickets relating to the traffic over the two lines had been forwarded to Mr Martin by his order . . . an account had been opened in the name of the Joint Committee at the National Provincial Bank, Newport, on the 22nd ultimo - and that certain sums had been paid in by Mr Simmons to the credit of the account since the above date; but there was no means of ascertaining the amount of traffic between the 20th December, when the Ryde Line was opened, and the 22nd February - the whole of these receipts having been paid over to Mr Martin . . .

Henry Martin responded that the accounts for the first two months were being made out and would be ready for the next meeting. The Directors were clearly unhappy that Henry Martin should have so much control over their affairs and on 5th April it was ordered that the whole of the accounts be transferred to the Secretary who was instructed to employ staff to maintain them. The station master at Newport was instructed not to make payments out of season ticket receipts and all bills for wages, etc. were to be submitted to the Joint Committee, for which purpose meetings would be held fortnightly in future.

The contract must have been profitable as on 16th April, 1876 Henry Martin indicated he was '. . . willing to continue to carry the traffic at the same rate'; others were apparently not so happy as Mr Petre was asked to go through his accounts. It had always been the intention of the two companies to take over the working of their railways from Henry Martin - this they did from 1st July, 1876. Following a decision to buy Henry Martin's rolling stock Joseph Bourne was asked to make a valuation. His enthusiasm alarmed Mr Martin who complained: 'Mr Bourne seems to be including in his valuation more than was intended by the Resolution . . . he was to value the Rolling Stock, and the Rolling Stock stores plant of which an inventory will be provided'. Joseph Bourne received £60 for his services and in December 1876 joined the CNR Board. The rolling stock was hired from 1st July, 1876 at a rent of £185 10s. 6d. per half-year.

The passenger service provided by Henry Martin consisted of seven trains a day in each direction between Ryde and Cowes; trains called at Ashey and Whippingham by request. By May 1877 the service had increased to eight trains each way with two additional return workings between Newport and Cowes; there were four trains each way on Sundays. On 20th October, 1875 the Joint Committee had decided that all Sunday trains were 'to have a third class carriage'. Third class tickets were available on other days for travel by the first train in each direction, but the return portions could only used by certain afternoon or evening trains. Tickets were of the familiar Edmondson pattern issued under the title 'R. N. & C. Ry.', although a printer's error resulted in the issue of single and return tickets to 'Hanen Street'.

Traffic in chalk from Mr Young's quarry seems to have begun shortly after a decision on 1st March, 1876 to set a rate of 1s. 6d. per ton from Ashey to any station; trains were not to exceed five wagons and the rate excluded loading and unloading. Destinations for the chalk included Ryde; the Ryde Pier Company sent a cheque for £171 13s. in July for carriage of chalk, of which £19 was owed to others for '. . . horse hire for haulage of wagons', presumably over the pier company's tramway.

Barely had the Joint Committee taken charge than Mr Simmons reported a series of minor accidents - there must have been many earlier mishaps but the Minute books failed to mention them. In July 1876 he wrote that a truck belonging to the RNR was broken in half when in the charge of the IWR; a bill was promptly sent for the repairs. On 28th September, 1876 a hurricane hit Cowes about which a local newspaper reported: 'At the railway station, the damage was very serious. One of the sheds was destroyed, a huge tank deposited on top of an engine, railings and walls torn down, nearly all the windows broken, and the whole place covered with bricks, tiles and straw . . . several carriages were blown over . . .'

On 25th October a train left the rails on the Ryde to Newport line due to 'insufficient action of the Points'. Two months later the Secretary was ordered to report to the Board of Trade that a man had been killed on 23rd November '. . . by one of the Committee's Engines near Smallbrook Junction.' A Mr Davidson failed in legal proceedings against the RNR claiming false imprisonment because of a late running train!

The financial position continued to be of concern. In October 1876 RNR Directors reported to shareholders that the company was not doing as well as expected. Operating costs were inflated by instalment payments to Henry Martin and others for the purchase of rolling stock leaving virtually no income to pay debts. This came to a head in January 1878 when the Joint Committee acknowledged that money had to be set aside to pay the CNR's rent charges of £2,000 per annum, and RNR debenture interest then amounting to £2,500 a year.

The appointment of Joseph Bourne as a CNR Director was not to the liking of Henry Martin. On 11th April, 1877 the two men were asked to consult about the arrangements for keeping the accounts with a view to securing '. . . a regular return of the receipts and payments of the two Companies'. A month later the meeting 'Ordered that the Traffic Audit be completely carried on at the Offices of the Isle of Wight Railway, Sandown, the Committee undertaking to provide one Clerk and to pay the Isle of Wight Railway at the rate of £100 per annum'. However, in October the Joint Committee refused to increase the wages of the clerk on the basis that he was an employee of the IWR and not the committee. Mr Bourne scored a point against Mr Martin when he wrote on 10th October, 1877 reporting a cash discrepancy at Newport station of about £20 and recommending that '. . . a good Booking Clerk be appointed in lieu of the little Boy now employed'. The audit work was taken back from the IWR at the end of 1878 and placed in the hands of the Secretary in London. Soon afterwards the IWNJ accounts were taken on. In January 1878 it was reported that Haven Street station had been robbed and £2 15s. 7d. taken from the till; despite not living on the premises the station master was dismissed for negligence. In August a fatal accident to a porter was reported to the Board of Trade.

The punctuality of trains was mentioned in July 1877 when it was decided to purchase two watches for issue to the guards but later that year it was decided to buy just one - '. . . the other guard having a Watch of his own'! The *Isle of Wight Times* mentioned an accident that took place on Sunday morning 9th December when the first train from Newport ran into a siding at Ryde station and collided with several wagons of stone - shaking but not injuring the passengers. Although the locomotive had its front end smashed in, the carriages were said to be 'not much damaged'; the wagons came off worse with one being broken in two.

Despite having ploughed much of his capital into the railway, Mr Young was billed for repairs to Ashey quarry siding in early 1878. The quarry was passing quite a quantity of traffic over the railway. Typical was a prison contract in December 1877 for 600 yards of sand at a price of 2s. 5d. per yard including delivery; the sand was the wrong colour for use in brick making but perfectly suitable for other building purposes. In November 1878 rates for the carriage of chalk to the jetty at Shamblers were quoted as 4d. per ton for haulage on the siding at Ashey, 1s. 4d. per ton to the jetty and 3d. per ton pier dues. This was evidently considered excessive as in March 1879 the matter was referred to Henry Martin '. . . to see if he can meet Mr Young's wishes' - he couldn't! When two wagons from the quarry collided with locomotive No. 4 hauling a Newport-bound passenger train in September 1879, the Joint Committee sent George Young a £125 bill for damage with a request that he provide his own wagons by the end of the year. This was ignored as in January 1880 Mr Rutherford, Mr Young's agent, complained of a want of wagons. A month later there was a claim for damage after another accident in the siding.

Deliveries of parcels around the town of Newport were made using a horse and cart owned by the railways; although a horse was bought in December 1879 for £30, more horses were acquired in April 1881 and February 1882 so they must have had hard lives! Mr Simmons was asked to see Joseph Bourne with a view to the production of a 'joint illustrated guide and time card'. In August another fire at Newport destroyed some carriage lamps but, after receiving payment from the insurers, it was discovered that the IWNJ rolling stock was not insured so premiums had to be increased to include them. Recipients of subsidies for road coaches from stations to locations not reached by the railways included Mr Dabell who operated the Blackgang Coach and Mr Cave who took visitors from Newport station to Carisbrooke on the 'Ryde, Newport and Cowes' coach.

Long-running problems with the refreshment room at Newport were first mentioned in December 1880. The rooms had been constructed in 1878 and let to a Mr G. Goodden (sometimes referred to as Godden) from 24th June, 1878 at a rent of £155 per annum for seven years. W. H. Smith had been given the contract for bookstalls and advertising at the stations in November 1876 but complained when Mr Goodden began displaying advertising outside the refreshment room. He was told to remove the offending material and when this met with no response the Joint Committee threatened to take proceedings and decided in June 1881 that he be given notice to quit. This was not carried out as in November he was offered a reduction in rent of £10 a year if he removed the advertising. The wily Mr Goodden graciously accepted the reduction but stated that he had sublet the space to a Mr Locke who refused to remove the advertising! A year later a refreshment room was built at Cowes station and let to Mr Goodden for £20 a year. Business did not prove very lucrative as in February 1883 he suggested that passengers alight from trains on the booking office side of the station adjacent to his room. When this was refused because the platform was too short on that side, he responded by deducting the first quarter's rent for Cowes claiming it had been spent in cleaning and preparing the new room. By June Mr Locke who had begun paying rent for the advertising at Newport was in arrears and a month later filed his petition for liquidation - at least this solved the problem with the advertising! Mr Goodden gave up his tenancy at Cowes in the autumn of 1883 and in the following January it was let to a Mr Edmund Webb for £20 a year - he lasted only until October 1884 when the room again became vacant. Meanwhile, after some brinkmanship, Mr Goodden renewed his lease of the refreshment room at Newport in 1885 for a further seven years at £145 per year.

The numbers of passengers carried during Joint Committee days showed no great increase probably because the battle for through traffic to Ventnor had already been lost to the IWR and the Portsmouth - Ryde ferry route. There was an opportunity to extend the through ticketing arrangements and, in a move clearly designed to embarrass Henry Martin, in August 1879 Joseph Bourne (who was a CNR Director and thus attended meetings of the Joint Committee) mentioned that the IWR was receiving its share from cheap tickets as if they had been paid at the full rates - Mr Martin was asked to report. It seems through running to and from Cowes was the exception rather than the rule, probably because of the short platform there. Joseph Bourne opined how the change of carriage at Newport was a great inconvenience and could be eliminated with a little reorganisation. The frequency of the service was limited by the absence of a crossing loop between Sandown and Newport and a train was usually timed to leave Newport for Sandown immediately after another had arrived in the opposite direction.

Following the opening of Medina Jetty in 1878 and the junction with the IWNJ a year later, there was a steady growth in goods traffic. The operating costs were still worryingly high as an acceptable percentage of expenditure in relation to receipts would normally be 50 per cent - the surplus of income over expenditure was quite unable to cover the burgeoning debts let alone pay for improvements. These figures include the IWNJ from 1882.

| Year ending 31 Dec. | Passenger traffic Numbers carried | | | Goods traffic | | Gross receipts | | Working expenses | % of expenditure in relation |
	First	Second	Third	Minerals Tons	General Tons	Pass. £	Goods £	£	to receipts
1876	27,496	162,710	69,335	2,040		10,128	161	9,347	91
1877	27,582	176,196	53,040	8,402		10,431	1,137	9,543	84
1878	27,670	174,284	64,601	2,916	11,801	10,381	1,539	10,504	88
1879	28,005	172,744	64,506	28,877	13,925	10,465	3,508	10,916	78
1880	29,395	171,471	69,995	34,357	17,962	10,758	4,494	10,833	71
1882	40,673	260,725	146,504	59,120	27,975	17,618	7,323	17,768	71
1884	36,149	238,543	179,362	66,964	23,762	16,357	7,618	17,341	72
1886	32,212	220,384	199,278	71,389	22,779	15,879	7,676	16,408	69

In October 1880 trains began running over the railway of the LSWR and LBSCR at Ryde, a somewhat later date than the IWR due to the incomplete state of platforms at the pier head. This greatly facilitated the carrying of passengers to and from the ferries at Ryde, but was probably a mixed blessing for the Joint Committee as more travellers would be attracted via Ryde instead of Cowes. The ability to board a train that ran direct to Newport and Cowes did at least give the Ryde to Newport route a clear advantage over that via Sandown. Goods traffic might have been higher if relations with the IWR had been better. Mention has been made of the problems between the IWNJ and IWR concerning the rent at Sandown and, more seriously, the additional terminal charges imposed for goods carried to IWR stations. In retaliation, the Joint Committee began charging 1d. a mile for IWR wagons running over any part of the system.

In 1882 a serious deficiency of £151 7s. 5d. in season tickets was discovered at Newport. This figure took into account season tickets '. . . found under the bottom of the safe at Newport'. There is no indication whether the booking clerk was ever prosecuted - the Directors were more concerned that the insurance company would pay no more than £100 to make up the shortfall! Perhaps the need to split proceeds between the Joint committee and IWNJ proved too complicated for the poor clerk. Whilst on the subject of tickets, a feature of the Island railways was the provision of family tickets allowing unlimited travel - apparently they were the first 'go anywhere' tickets to be issued in Britain. Joseph Bourne proposed such a ticket covering all the Island railways in June 1881, but the IWR refused to split the income equally after deducting the LSWR and LBSCR Companies' share. The outcome was the issue of separate tickets for the IWR and Joint Committee's lines. In May 1883 Herbert Simmons reported that from 1st June the IWR would extend the availability of third class return tickets for return by any train on its system instead of just two a day - he was instructed to do the same.

The majority of passengers travelled between Newport and Cowes, Sandown or Ryde and the intermediate stations saw little traffic. This was certainly the case at Whippingham where the station was some distance from habitation, including the Queen's residence at Osborne, but it was somewhat closer to Whippingham Church. The church was patronised by the royal party whenever they were in residence and in 1885 there was a royal wedding when one of the Queen's daughters, Princess Beatrice, married Prince Henry of Battenburg; the Joint Committee ran a number of special trains carrying all and sundry. The station had another brief period of feverish activity a few years later for the internment of the prince at the church.

Activities at Ashey quarry surfaced afresh in April 1883 when a letter was read from Mr Begbie, who had taken on Ashey estate and quarry, asking for a reduction in rates. It was agreed to quote 1s. a ton for three months in an effort to encourage the carriage of chalk from Ashey to Medina Jetty. Mr Begbie was asked to make sure his men were more careful in loading the wagons '. . . as there is much damage done at present', but within three months £17 worth of damage was done to three wagons in the quarry. Mr Begbie complained of a neglect of the chalk traffic on the Committee's part and in February 1884 Herbert Simmons reported the railway was being charged 2s. a ton for chalk, a rate he thought was excessive. There matters remained for the time being.

Amongst other complaints that appeared in the Minutes of the Joint Committee was one for 26th April, 1882:

Read letter from Mr Blake of 11th inst claiming compensation of £5 for injuries to his client Mr Cole received in alighting from a train at Cowes; - Mr Simmons letter of 24th April was also read, recommending that the claim should not be entertained on the Grounds that Mr Cole fell asleep in the train and remained there after the train had been put away for the night until about 2 o'clock in the morning and on awaking he attempted to alight, fell to the ground and found his way home the Company therefore not being responsible, and the Secretary was instructed to write Mr Blake refusing to entertain the claim.

More seriously, an accident at Medina Jetty in April 1882 resulted in the death of one Henry Urry and the eventual payment of £140 to his wife and children. Separately, the local population at Cowes had evidently been up to no good as in August 1882 it was decided to fit locks to the gates leading to Granville bridge and the accommodation crossing at Shamblers. Granville bridge was a private footbridge close to Cowes station that connected Ward's land - it was used as a Right of Way by local people although '. . . security is considered necessary to lessen the risk of accidents, to prevent nuisances and the other objectionable purposes to which the Bridge is exposed'. Cowes was the scene of an accident in July 1883 following which payments were made to the local doctor for his services and compensation to a lady passenger. There was discussion of a letter from the wife of the train guard asking for compensation for the loss of her husband and, ever generous, the committee authorised Mr Simmons to settle for a sum not exceeding £25. The accident was sufficiently serious for the Local Board to threaten to have the station inspected by the Board of Trade. The CNR Board received a letter from the Revd J. Bower respecting '. . . the bleating of Calves opposite his house at Cowes station'; Mr Simmons had to reply stating 'why the Calves were generally tied up at this particular spot'. In November 1884 £9 was paid for '. . . damage to a platelayer from a timber truck' but since the accident was caused by alleged bad loading by IWR employees at Ryde the IWR was asked for reimbursement.

In February 1885 the wing wall of Briddlesford bridge between Wootton and Haven Street collapsed; it took six months to let a tender for its repair. Mr Begbie wrote in November that he proposed to plant trees at Ashey station and asked that the approach road be repaired; after some delay it was established that the railway was liable for the repairs and in exchange Ashey got its trees, a feature of the station still. Chalk for the work was railed from the quarry but this resulted in a dispute about the amount supplied; a wagon was measured and found to hold 5 yds 11 ft of sand whereas a larger wagon held 7 yds.

At nearby Haven Street, John Rylands, a Lancashire textile manufacturer, funded the construction of a gasworks adjacent to the station; the retort house, which still survives, bears its date of construction in 1886 and Mr Rylands' initials. The railway collected £10 per annum for giving him a 999 year lease on the necessary land and constructed a siding to which coal was delivered for the new enterprise.

Capital authorised and paid up as at 1886-1887

Year ending 31st Dec	Authorised Capital		Capital Paid up					Loans outstanding			
			Ordinary			Preferential		Debenture Stock		Debenture	
	Shares	Loans	Capital	Dividend	Capital	Dividend	% paid	Stock	Dividend	Stock	Dividend
Cowes & Newport Railway											
1886	90,000	29,800	30,000	nil	20,000	5	½	nil		29,800	5
					10,000	5	nil				
					30,000	5	nil				
Isle of Wight (Newport Junction) Railway											
1886	181,000	87,545	78,100	nil	50,000	6	nil	100	4½	29,384	4
								3,800	5	47,005	4½
Ryde & Newport Railway											
1886	185,000	61,600	65,000	nil	105,460	5	nil			51,800	5
										3,040	5
Isle of Wight Central Railway											
1887	282,000	287,000	80,460	nil	193,055	5	nil	7,964	5	91,983	3
										116,505	4
										52,305	4½

Capital and loans issued in exchange for capital and debts of the old companies

'A' Debenture Stock paying 3% per annum issued in exchange for:
CNR   Outstanding land purchases, if any.
        Debenture stock paying 5% per annum, exchanged at par.
        Rolling stock, tools and plant, at par valued at £10,000.
        Advances for land and compensation, at par £7,000.
        First Preference stock paying up to 5% per annum, exchanged at 50% of par.
        Second Preference stock paying up to 5% per annum, at 40% of par.
        Third Preference stock paying up to 5% per annum, at 30% of par.
        Ordinary stock, exchanged for the remaining 'A' debenture stock.
'B' Debenture Stock paying 4½% per annum issued in exchange for:
IWNJ   'A' Debenture stock paying 4½%, exchanged at par.
        Rent charge for Newport station works, up to £ 12,000 of stock in exchange for the rent charge.
'C' Debenture Stock paying 4% per annum issued in exchange for:
IWNJ   'B' Debenture stock paying 4%, exchanged at par and £6,000 arrears of interest on that stock.
RNR   Debenture stock paying 5%, at par and £7,000 arrears of interest on that stock.
        Other creditors were owed £26,000.
First Preference Stock paying up to 5% per annum issued in exchange for:
IWNJ   First Preference stock paying up to 6%, exchanged at par.
RNR   Preference stock paying up to 5%, at par.
Second Preference Stock paying up to 5% per annum issued in exchange for:
IWNJ   Ordinary stock, exchanged at par.
        Second Preference stock paying up to 6%, at par.
RNR   Ordinary stock, at par.
Ordinary Shares issued in exchange for:
RNR   Fourth Preference stock paying up to 5%,   }   £10 of new stock for every £10 of old.
        Ordinary shares

Holders of debenture stock could expect payment of interest irrespective of the company's performance. If there had been sufficient profits, a dividend might be declared to holders of all stock or only to holders of one or more classes of Preference stock.

Chapter Nine

The Birth of the Central Railway

It was obvious to everyone that there were just too many railway companies in the Isle of Wight. The CNR, RNR and IWNJ were in a poor financial state. Each had its own Board of Directors and chief officers that served only to add to costs and duplicate effort. Complaints and bills were frequently passed amongst them - each denying responsibility. A first attempt at amalgamation in 1875 has been mentioned but the matter surfaced again in 1877 when the South Western and Brighton companies agreed to build a railway at Ryde from the IWR station at St Johns Road to the pier. Discussions between various individuals and representatives of the mainland companies took place on several occasions during the late 1870s and early 1880s when proposals to lease or purchase the Island companies were put forward on both sides only to be rejected. Following an exchange of letters during October 1882 concerning a proposal to lease the CNR, RNR and IWNJ, the LSWR included clauses in a Bill before the next Parliamentary session for the necessary powers. However, the Island companies refused to hold meetings of their shareholders, claiming that no acceptable agreement had been reached, and the proposal was abandoned.

The next scheme for amalgamation was put forward in 1884 by Roderick MacKay, a Director of the RNR and an auditor for the IWR. A Bill was placed before Parliament in the 1885 session proposing to amalgamate the CNR, RNR, IWNJ and IWR; it also included powers to sell or lease the railways to the LSWR and LBSCR. Firstly provisions relating to the IWR were taken out of the Bill whilst negotiations amongst the other three companies continued in the hope of reaching a settlement; in June 1885 the Bill was withdrawn after the IWNJ demanded an arrangement unacceptable to the other companies.

In October 1886 William Abbott, a London stock and share broker, announced that he had been encouraged to embark on fresh negotiations for amalgamation by some of the larger stock holders. He was joined by Roderick MacKay and supported by the *Financial Times*. The Isle of Wight Railways Bill that appeared before the next Parliamentary session proposed to bring together the CNR, RNR, IWNJ, IWR and the railway of the BHIR company. Clauses relating to the IWR and BHIR were soon deleted but the IWR nevertheless petitioned Parliament in opposition to the Bill.

Horace Tahourdin, the IWR Chairman, gave evidence to a committee of the House of Commons on 29th June, 1887. He claimed that it had always been intended that the IWR would work the IWNJ and although this had not come about, the IWR Manager had managed the line. He commented that 'it was a great misfortune to the Island that both those lines [the RNR and IWNJ] should have been granted' and implied that the amalgamated company would reduce or discontinue the service between Ryde and Newport. The IWR wanted clauses inserted in the Bill which obliged the new company to agree through passenger and goods rates via Sandown and run a minimum number of trains between Newport and Ryde - this was to safeguard IWR income from the use of Ryde station. Under cross examination he gave as good as he got:

> . . . those lines at present are in an utter state of disrepair, their carriages are rotten and ready to fall to pieces almost; they have to be continually patched up and kept together. The whole business is worked as badly as it could possibly be, and certainly under one management I do expect that they will put their lines in a good state of order, renew their carriages, and have a considerable economy in working their line properly.

T. Dolling Bolton, the IWNJ Chairman, then appeared before the committee. He stated that the amalgamated companies could not close the RNR without the sanction of the Board of Trade nor did they intend to do so. They sought economies by the creation of one Board (although only one of the three companies paid Directors' fees), Secretary, solicitor, etc. After deliberation, the committee ordered the insertion of clauses to require the running of at least seven passenger trains a day (except Sundays) between Ryde and Newport. The Bill creating the Isle of Wight Central Railway became law on 19th July, 1887 - the company name was settled only a few weeks earlier.

The IWR promoted its own Bill before the same session of Parliament following discussions between the IWR and IWNJ Boards. Entitled the Isle of Wight Railways (Amalgamation and Transfer) Bill, it differed by including the Shanklin & Chale and Freshwater, Yarmouth & Newport railways and permitted the lease or sale of all the Island railways to the LSWR and LBSCR. The Bill met with opposition and was withdrawn after the IWNJ alleged that the interests of debenture holders were not sufficiently protected - one IWNJ Director held a significant number of debentures. The passing of the IWC Act was followed by a sudden drop in the value of IWR shares although *The Standard* said: 'The fall registered yesterday in that stock seems to have been the result of a mere trick, and it has been impossible today to buy the stock at the lower quotation'. The IWR Chairman claimed that the scare had been designed to benefit the CNR, RNR and IWNJ at his company's expense - small wonder the animosity that coloured relations was destined to continue.

The Isle of Wight Central Railway Act authorised the creation of the company with a Board of six Directors: John Winterbottom Batten, Thomas Dolling Bolton, Henry Daniel Martin, Roderick MacKay, Percy Mortimer and Andrew Gibson Gibson. The majority of the Act was given over to a listing of the terms by which holders of shares, debentures and other debts of the three companies would receive shares and debentures in the undertaking. The CNR, IWNJ and RNR together paid over £14,500 a year in debenture interest but, by rearranging the capital, the IWC reduced this to just over £10,000. There was an additional liability of £400 a year in rent charges granted by the IWNJ and RNR to various landowners. The total cost of the amalgamation was quoted as £1,037 11s. 1d. although this probably excluded some of the legal fees. The company came into being on 1st July, 1887.

Henry Martin held the majority of the CNR shares and debentures and was a clear beneficiary because his CNR ordinary and Preference shares were exchanged for debentures. Next in priority were the IWNJ shareholders leaving holders of the RNR shares at the bottom of the pile. Thomas Bolton, Chairman of the IWNJ, became Chairman of the IWC; he had (in 1886) become the Liberal Member of Parliament for North East Derbyshire and at various times was a member of Windsor town council, where he lived, Chairman of Neuchatel Asphalte Company and a Director of the Brecon & Merthyr Junction Railway, the Worksop Waterworks Company and others - quite an active individual.

Almost all meetings of the Board and the six-monthly meetings of shareholders were held at 3 Lothbury, London, the offices of the Secretary Mr Beard. A feature of the Chairmanship of Thomas Bolton was the insistence that every matter be put in writing; a Board meeting would consist of a reading of numerous letters to which the Secretary had to write replies. Attendance by the Manager or his staff was positively discouraged and personal contact between the Manager and Board was sporadic. The Board's preoccupation was with money - or rather, a lack of it. On several occasions the Manager was instructed to provide additional information or obtain tenders, sometimes more than once, that had to be studied and discussed before any decision was reached. A consequence might be an instruction to order fewer wagons than were needed leading to a further request a few months later. Contacts between the Board and management were not, however, as remote as these arrangements imply. At least one of the Directors was usually an Island resident and the Chairman made frequent inspections, sometimes accompanied by a fellow Director. The visits cannot always have been happy events as the Board occasionally found fault with a matter on which the Manager had been pressing them for months. This parsimonious attitude spread to the Central's dealings with other railway companies, local organisations and the population.

The first meeting of the Board took place in London on 17th July, 1887 when the Directors resolved to re-appoint the existing Manager and Secretary to their posts; Frank Stileman remained Engineer but he died in 1889 as did Roderick MacKay. A new seal had been made, the design of which was similar to that used by the IWNJ. Herbert Simmons was asked to prepare a detailed report summarising economies effected and possible, an estimate of what capital expenditure was necessary and how the traffic would be worked. Realising that a tight control of money was critical to the company, a Finance committee was created; there was also a short-lived Works committee. On 18th September, 1887, after a decision was made to transfer the traffic audit work from the Secretary's office in London to the Island, George Henley was appointed chief audit clerk on a salary of £110 per annum - he had been with the IWR since 1870 and worked in the General Manager's office before moving to the IWC. A month later the Board decided to employ a Mr Crowford in Mr Henley's office and '. . . the lad from the Isle of Wight Railway's office . . . at 12s. per week'. The salary of Mr Simmons, the manager, had risen to £350 per annum.

The next months were mainly taken up with the issue of shares and debentures. An agreement was made in December 1887 with Sir Richard Webster for the issue of £931 'B' debenture stock in exchange for the abolition of rent for sidings at Alverstone, Merstone, Blackwater and Newchurch - he also got a free pass. A number of debts were settled, particularly those in respect of locomotives and rolling stock.

Surprisingly, the Minutes contained no reference to the adoption of standard colours for the new company's stations, locomotives, etc. - perhaps there had been an element of standardisation prior to 1887. By the 1890s stations were liveried in a red colour that was similar to that carried by IWC locomotives. Photographs of Cowes and Newport stations taken at the turn of the century show that platform coverings were painted in stripes, probably red and cream. This would give weight to a statement in the *Railway Magazine* that railmotor No. 1 was in 'the railway's standard colours' when delivered in 1906 and in direct contrast to the impression that the Central was wedded to black, a colour that made its appearance on locomotives only after 1911.

The company inherited a number of working agreements from its predecessors, including two with the IWR for the use of the stations at Sandown and Ryde. In December 1887 a new agreement permitted the IWC joint use of Sandown station for 21 years from 31st December, 1884 at a rent of £350 per annum. The IWR undertook to pay the wages of staff at the station, employ signalmen to work the points and signals, paint and maintain the station 'Provided that if the Overbridge at the said Station or the roof over the platform used by the Central Company shall require renewal during the terms of this agreement the expenses of such renewal shall be borne jointly by the Companies'. In a reference to past disputes, the IWR also agreed to '. . . provide and supply oil and grease for the station points . . . and shall also clean one train of carriages daily of the Central Company running into Sandown Station'. IWC staff had to observe IWR rules when in the station and 'The Isle of Wight Company shall be responsible for any accident that may happen through the neglect, default or omission of their servants'.

An agreement to pay rent for use of the station at Ryde proved more difficult to achieve, and in December 1888 the IWC Board threatened to take the dispute to the Railway & Canal Commissioners in an attempt to win a fair settlement. The Railway Commissioners had a busy time dealing with Isle of Wight matters as the IWR secured a ruling in June 1888 that equal rates had to be charged between Ryde and Cowes, Mill Hill, Newport and Shide by either Smallbrook or Sandown. The IWC unsuccessfully tried to secure equal rates to Ventnor via Sandown or Ryde.

The Central inherited a commitment that it might have preferred to do without. In 1880 the Freshwater, Yarmouth & Newport Railway obtained an Act for a railway connecting the western end of the Island with Newport. The Directors had no connections with other railways and several years passed before anything tangible was achieved. On 5th March, 1886 a provisional agreement was signed with the CNR and RNR whereby the CNR, presumably as the senior partner in the Joint Committee, undertook to work the line if it was completed before 26th August, 1888. Major General Hutchinson on behalf of the Board of Trade made inspections in May and June 1889 but could not sanction opening because the working agreement had lapsed. The railway finally opened to passengers on 11th July, 1889 after a reluctant IWC agreed to staff and operate the line as part of its system for 55 per cent of gross receipts provided the Freshwater company maintained the structures and permanent way.

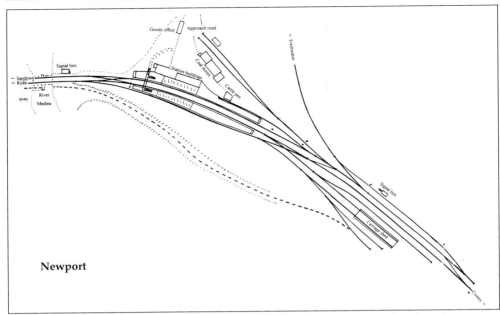

This track plan of Newport *circa* 1889 shows alterations made to accommodate the railway to Freshwater. Within two years there were more additions in the shape of a locomotive shed and workshop.

Track plan of Cowes in 1892.

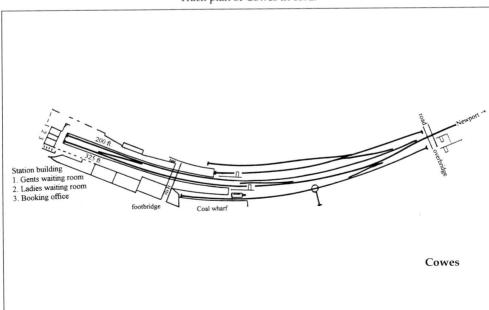

Mr Elliott Cooper, the Engineer, prepared drawings for a brick-based water tower, the Board complained about the cost and he was told that '. . . what was wanted was a timber construction with a tank above'; in the end they compromised by having a steel tank atop an angle iron frame! The station was inspected by Major Addison in June 1895; his report read:

At Merstone (Sandown to Newport line), the junction with the Merstone, Godshill and Ventnor Raily, a new station has been built; with an island platform and good accommodation and conveniences for both sexes. The access to the Station is at present very bad, but a subway is about to be constructed to improve matter: this will require to be inspected when completed. The general arrangement of the station was, I understand, approved by Genl Hutchinson before the work was commenced. The signal cabin contains 28 levers, all in use, and they are correctly interlocked. There is also a wheel, in the cabin, to work the gates of the level crossing.

The transfer of the locomotive shed and workshops to Newport coupled with alterations at Cowes permitted several changes in the pattern of services. Newport became the centre of operations and passenger trains would depart or arrive within minutes of each other for Cowes, Ryde, Sandown and Freshwater. The Ryde, Sandown and Freshwater lines generally had a single train shuttling to and fro although a train from Sandown might continue to Freshwater or vice versa; every other Ryde train ran through to Cowes. During July and August 1894 there was an extra return trip from Newport to Ryde at lunch times and early evenings, crossing at Ashey; it might be the same train that worked to Freshwater during the afternoon. Naturally there were fewer trains outside the peak season but the reductions were not drastic and the number of locomotives in steam cannot have been much less than in the summer. Journey times from Newport averaged 15 minutes to Cowes and 30 minutes to Ryde or Sandown; trains stopped by signal or prior notice to the guard at Ashey, Whippingham and sometimes Haven Street on the Ryde line and Blackwater, Horringford, Newchurch and Alverstone on the Sandown line. Depending on the capabilities of the locomotive, wagons were attached to the rear of passenger trains. The best of the Central's stock worked a through train between Freshwater and Ryde.

Passenger services were publicised by means of large poster timetables containing views of attractions served by the railway. Tables listed the times of trains on each of the company's lines, and connections with the ferries and trains to and from London via the LSWR and LBSCR. Third class tickets were available for travel on very few trains but during the summer months excursion fares were offered to tempt visitors and residents alike. From 1st June, 1892 weekly 'tourist' tickets were introduced giving unlimited travel over the IWC and FYN for 10s. first class or 7s. 6d. second; again, the IWC seems to have been the first railway in the country to offer this facility. In March 1893 the IWR got in on the act when IWR stations could be included for 16s. first and 12s. 6d. second class.

Before the 1890s Britain's railways charged a bewildering array of goods rates set out in about 900 Acts of Parliament; the IWC alone had three different sets of charges laid down in the Acts of its predecessors. This discouraged traffic and inevitably there were calls for a rationalisation of rates and the creation of commissioners to settle disputes between railways and traders. In 1888 the Railway & Canal Commissioners came into being and soon afterwards the Board of Trade drew up revised schedules of charges for incorporation in confirmation Acts - a common set of rates applying to all railways in the Isle of Wight became law in 1892.

By 1887 ownership of Ashey Quarry had passed into the hands of Andrew Gibson, George Young's son-in-law; he complained in April 1888 of a want of trucks, to which the Board responded that it would help if he could arrange for a steady production of chalk. The quarry seems by then to have been largely worked out and Ashey was soon eclipsed by another source of supply; the quarry fell into disuse during the 1890s.

During 1892 there was correspondence concerning the provision of a siding at Shide for J. W. Alexander, a gravel, sand and builder's merchant who leased a pit there. Despite not receiving a guarantee that Mr Alexander would give the railway sufficient traffic to justify its construction, Mr Simmons was authorised to go ahead with its provision. This was in marked contrast to an entry 10 years previously when Mr Martin did not consider it advisable '. . . to make a fresh siding' there. By 19th October, 1893 traffic was evidently passing in quantity as complaints were made about the Central's inability to supply enough trucks; although the matter went to the Railway & Canal Commissioners, they could only recommend that the complainant provide his own wagons. In 1895 Charles Francis Son & Co. leased part of the chalk pit at Shide and on 30th January concluded an agreement with the IWC for the haulage of chalk in the cement company's wagons from the pit to the mills at a rate of 5d. a ton, subject to a guaranteed traffic of 30,000 tons a year. Trains had to consist of a minimum of six wagons and the Central was under no obligation to carry out any shunting at either end of the journey. A spur was laid from the railway's siding uphill through a deep cutting and a short tunnel into the pit itself; at the cement mills an existing siding was extended and a run-round loop provided. In practice, the locomotive propelled loaded wagons from Shide to the mills, often with a goods train in tow. The cement company amalgamated with 26 others in 1900 to form Associated Portland Cement Manufacturers Ltd.

Receipts from passenger and goods traffic had grown steadily. The formation of the IWC had been followed by reductions in management costs but the company's financial performance was still inferior to the IWR and most mainland companies. (From 1889 the figures included the FYN.)

Year ending 31 Dec.	Passenger traffic Numbers carried			Goods traffic		Gross receipts		Working expenses	% of expenditure in relation
	First	Second	Third	Minerals Tons	General Tons	Pass. £	Goods £	£	to receipts
1887	28,432	217,737	189,833	70,423	20,905	16,017	8,287	15,434	64
1890	36,124	221,266	404,563	76,816	24,637	23,683	9,938	19,270	57
1895	33,575	238,043	385,538	97,159	30,457	25,056	11,482	26,380	62

A reason for the company's difficulties was the condition of the permanent way inherited from its predecessors:

Company	Year	Rail length	weight	pattern	fixings
CNR	1862	18 and 21 ft	60 lb.	FB iron	spikes and bolts
IWNJ	1872	about 16 ft	72 lb.	DH iron	cast iron chairs
IWNJ	1875	not known	not known	Vignolles FB iron	spikes and fang bolts
RNR	1875	24 ft	72 lb.	FB wrought iron	fang bolts

FB = flat bottom, DH = double headed (similar to bull head).

Permanent way renewals had been carried out on the CNR in 1878, a few steel rails had been laid on the sharply curved IWNJ viaduct at Newport and more were purchased by the IWNJ during the early 1880s. Of the remainder, the company could not afford a wholesale replacement of the permanent way and renewals had to be spread over many years. When Col Sir John M. Burgoyne complained to the Board of Trade in October 1894 about the state of the rails between Cowes and Newport, Herbert Simmons reported that since December 1893 1 mile 24 chains of track had been relaid, making 11 miles 26½ chains renewed and leaving 9 miles 23 chains to be attended to. Pressure from the Board of Trade forced the company to place further orders in 1894 and 1895, but this had such a disastrous effect on the finances that in February 1895 the IWC had to issue Lloyds Bonds to the suppliers of rails and wagons in part payment of their bills. Given that many of the locomotives and rolling stock were also worn out, it was hardly surprising that the railway had an appalling reputation in the eyes of the local community. We shall read more of this in the next chapter.

Chapter Ten

Accidents, Complaints and the Board of Trade - The 1890s

On 12th June, 1889 an event took place near Armagh in Ireland that had a profound effect on Britain's railways, including the IWC. An excursion train stalled on a steep gradient but after the train was divided the rear portion ran back and collided at speed with a following train killing 80 people. Such was the accident's effect on public opinion that on 30th August, 1889 legislation was passed giving the Railway Department of the Board of Trade powers to order companies to improve their railways for public safety. Francis Beard, the IWC Secretary, wrote to the Board of Trade asking for time to satisfy the requirements of the Act and claiming that the company was in a 'pecuniary position' '. . . the average mileage run is about 2¼ miles and the running is at a very slow speed averaging barely 17 miles per hour, further the trains consist of only three ordinary carriages one of which is a composite brake carriage'.

In an order issued in 1890, the Board of Trade told the company to install block working on all lines within two years; six months later they had to complete the interlocking of points and signals along with the fitting of continuous brakes to locomotives and rolling stock used in passenger trains. Mixed trains had to stop at all stations, could not exceed 25 mph, consist of no more than 25 vehicles and carriages had to precede wagons with a brake van at the rear.

The IWC Directors had no money to spare for work that would not bring any additional income to the railway and it was several years before they could be persuaded to make the improvements demanded by the Board of Trade. The company's attitude to the provision of continuous brakes had been known as long ago as 1880: '. . . as no efficient brake had been discovered, nor had the Board of Trade recommended one, the Company were at a loss to select one'; they possessed a few NLR carriages fitted with a primitive chain brake but that was more by accident than design. Some LBSCR carriages carried the Westinghouse brake when purchased in October 1889 and this prompted the Board to resolve that the railway adopt the brake, if and when it possessed the necessary capital.

The fallacy of the company's attitude to safety can be seen in a series of accidents that peppered its history during this time. On 21st April, 1888 the *Isle of Wight County Press* mentioned an incident that took place at Merstone the previous Saturday night. After the regular passenger service ended an extra goods train was dispatched from Newport but the intermediate stations were not informed and the train demolished the crossing gates at Merstone. The deputy coroner called an inquest at Wootton following an incident on 19th May when a passenger train heading for Ryde knocked down and killed an 80-year-old man who was crossing the line at Woodhouse crossing; a verdict of accidental death was recorded. On 6th April, 1889 Newport magistrates fined the company for delaying the vessels *David* and *Swift* for an hour and 40 minutes before opening the bridge to allow them to pass. In retaliation, on 25th September, 1889 the Board considered prosecuting the captain of a vessel that delayed the train service; they bided their time until 29th September, 1892 when the vessel *Orlando* grounded under the bridge - a prosecution of the owners gained damages and costs for stopping trains on the Ryde line.

On 13th August, 1889 passengers on the 2.40 pm mixed passenger and goods train between Newport and Ryde were 'alarmed' when an axle of coal wagon No. 24 broke beyond Ashey derailing some wagons. The *Isle of Wight Herald* published details of a more serious accident at Cowes on 7th September:

A very alarming accident occurred on Saturday afternoon last at the Cowes Railway Station, and it is remarkable that no fatalities or injuries to life or limb were caused thereby. It appears that five carriages which were to form the train from Cowes to Newport at 2.40 pm were being run down the incline into the station as is usual, but on the guard (named Williams) proceeding to apply the brake, he found that it would not act, and the carriages therefore ran into the station with considerable speed. Seeing the danger, Williams jumped out of the brake van onto the platform, and the carriages dashed against the buffers at the High Street end of the station, and having demolished this obstruction, they ran on until the front carriage struck the wall at the top of the staircase leading to the street where it reared partially on end, smashing the clock and some of the station woodwork. Part of the carriage was left hanging over the staircase with its top forming an incline back to the rails. The van from which the guard jumped was crushed entirely out of shape, and if he remained in the carriage he must have been killed or terribly injured. The body of the carriage was torn away from the underframe. The Station Master, Mr Greenwood, at once set a gang of men under Mr Hindmarsh to clear away the wreck, and the other carriages having been run out of the station, the injured one was covered in tarpaulins, and the station reopened. Late in the evening, the debris was entirely cleared away, and by a little manoeuvring all traces of the accident was put out of sight. It was a mercy no-one was injured, as several people were standing on the side platform, and a number are generally to be found where the smash-up occurred. A passenger for the boat was going downstairs at the time, and was very much frightened by the occurrence. Some years ago a similar incident took place (although not to the same extent), and then the bookstall, which used to stand at the top of the stairs, was knocked down and the contents sent flying in all directions.

In October 1889 a goods brake van ran away and demolished the crossing gates at Alverstone. The crank axle of the locomotive *Precursor* broke on 31st December, 1889 just beyond Newchurch whilst working the 8.30 Sandown to Newport train. Three heifers strayed onto the railway near Haven Street on 28th June and although the driver of the 12.40 pm train from Ryde slowed down he knocked one down that had to be finished off by the station master - it was not said how!

Not all publicity was negative as the *Isle of Wight County Press* mentioned the satisfactory running of three special trains, the first of which ran on 11th February, 1888 from Whippingham to Ventnor and back for the opening of the National Consumption Hospital:

Driving from Osborne to Whippingham Station, where a carpeted footway had been laid down from the carriageway to the platform, the Queen entered the special train made up of an engine, five carriages and a guard's van belonging to the Isle of Wight Railway Company. With the Queen were HRH Princess Beatrice, and Princess Victoria of Schleswig-Holstein, with the Countess of Errol, Miss M. Cochrane and Miss Fitzroy in attendance.

The train was in the charge of Mr H. Simmons, the manager of the Isle of Wight Central Railway as far as St Johns Road, when Mr Day, the newly appointed manager of the Isle of Wight Railway took over the direction . . . [19th February, 1888]

Despite the pouring rain which interfered with the traffic on the day of the Cowes Town Regatta (11th August), as many as 22,633 passengers were carried on the Isle of Wight Central Railway, and receipts amounted to £968 for the week. [17th August, 1889]

On Tuesday morning (18th February) HRH Prince Henry of Battenburg left Mill Hill Station by special train for Wroxall. The train, which was in charge of Mr Herbert Simmons, was made up of two new saloon carriages, and we understand that His Royal Highness was satisfied with the arrangements. PC Targett was on duty at the station, but as the train left at 9 o'clock, the event was not known to any beyond Mr Thomas, the Station Master, and the officials. [22nd February, 1890]

In 1891 it was the turn of the elements to disrupt services. The *County Press* reported:

The very severe blizzard which caused widespread disruption throughout the South West caused considerable inconvenience to the Central Railway. The last train from Sandown to Newport on 9th March became stuck in a snowdrift near Merstone. Fortunately there were only about six passengers, and these were accommodated in the Station Master's premises at Merstone - the first time such an occurrence has ever happened on the line. Two engines were dispatched from Newport to Merstone to dig out the disabled train, and the leading engine derailed on hitting the drift. The train was dug out overnight, and the engines and train eventually reached Newport about 9.00 am. The clearing gang then returned to Merstone, and the line was reopened through to Sandown at about 11.00 am. The Ryde and Cowes lines had also been blocked, and these reopened about 11.00 am. [14th March, 1891]

An accident occurred to the 7.37 pm train from Newport on Tuesday evening [13th October] last. Nearly the whole train left the rails at a point shortly before Marvel. In consequence of the storms the river was in full flood. A distance of 100 yards was covered before the train could pull up. It was found that 15 carriage wheels and three engine wheels were off the rails. Fortunately, the train remained on the sleepers, otherwise it would have overturned into seven or eight feet of water. There were no injuries but it was a very narrow escape. [17th October, 1891]

On 7th November, 1891 the 10.30 am Newport to Ryde mixed train was delayed when a wagon left the rails near Whippingham. In 1892 the IWC Board agreed to contribute two guineas to a subscription for an employee of Pring Bros, who had his right arm amputated following an accident at Medina Jetty. A slight collision at Newport on 1st August, 1892 passed by almost without comment but on 15th October the *County Press* reported a more serious derailment of an evening goods train on the nearby viaduct:

Last evening an alarming accident occurred . . . the train consisted of six loaded trucks drawn by the locomotive *Precursor*. One of the rails just beyond the points and about 20 yards before the parapet of the bridge gave way, snapping about a yard from the end as the engine passed over it. The engine was naturally thrown onto the permanent way and proceeded about 40 yards before it could be stopped. The engine was now on the drawbridge and sank into the woodwork up to the level of the axles. Fortunately, the engine, which weighs about 16 tons was over one of the massive longitudinal girders which run under the length of the rails, and this alone prevented it being precipitated into the river. Five trucks left the rails with the engine.

No real attempts were made to comply with the Regulation of Railways Act except at Sandown where the IWR had responsibility for alterations at the station, subject to agreement with the IWC. In addition to the construction of a junction at the southern end of the station, the IWR also thought it necessary to widen the island platform, provide new signalling and replace the wooden footbridge with a subway. Who paid for the improvements was not agreed as in 1889 the IWC claimed it was liable only for renewals and on 21st October, 1891 went so far as to declare it did not approve of any of the proposed changes. Second thoughts prevailed and after a meeting of the two managers on 28th September, 1892 the IWC agreed to contribute £862, including £210 for the southern junction and £147 for an island platform covering and waiting room.

The reason for the Central's delay was, of course, a lack of finance. This should not have been a problem because companies were given powers to raise additional capital subject to the approval of the Board of Trade. The IWC Board discussed the matter on several occasions during 1892 when the sum needed was repeatedly revised upwards. On 14th June, 1893 the Secretary wrote to the Board of Trade asking for authority to raise £7,355 by the issue of 'A' debenture stock for equipping 22 miles of line with the Electric Block system, interlocking points and signals at 10 stations, and fitting continuous brakes to seven locomotives, 40 carriages plus four carriage and cattle trucks. The dilatoriness of the IWC in applying for the capital was noted and they were asked to explain how much progress had been made. On 23rd August Mr Beard repeated that the company possessed no unissued capital and could only fund improvements out of income generated from working the railway. This had the desired effect, the issue of the additional capital was authorised and it was placed with investors in October.

In view of the length of time since the passing of the Act, the IWC was asked to send in monthly progress reports but they were tardy in coming and not to the liking of the Board of Trade. In February 1894 the Secretary managed to confuse everyone by adding several stations to his previous lists of those awaiting upgrading. Two locomotives, 21 carriages plus three carriage and cattle trucks then had continuous brakes. A month later the fitting of continuous brakes '. . . has now been completed' to the relief of all concerned.

There had been no let up in the numbers of mishaps. A ballast wagon left the rails between Wootton and Newport on 28th February, 1893; later that year 'mischievous boys' unchained a number of wagons in Ashey quarry and let them run away onto the main line where they collided with a locomotive pulling a ballast train. In August there was an '. . . accident to a man named Osborne at Cowes on the evening of Friday 11th caused by him falling from the platform under the train and sustaining injuries which necessitated the amputation of his left arm' - he was later refused any compensation. Two heifers were killed by a train between Newchurch and Alverstone on 21st March, 1894 for which the farmer accepted £20.

Given the forgoing, it was hardly surprising that there were frequent letters of complaint to the local newspapers. Allegations were made that the company was a bye-word for mismanagement, high fares, unpunctuality and the appalling state of the rolling stock that was badly lit and sometimes leaky - 'the dustbin on wheels' as one writer put it. Some of the myths perpetuated about the company were quite comical in their telling; the need to wait at Ashey whilst the 'stick' was brought from Newport by horseback is well known, but there was also the legend of the dog that fell out of a carriage at Whippingham but was waiting for its master when the train arrived at Haven Street!

The Central's problems had also reached the ears of Island politicians. In January 1893 the *Isle of Wight County Press* reported a meeting of Newport Borough Council when it was said that second class passengers were being unfairly treated as their carriages were used to carry those paying third class. Later reports mentioned the overcrowding and decrepit carriages that were no better than the trucks and vans! Local newspapers published the admission that the IWC was running mixed passenger and goods trains. Since none had been authorised by the Board of Trade, there ensued a further bout of correspondence until July 1894 when the running of mixed trains was authorised; there were usually three a day each way on weekdays and one on Sundays.

Estimates for the provision of block working had been obtained in April 1893 but the Board deferred a decision because of the cost. The IWR was aware of this and wrote to the Board of Trade asking if the delay had been sanctioned. When the IWC was asked for its comments, on 24th October, 1894 Mr Beard curtly replied: 'I was instructed to inform you in reply that they cannot see any reason why your Board should give the information to the Isle of Wight Railway Coy who have always been hostile to this Compy; nor do my Directors understand on what ground the Isle of Wight Ry are entitled to the information asked for'.

Dr Dabbs, a prominent Shanklin medical practitioner, persuaded the Isle of Wight County Council to set up a special committee to investigate the state of the railway under its powers in Section 15 of the Local Government Act. Speaking years later, he commented that when passengers '. . . left home in the morning they never knew how much money they would want, as the fares seemed to be altered daily, and the trains seldom ran to time'. In a report to the County Council on 21st November, 1894 the committee listed the following complaints:

1. The general feeling of the public that the permanent way was in an unsatisfactory condition and rolling stock was insufficient.
2. The regulation of the bridge over Newport Town Quay was not worked to suit the general wants of the public and traders.
3. The structural state of the railway jetty at Shamblers was unsatisfactory.
4. A survey and general inspection of the permanent way and stock by a proper qualified Engineer was urgently needed.
5. The management of the Freshwater line in connection with the Newport and Cowes line was unsatisfactory.
6. The passenger footbridge erected at Newport Station was a source of annoyance and danger to passengers because it had no covering to keep out the rain.
7. The approach road to Newport Station was kept in an imperfect state.
8. The fares charged were unequal, there were insufficient third class and Parliamentary trains and that the market train fares should be reduced to their original charge.
9. The charges were inconsistent and unfair to the public generally.
10. Delays occurred at Newport and other stations because goods trucks were being hauled by passenger trains.
11. The train service to Yarmouth in connection with the Lymington boats was inadequate and failed to meet the requirements of the public travelling to or from the mainland by that route.

One does wonder just what, in the opinion of the Council, the railway was doing right! The Central Chairman, Thomas Bolton, took a robust attitude by demanding dates and events as proof of the company's wrongdoing. It should be borne in mind that the complaints coincided with the creation in 1894 of the County Council and Urban District Councils in the more important towns - the IWC was a sitting target for aspiring politicians. It seems more than coincidence that in May 1894 market fares were increased to help offset demands for rates from the councils. Market fares, first introduced by the IWNJ, had become a veritable institution by the manner in which they encouraged traffic to the twice-weekly market at Newport; even the most minor station would be crowded with local people anxious to experience an uncomfortable journey aboard one of the Central's trains.

In January 1895 Cowes UDC complained that the rolling stock and permanent way might be greatly improved, foot warmers were not provided and the arrangements at Shamblers and Smithards crossings were unsatisfactory. The crossing at Shamblers was not protected whilst at Smithards the road traffic was being obstructed '. . . as there was only a woman in charge'. On 11th May a meeting took place between the IWC Board and a sub-committee from Newport Corporation. The complaints repeated those expressed by the County Council but with special emphasis on Newport matters. Mr Bolton again demanded specific instances and maintained that Medina Jetty was perfectly safe! In the face of such a performance the committee went away empty handed. The IWC Board could not be so dismissive towards the Board of Trade and the Secretary wrote to explain that construction of the Newport, Godshill & St Lawrence Railway (*see Chapter Twelve*) had delayed progress in complying with the 1889 Act. It was estimated the work would be completed within three months so another extension of time was granted.

On 8th January, 1895 an accident between Alverstone and Sandown brought the railway's dubious working practices to the attention of the Board of Trade. A special goods train of four wagons was dispatched from Newport to Sandown at 7.40 am, 10 minutes in advance of the normal passenger train. The goods train had been due to leave at 7.30 but was delayed as the relief guard was late coming on duty. It seems a separate goods train was necessary because the available motive power was incapable of pulling a mixed train of just three carriages and four wagons! Despite an undertaking that the line would be worked with one engine in steam, the IWC was actually using the Staff and Ticket system but in the absence of a telegraph at all stations it also operated the time interval system. The rule book explained: 'At stations where the signal telegraph is not in use . . . the danger signal is to be shown for five minutes after the departure or passing of each train or engine, in order to stop any following engine or train. After this time had elapsed a caution signal will be exhibited for five minutes more, to complete a ten minutes precautionary signal'.

Such was the poor condition of the goods engine, thought to be No. 3, that it was unable to pull all four wagons up the 1 in 54 gradient approaching Sandown station. The train was split and the first two wagons were placed into the sidings at the station. An IWR porter, who was in charge of shunting, arranged for a wagon loaded with cans of oil to be drawn out and run back onto the wagons on the main line setting them off downhill in the direction of Alverstone. Although the oil wagon was stopped, the others careered into a three-coach passenger train drawn by locomotive No 1. The *Isle of Wight County Press* added:

Fortunately, the driver was appraised of the danger, and was able to stop before the impact . . . The passengers obeyed the instructions to stay in their seats, and prepared for the shock of the collision . . . The force of the impact was considerable, and a number of the passengers were badly knocked about and shaken, several seriously enough to require medical attention . . . Mr C. Varty of Newport sustained head injuries and has required medical treatment ever since, and Mrs Watson of the same town received such injuries that medical treatment was necessary.

The IWC Board attempted to pass the blame onto the IWR but after a futile exchange of letters, counsel's opinion was obtained and £15 7s. 6d. paid to injured passengers. Two men who warned the driver of the passenger train each received £1 and it cost another £16 3s. 9d. to repair the rolling stock. In his report on the accident Major Addison, the Board of Trade Inspector, stated:

> The omission of a brake van for goods trains of less than six wagons is contrary to custom, and is a most dangerous practice . . . In the absence of proper modes of working, and proper rules for the instruction and guidance of the Company's servant, I am not disposed to put any blame for this collision on the man in charge of operations which led up to it . . . the Company had not adopted the Clearing House rules for management of railways and their book of rules contained none of the usual precautions . . .

To make matters worse, just months later on 30th March, 1895 the 1 pm passenger train was derailed shortly after leaving Newport for Freshwater. It was already an hour late owing to an engine failure on the Sandown line from whence the train had come. This time a carriage left the rails because of the poor condition of the permanent way, the responsibility of the FYN. The IWC did not escape criticism as the Inspector considered the hours of duty of staff to be excessive: the driver came on duty at 7.50 am and was due to work until 9.40 pm whilst the guard was expected to work from 7.15 am to 10.30 pm. The Regulation of Railways Act 1893 placed restrictions on the working hours of guards, but Herbert Simmons had neither submitted returns to the Board of Trade nor made any attempt to comply with the legislation. The IWC took the hint and at the next shareholders' meeting on 28th August, 1895 it was announced that: 'The decrease in passenger receipts is mainly attributable to the long and severe winter. The increase in expenditure is mainly due to relaying various portions of the permanent way, to necessary repairs to engines, and to the increase in wages necessitated by the employment of extra men owing to the agitation for shorter hours of duty'.

Major Addison visited the Island and made an inspection of the IWC to see what progress had been made in satisfying the requirements of the Regulation of Railways Act. On 25th June, 1895 he noted that absolute block working had just been introduced between Cowes, Newport and Sandown linked to the Staff and Ticket system. The interlocking of points and signals at the smaller stations had not been brought up to modern Board of Trade standards and in several places the permanent way was in poor condition - at least the new crossing loop at Merstone was ready for use. In a note to his staff, Major Addison wrote that the company had no response to 'the serious defects . . . the only way to get anything done by this Coy is to keep pegging away at them!' This time the Board of Trade was successful as in October 1895 the IWC Board considered tenders for the work necessary to bring the interlocking of points and signals up to date: A tender from the Railway Signal Company was accepted after Mr Simmons had beaten them down to £1,178 18s. 3d.

The catalogue of accidents continued. The IWC paid the funeral expenses of a labourer killed at Newport on 10th July. The 'discovery of a large hole in the middle of the line between Cement Mills and Newport' in August probably did not come to the ears of the Board of Trade, but another incident at Newport on 20th November certainly did. Part of Lt Col Addison's (he had been promoted) report read:

> On the 20th ult., the bridge of the Ryde line had remained shut for some hours and had been passed over by several trains previous to the accident, but when a light engine came to a stand upon the bridge the latter went down at one end and it was found that the cams had moved i.e. lowered themselves whilst the stud on the locking lever (from the Signal Box), which fits into a slot in the boss of the cam when the latter is raised was broken off.
>
> It is impossible to say for certain how this occurred, but it clearly shows some alteration to be necessary and there is evident defects in the present arrangements. When trying the other bridge I found that, owing to defects, the locking lever could be moved and the signals thus released before the cams were in position. The electrical contact, for the completion of the block circuit I also found to be made before the cams were absolutely in the proper position for trains to run over the bridge.

another, passed to his two surviving sisters. A similar link can be seen in the Gibson family who were descendants of George Young. In 1899 Lt Col John H.C. Harrison RE became a Director but two years later the death was reported of John Batten.

There was a continuing need to spend considerable sums on rebuilding bridges, most of which were wooden structures dating from the opening of the railways; in April 1898 a culvert near Dodnor collapsed and had to be completely rebuilt. Such was the expense during that year that the repainting of bridges at Granville (on the approaches to Cowes station), Cement Mills and Pinnocks (an underbridge at Binfield) was deferred; only that at Coppins Bridge was done as its condition was giving cause for concern. It was not the only one because in January 1899 the Chairman, when inspecting the railway, ordered that Granville and Fatting Park bridges be dismantled because they were unsafe. The removal of the bridge at Fatting Park caused the most problems: at first the company tried to avoid building a replacement but the local authority refused to permit this and, after encountering the Central's usual delaying tactics, took court action. In May the Board accepted a tender from Mr Firbank for £543 8s. 2d. but had cause to regret it because it did not include the cost of building the abutments. Although the bridge seems to have been completed by the end of the year, a dispute with the contractor over the extra work delayed payment of his £780 bill until June 1900.

Other matters were just as pressing. On 19th January, 1898 the Board read a letter from Mr Conacher reminding the Directors of the need to renew the permanent way between Ryde and Newport. This met with the curt response that such a heavy expenditure would have to be incurred by degrees; a similar attitude prevailed in the replacement of fencing. The Chairman did sanction the purchase of trees for £2 for a windbreak at Merstone, probably a bonus from the sale for £40 of 28 tons of hay harvested by the permanent way men. Even some single line tablet instruments purchased for use between Ryde and Ashey had to be paid for by instalments of £10 per annum over six years; the Tyer's No. 7a electric tablets came into use in the early months of 1899 and seem to have been linked with changes to the signalling at Ryde St Johns Road. On 28th December, 1898 the Board heard that the weighbridge at Medina Wharf was faulty; its repair was a minor matter when compared with the payment of compensation to the coal merchants. In December 1899 Mr Conacher asked for an additional siding at Newport but it had to be refused until the purchase of the necessary land could be afforded. Even a £38 estimate for gravelling the road and path of the approach road was rejected as it was considered too expensive. Pan Mill had been enlarged during the 1880s but lacked rail access; this was put right when a siding was built for J. Thomas & Co. Ltd only because the firm paid for its construction - Col Von Donop sanctioned its use in June 1900. Another siding was provided at Newport in later 1901 for Messrs Edmundson, who traded as the Isle of Wight Electric Light Company. The electric light company had originally been formed in 1899 to generate and distribute electricity within the town of Ventnor but subsequently expanded its operations to Newport where a power station was built between the railway station and river. Also at Newport, a siding to the nearby brewery of Mew & Co. had been rejected years before and Mr Conacher was equally unsuccessful in getting one built for their rivals Messrs Whitbread - the £195 cost was evidently too high.

Mundane matters mentioned during 1899 and 1900 included the renewal of a lease on the refreshment room at Newport but attempts to let the one at Cowes fell through. Similar difficulties were encountered in letting the rooms on the lower floor of Cowes station and Mr Ball refused a request for an increase in rent. Eventually, Mr Beaven, proprietor of the local newspaper *Beaven's Advertiser*, was persuaded to pay £25 a year for the rent of a large room, two small rooms and lavatory. In a typically parsimonious response, the Board refused requests to contribute to the advertising budgets of Ventnor and Ryde claiming that large sums were already being expended in advertising. Far from subsidising the operation of a horse bus between Newport and Carisbrooke, the IWC charged its owners £2 a year for the use of Newport station yard and refused to reduce the £5 a year rent for the town bus. An offer from Messrs Pickford & Co. to advertise the railway on its vans in exchange for a reduction in charges for advertisements in second class carriages was accepted. The Picture

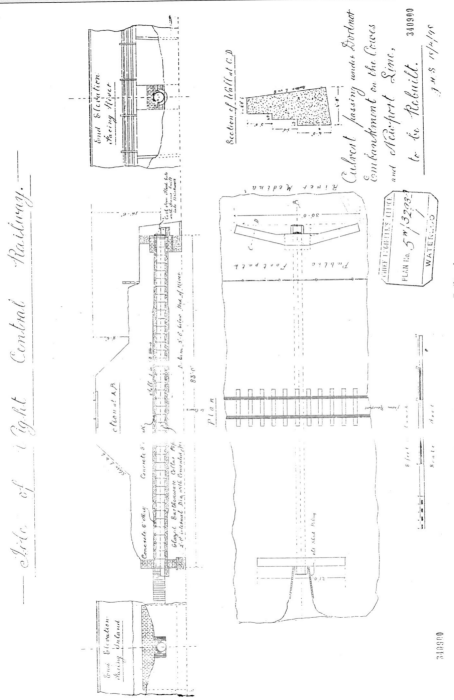

Drawing of the new culvert under the railway at Dodnor 1898.

Railtrack

Postcard Company was allowed to place its automatic machines at stations for £2 a year per machine - they were not a success and an agreement was later concluded with another firm. A donation of six guineas was made to Ashey races and one guinea towards the provision of a volunteer encampment at Ashey; the latter was served by a temporary station at Green Lane. The first telephone was installed in the offices at Newport.

The number of accidents to the public and employees had not reduced to any great extent but every injury, however minor, now had to be reported to the Board of Trade. The Board refused to accept liability when a cow was reported killed near Sandown on 17th January, 1900. More seriously, on 27th January the *Isle of Wight County Press* reported the derailment of locomotive No. 8 with a train at Mill Hill. A fatal accident at Newport on 24th February was followed by a less serious injury in April for which a porter was awarded 10s. a week. After a Mrs Kelly was injured at Newport station, it was suggested that a local doctor be appointed as Medical Officer but, ever cautious, the Board asked for details of his proposed duties before agreeing to issue a free pass in payment. Apart from three fires caused by sparks from locomotives, the only significant accident during the summer occurred on 14th June. The *Isle of Wight County Press* reported:

> The derailment occurred about 7.30 pm. The train consisted of 21 wagons and three empty carriages. A wagon in the middle of the train collapsed near Sandown Waterworks, throwing the rear eleven wagons into utter confusion, and damaging about 300 yards of permanent way and a bridge. The rear two carriages stayed on the rails.

The South African War broke out on 11th October, 1899. Such a distant event might be thought to have little effect but a number of IWC employees were reservists and they were called to their regiments. One long serving employee was awarded 4s. a week in his absence and promised a job upon his return - there were probably others that were not mentioned in the Minute book. Mr Seymour, the locomotive superintendent, departed to South Africa and whilst the IWC coped through the 1900 season, by the autumn the Board was being pressed to engage a replacement or sanction the loan of a suitable man from the LBSCR or LSWR - this became essential when the leading fitter fell ill. Fortunately, the end of the main campaign in September 1900 permitted the release of Mr Seymour from his South African duties, although it was May 1901 before he was back on the railway. The effects of the war and its aftermath added to the cost of living and led to a series of pay rises. In 1901 the Board refused to recruit another clerk for the General Manager's office stating '. . . that arrangements should be made for clerks to take their holidays at the less busy season of the year'; they relented a year later and also bought a second-hand typewriting machine.

Following the death of Queen Victoria in 1901 many Islanders travelled to Whippingham and Cowes on 1st February to see the funeral cortege travel from Osborne through the streets of East Cowes to Trinity Pier; special trains had to be put on to cope with the traffic. Employees were granted one half day's pay on the occasion of the coronation of Edward VII whilst two guineas were donated towards the cost of Queen Victoria's memorial in Newport. Some of the employees were becoming advanced in age and in failing health: two platelayers were granted pensions of 5s. a week and another employee who had lost a leg received a contribution towards the cost of an artificial replacement!

Despite Conacher's efforts, the company continued to receive complaints about late trains, the poor condition of rolling stock and a lack of third class fares on all services. E.A. Wane of Newport wrote about the overcrowding of the 2.30 pm Sandown to Newport train on 21st August, 1901; Charles Conacher responded that two extra carriages were available at Merstone but the station master failed to add them to the train. At the instigation of Mr Gibson, members of the local Gun Club at Ashey were given reduced fares on the same basis as those given to golf clubs. Disputes broke out with the local coal merchants and threats were made to divert traffic to the IWR quay at St Helens - one firm with premises at Ventnor actually did this.

The races at Ashey received a mention during 1901, not in IWC documents, but in correspondence written by Henry Day, manager of the IWR. It was practice to rent several of the IWR's Oldbury carriages which, after replacement of their armchairs by tables, would be left behind the grandstand on Ashey race days for use as dining saloons. Here are extracts from two of Mr Day's letters:

23rd April, 1901. To Mr Wetherick, Station Master at Ventnor
Your memo of the 22nd inst. as to reserved saloon for Mr Judd for Ashey Races both days.
We will do what is required but there appears to be some doubt as to Mr Conacher being able to place the train in the same position as in previous years, as the siding is not in good order but I think Mr Conacher might do so if Mr Judd wrote him to the effect that he was prepared to relieve his Company from all liability as far as he and his party is concerned if any accident should arise. Let Mr Judd know this early. [This was the siding to the quarry.]

24th April 1901. To Inspector Wheway, Brading
Please note we have loaned the Central Co. 3 open 2nd class carriages and these must be attached to their 8.5 pm train to Newport *this evening.*

In September 1901 an inspection of the railway bridge at Coppins Bridge was followed by orders that two locomotives must not cross it at the same time pending repairs - they were soon put in hand but to no long term effect. Conditions at Newport station must have been grim as complaints were received from the town clerk and the County Council about, amongst other things, the state of the water-closets.

An improvement in the financial climate following the end of the South African War cleared the way for the raising of additional capital. In 1902 the Isle of Wight Central Railway Act became law giving the company powers to issue £50,000 'A', 'B', or 'C' debentures. A start was made on paying off the debt to the Southern Counties Rolling Stock Company, but it was not until 1906 that the final payments were made and the rolling stock company wound up.

Dealings with traders during 1902 included the granting of a wayleave over railway land to Cowes Co-operative Society in lieu of the construction of a private siding - coal deliveries to the Co-op by this means began soon afterwards. Six months later the Board refused a request from the executors of J. W. Alexander that the railway carry gravel from Blackwater at the same rate they charged from Shide.

Some accidents to employees may have been attributable to their lengthy working hours and the impression is given that staff were expected to work such hours as a matter of routine. From 1889 the Board of Trade required regular returns of excessive hours but whilst other railway companies took the hint and reduced working hours, this did not happen with the IWC. In 1902 Charles Conacher reorganised duties but returns for December of that year showed that footplate men and guards were still working well in excess of 12 hours a day.

The contents of the Railway Employment (Prevention of Accidents) Act that became law in July 1900 were considered by the Board in early 1902. It was decided to install ¼ mile posts, issue a new Rule Book and make a number of purchases including boiler gauge protectors for the locomotives and three goods brake vans from the LBSCR. In June 1903 instructions were issued for the protection of platelayers and governing tow-roping (the use of ropes when shunting wagons in and out of inaccessible sidings) and the propping up of wagon doors. The standard Railway Clearing House by-laws were adopted in May 1905, prompting a fresh round of correspondence with the Board of Trade, and on 1st September, 1906 new rules were finally brought into use. Meanwhile, virtually nothing had been done about the excessive hours being worked by employees. Matters came to a head in 1907 when, following a decision in Parliament, the IWC received a visit from Col Von Donop and then a written instruction from the Board of Trade that staff must work no more than 12 hours a day - the company was forced to comply.

Improvements to electricity, gas and water supplies frequently figured in Board meetings. On 30th July, 1902 the electricity company asked IWC Board for permission to lay a power cable along the railway from the power station at Newport to a point near the site of Granville bridge, Cowes. The railway company extracted £50 a year for five years and £25 annually thereafter for the privilege. Cowes got its electricity supply by this means the following year; the cable along the railway was a prominent feature of photographs and remained in place, long disused, until the railway closed in 1966. The provision of lighting in goods yards had become a Board of Trade requirement and in 1902 a quotation was accepted from the Isle of Wight Electric Light Company for the provision of two lights in Newport yard. After the Directors decided that just one light was necessary, there ensued a lengthy wrangle over the necessity for and methods of lighting needed. The availability of an electricity supply near Medina Wharf meant that it was one of the sources of power considered for new lighting in October 1903:

Incandescent gas - cost of installation £80, running cost £69
Electric light - installation £10, running cost £68
Acetylene gas - installation £106 15s., running cost £111
Kitson's incandescent oil - installation £100, running cost £60

Although the Board decided to adopt the electric light, the work was deferred despite the decision that four lamps would be sufficient instead of five. Six months later electric lighting was provided at Cowes station and in December 1904 its use was proposed in the workshops at Newport.

Meanwhile, in March 1904 the Board sanctioned the connection of Alverstone station house to the public water supply along with Horringford and Blackwater when a supply reached there. In August Newport Corporation agreed to supply mains water at 15s. a year to the crossing keeper's house at Pan Lane. The Board also agreed to the construction of a siding to the waterworks near Sandown paid for by Lord Alverstone, alias Richard Webster, who owned the land. Lt Col Von Donop reported on the siding on 15th May, 1905 and it came into use shortly afterwards. However, rather than use the IWC it was proposed that traffic be worked from the IWR at Sandown - naturally the Board wanted to charge the maximum for the short journey over the Central's metals.

Some useful positive publicity was obtained from the most minor of events - the 1903 Cowes Regatta was one such occasion. Locomotive No. 9 hauled a special non-stop express of a modest two bogie and two four-wheel carriages from Cowes to Sandown. It left Cowes at 5.5 pm and took 22½ minutes to run the 13¾ miles to Sandown where it arrived at 5.27½. Less publicity was given to a letter from Charles Conacher on 10th August, 1903 explaining that the five minutes allowed for interchange between trains at Sandown was insufficient and as a result he had refused to issue through tickets to stations on the IWR. Although this had been a long standing problem, no attempt had been made to improve connections because a train with its crew standing at a station earned nothing whereas extra journeys squeezed into the working day would bring in some income. Even so, a request for an additional train to Sandown at 6.30 pm was refused on the grounds that the traffic did not warrant the expense.

Accidents to two employees were mentioned in September 1903. G.W., an electrician, had his doctor's bill and full wages paid for a month. Following an inquiry by the Board of Trade into an accident to craneman S. at Medina Wharf, a shield had to be put over the lifting pinion of each of the steam cranes. In April 1903 Mr Conacher celebrated a long awaited pay rise to £400 a year. The *Railway Magazine* reported on a short ceremony in the offices at Newport on 12th November when he was presented with a pair of bronzes and a dining room clock bearing the inscription 'Presented to Charles L. Conacher, Esq. by the staff of the Isle of Wight Central Railway Company, on occasion of his marriage, October 14 1903'.

In November 1903 Mr Conacher reported that the Ryde line badly needed replacement rails. Tenders from several suppliers for 100 tons of rails plus sleepers and crossings were put before the Board in January 1904 who agreed to place orders. The permanent way through Newport station also required renewal, although in this case second-hand materials could be used. Attempts were made to buy suitably cheap rails from the LSWR, LBSCR and from the NGStL who had a spare stock stored at Ventnor. To add to costs, heavy rain during February caused earth slips at Wootton, Fatting Park and Mill Hill.

In January 1904 the refreshment rooms at Newport and Cowes were let to the Portsmouth United Breweries; notice was given to the existing tenant - presumably he was unable to match the rent! In March Pickfords agreed to take on the delivery of parcels in Newport; £30 was accepted for the cart, horse and harness. Following complaints about high fares the Directors decided that the excursion fares needed to be publicised more widely; they refused a proposal to make Ryde - Newport return tickets available by either route but LSW and LBSC through tickets were given wider availability. Booklets were issued jointly with the IWR containing details of train times, connections with ferries to the mainland and trains by all routes to London and other parts of Britain. A large number of pages were devoted to the special and excursion fares that were available during the summer - one such booklet ran to 78 pages. Confusion was not confined to the public; Miss Mary Evans, a Ventnor resident, wrote:

Early in the 20th Century, the vagaries of the Isle of Wight Railways were made fun of in *Punch* but even then the real facts were funnier. I walked with some friends across Appuldurcombe Park on a Tuesday to Godshill Station, I then asked the porter whether it would be cheaper to take a return or a single ticket to Ventnor knowing that it was not cheap return day on the railway. The man said reflectively 'Let me see what day of the week is it?' Before I could answer he said, 'Oh its Wednesday it will be cheaper to take returns'. 'No it isn't', one of my friends said 'Its Tuesday'. 'Oh then' the man said, 'it will be cheaper to take singles'.

On another occasion my brother and his wife bicycled to Carisbrooke but as it turned into a wet afternoon decided to return by train from Newport. My brother had 7s. 6d. in his pocket but though the distance by train to Ventnor was only 9 miles it was not enough to take the two passengers and cycles, so when he asked the booking clerk what could be done, the latter said, 'Though you haven't enough money for single tickets perhaps you have for returns' and that proved to be correct!

At Newport a porter opened the door of a crowded railway carriage and asked 'Are you all Cowes?' When I wished to go to that town I was not sure whether I had to change at Newport or not, one official said Yes and another No, so I got out of the train and asked the actual engine driver where he was going, and found I had not to change after all.

As the following figures show, passenger and goods receipts had shown a healthy increase although working expenses remained stubbornly high:

Year ending	Passenger traffic			Goods traffic		Gross receipts		Working	% of expenditure
	Numbers carried			Minerals	General	Pass.	Goods	expenses	in relation
31 Dec.	First	Second	Third	Tons	Tons	£	£	£	to receipts
1897	36,278	238,880	473,681	108,948	35,009	26,736	13,072	26,118	66
1900	40,648	210,774	658,034	118,851	44,287	29,080	14,975	29,903	68
1904	43,804	237,167	711,902	127,845	57,755	33,074	16,160	32,540	66

Having taken our history up to 1904, we must now go back a few years to chart the company's involvement in the promotion, construction and opening of the last railway in the Isle of Wight, the Newport, Godshill & St Lawrence Railway.

Chapter Twelve

A Railway from Merstone to Ventnor

The story of the Newport, Godshill & St Lawrence Railway has been told elsewhere* but the railway's history was so intertwined with the Isle of Wight Central Railway that it cannot be excluded from this book.

As we have seen, desires for a railway connecting Cowes with Ventnor dated back to the earliest proposals for railways in the Isle of Wight. Construction of the CNR, IWNJ and IWR created a continuous length of rails between Cowes and Ventnor but the IWR never permitted the running of through trains. In 1882 events on the mainland gave a fresh impetus for renewed railway construction when the Swindon, Marlborough & Andover Railway (soon to become part of the Midland & South Western Junction Railway) proposed the construction of a branch to Stone Point opposite Cowes. It was claimed that steamers would ply between the two points in about 10 minutes. Although the company obtained Acts in 1882 and 1883 for a railway and pier, the scheme was finally abandoned in 1893.

In 1885 the Shanklin & Chale Railway Company was formed to improve access to and develop a part of the Island singularly lacking in good transport links. The company secured its Act of Incorporation on 14th August, 1885 for a line branching from the IWR at Winstone between Shanklin and Wroxall before meandering through open country to a terminus near Chale. Running powers over the IWR to Shanklin station were granted subject to IWR agreement. The first Directors were named as Harry Francis Giles, A. Curzon Thompson and Philip Powter.

At this point, two individuals took an interest in the proceedings of the Shanklin & Chale Railway - William Bohm and Harry Magnus. It is not generally known that they were either relatives or close friends of the Martin and Petre families, e.g. William Bohm was a nephew of Henry Martin. They found that the authorised railway was not long enough to be worked profitably, either by the IWR or as an independent concern and it made sense to build an extension along the old Military Road to Freshwater. Such a railway had been authorised by Parliament in the 1870s but was abandoned before construction began.

In December 1885 the *Isle of Wight County Press* reported that a Bill had been placed before Parliament by the Shanklin & Chale Railway for a 10½ mile railway from Chale to Freshwater. It would have run along the Military road from Chale to Compton Bay, climbed steeply onto Afton Down with 30 ft cuttings before approaching Freshwater on 15 to 20 ft high embankments to a terminus close to the high road. The promoters gained War Office support for the use of the Military road but not from Lord Tennyson, the Poet Laureate, who wrote a letter of complaint to *The Times*. Whilst the Bill passed both Committees of the Houses of Parliament without difficulty, Mr Chamberlain objected to it at the third reading in the House of Commons on 24th June, 1886. He said there was little or no potential traffic and the line would run over and ruin some of the most attractive scenery in the Island. He was joined by members of the Commons Preservation Society, who claimed the railway would pass over land near Freshwater where the public had been allowed to picnic although it was not officially common land. Together they succeeded in having the Bill voted out.

Having failed to extend the railway in one direction, in 1887 the promoters placed a third Bill before Parliament. By the construction of two short spur lines and the granting of running powers over the IWR they hoped to create a through route from the IWNJ at Merstone to Ventnor. Although the lines were authorised, the running powers were struck out; it was clear that the IWR would never allow another company to gain access to Ventnor over its railway.

That year (1887) the CNR, IWNJ and RNR had amalgamated to form the Central Railway. Its Directors were acutely aware that without an independent railway to Ventnor they would

* *The Ventnor West Branch* by P. Paye, Wild Swan Publications 1992.

be unable to capture more than a fraction of the traffic. In 1889 a fourth Bill appeared for a railway from Merstone to a terminus near St Lawrence church in substitution for the authorised lines. A change of name was proposed to the Isle of Wight Central and St Lawrence Railway Company but by the time the Bill became law this had been amended to the Newport, Godshill & St Lawrence Railway Company; an agreement with the IWC was included as a schedule to the Act. The NGStL was obliged to complete the line to the satisfaction of the IWC and, in exchange for 55 per cent of the gross receipts, the IWC undertook to work the railway and maintain the permanent way, etc. once the contractor's responsibilities had expired (12 months after opening). The agreement was sanctioned by the IWC shareholders at a meeting on 27th February, 1889. In exchange for three seats on the NGStL Board, the IWC guaranteed a minimum payment of £900 for every half year in which the Godshill Company's share of the gross receipts fell below that amount; this guarantee was incorporated in the two companies' Acts of 1890 and 1892.

In 1892 the Godshill company returned to Parliament seeking powers to extend the line from St Lawrence to a point immediately west of the Steephill Castle Estate on the edge of Ventnor; it was not proposed to purchase the castle but a steeply graded access road to the terminus would have passed over estate land. A committee of the House of Commons met on 14th and 15th June, 1892 to hear evidence for and against the Bill. Much of the rhetoric was aimed at forestalling attempts by the IWR to cast doubts on the need for, viability and safety of the extension along the Undercliff - they had not opposed the 1890 Act but evidently this extension was rather more of a threat. Those giving evidence in favour of the Bill included Thomas Bolton, Chairman of the IWC. He explained that it was desirable to get the railway closer and on the same level as the town in order that it might compete with the IWR line, his company did not pay any dividends on the ordinary or Preference stock and he was sorry to say he was one of the largest shareholders. Mr Bolton was asked 'With regard to your not paying a dividend, what you want to see is a good independent terminus of your own at Ventnor?' He responded: 'I should like to see a dividend (laughter), and I should think this would help the dividend'. Ventnor residents continually blamed the IWR for high fares and goods rates that were said to have strangled the town's development and this evidently prompted another witness to state that '. . . all sensible people of Ventnor were in favour of the proposed extension'.

Evidence in opposition to the Bill came mainly from landowners who expressed concern at the manner in which the railway would spoil the peace and beauty of the neighbourhood. F. S. Judd speaking on behalf of the trustees of the Rt Hon. Evelyn Cornwallis Anderson Pelham said the railway would have an adverse effect on his land near St Lawrence, it being laid out for residential purposes. Henry Sewell stated that he had bought Steephill Castle in 1887 for its quietness and repose - he owned about 50 acres. He believed that the value of the property would depreciate, the railway would be a source of serious annoyance and as a result he was already eager to sell the estate. Dr John G. Sinclair-Coghill, senior physician to the National Consumption Hospital at Ventnor felt the railway would be '. . . injurious to the hospital, and detrimental to Ventnor generally'. Although the Bill went on to become law, the poor location of the terminus, its difficult access and restrictions that prevented the company from handling goods traffic at the station were considerable handicaps.

A contract for construction was signed by the Directors of the NGStL with Messrs Westwood & Winby of London in August 1891. Payment was mainly in shares, in exchange for which the contractor undertook to pay certain incidental expenses. The Engineer was Robert Elliott Cooper who acted as consulting Engineer to the IWC for many years; structures that he designed for the IWC and NGStL had marked similarities with others on the Great Northern lines in West Yorkshire for which he was Engineer in the 1890s. On one occasion he instructed the contractor that the crossing keeper's house at Dean be built 'Similar to those on the Lancashire, Derbyshire & East Coast Railway'. Plans for the stations and every structure on the NGStL had to be submitted to the IWC Directors who, not having to pay for them, insisted on additions that made the railway the most lavishly equipped part of the IWC.

Pegging out the route of the railway began in September 1891 but it was April 1893 before the *Isle of Wight County Press* reported the cutting of the first sod:

Merstone kept high holiday on Tuesday (18th April) for on that day was taken the first step of elevating that pleasant hamlet to the position of 'junction'. In perfect weather conditions, the first sod of the new railway was ceremoniously cut by Miss Beatrice Kate Martin, niece of Mr H. D. Martin, who may almost be called 'the father of Island Railways'. The village was decorated with bunting, and the neighbourhood of the junction was especially gay with flags. The interesting proceedings attracted a large gathering, most areas of the Island being represented. Very gracefully and expertly did Miss Martin perform the task allocated to her. With a mahogany-handled silver-bladed spade she turned the first sod - several sods in fact - placing them in a mahogany silver-mounted barrow, and wheeling them along a plank to their appointed destination, and returning along the same narrow way without once 'running off the line' - a fact which the spectators loudly cheered. The blade of the spade bore the following inscription:
'Presented by Messrs Westwood & Winley* to Miss Beatrice Kate Martin on the occasion of her cutting the first sod of the Newport, Godshill & St. Lawrence Railway. Merston, 18 April 1893'
On a silver plate at the back of the barrow was Miss Martin's monogram, with the name of the railway and the date of the ceremony. The spade and the barrow, which were very handsome, were made by Messrs Mappin Bros of London.†

The promoters spared no expense in holding the ceremony and providing lunch in a marquee for their guests - local children who attended the event each received a bun!

It was 1894 before a significant amount of construction took place. The works progressed satisfactorily apart from a cutting north of Whitwell where blue slipper clay was encountered; the tunnel was cut without difficulty - the greatest problem was in securing sufficient land on which to tip the waste. Where the line passed along a narrow shelf near St Lawrence there were several falls of chalk, including a fairly serious one on 21st June, 1897 when two wagons were smashed.

The contractor's financial position took a turn for the worse during 1894. In July 1894 a variation to the contract was signed providing for the issue of part paid up shares rather than fully paid up shares - evidently their value to investors was not what had been expected. Difficulties in selling on the shares became evident a few weeks later when the NGStL Board complained that the contractor had failed to pay a number of expenses incurred. In early 1895 the issue began of 4 per cent debentures at the instance of certain Directors, including Messrs Dunstan and Toleman, who had connections with the contractor. The action of the Board was too much for certain shareholders and after a court action, an injunction was issued preventing the contractor receiving £500 of the debentures. Towards the end of May, between 60 and 70 navvies working at Whitwell downed tools when the contractor refused to increase their pay from 4¼d. per hour to the rate of 5d. that certain other men employed on the line were receiving. The strikers drifted away to other work but during June it emerged that the contractor had been borrowing money left, right and centre; Henry Martin claimed he had been promised £12,462 10s. in debentures in exchange for money borrowed from him. Westwood & Winby went into receivership and all work stopped. Construction resumed in November in the hands of Charles Westwood trading under the name of C.J. Westwood & Co.

Meanwhile, on 24th November, 1894 the *Isle of Wight County Press* carried an official notice that the Ashey & Horringford Railway Company intended to place a Bill before Parliament in the forthcoming session. Its railway would have branched from the Ryde to Newport line about 125 yards west of Ashey station, climbed at 1 in 57 before passing through a 200 yard tunnel below the chalk ridge, then descending at 1 in 55 to join the Sandown line about 61 yards north east of Horringford station - a triangular junction at Merstone would have allowed though running to the Ventnor line. The proposals were a thinly disguised attempt to draw off traffic from the IWR. The County Council lodged objections on the grounds that third class passengers would not be carried on all trains and that the level crossings lacked

* The partnership was actually Westwood & Winby, the latter being a Mr F.C. Winby.
† An illustration of the barrow and spade appeared in the *Illustrated London News*. They were kept for many years at the family home - Halberry House, Newport.

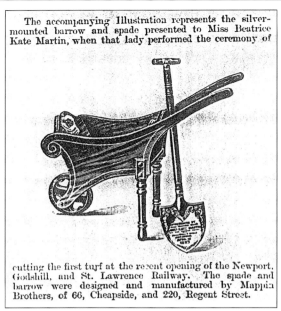

The accompanying Illustration represents the silver-mounted barrow and spade presented to Miss Beatrice Kate Martin, when that lady performed the ceremony of

cutting the first turf at the recent opening of the Newport, Godshill, and St. Lawrence Railway. The spade and barrow were designed and manufactured by Mappin Brothers, of 66, Cheapside, and 220, Regent Street.

Illustrated London News extract, 1893.

The men employed to construct the Ventnor extension of the NGStL were brought together for this photograph. The location is presumed to be the run-round loop east of St Lawrence station and the locomotive is *Godshill*. The water tank spanning one track supplies water to the locomotive by means of a wooden chute.   *IWSR Collection*

sufficient protection. Anxious not to spread the indiscriminate use of third class to its trains, the IWC Board gave notice that it would not work the line and that was enough to see the project die.

During 1896 the NGStL secured an Act of Parliament for an extension to a more convenient terminus and the removal of restrictions on the handling of goods traffic. The IWC increased its guarantee to £1,000 per half year upon completion to Ventnor; this helped the Godshill company raise more capital.

Charles Conacher arrived about a year before the railway to St Lawrence was completed so he had the pleasure of organising and publicising the opening of the line. In July 1897 Lt Col Addison conducted an inspection of the section between Merstone and St Lawrence on behalf of the Board of Trade. Part of his lengthy report read:

> The total length of single line now submitted for inspection is 5 miles 55 chains. The width at formation level varies from 16 ft to 18 ft, and the permanent way has steel rails, weighing 67 lbs per yard, secured to 8 ft 11 in. x 10 ft x 5 ft sleepers by iron spikes and fang bolts. The ballast is stated to consist of broken stone, although in many places it can hardly be distinguished from chalk ballast.
>
> The fencing is of iron wire, with a top strand of barbed wire. The steepest gradient has an inclination of 1 in 55, over half a mile in length, and the sharpest curve has a radius of 12 chains - the curves on the whole being easy. The line is generally either in cutting or on embankment, the former having depths of 25 ft, 29 ft and 39 ft and the latter heights of 22 ft, 23 ft and 25 ft. On the St Lawrence side of the tunnel a very extensive slip occurred quite recently, of the cliff, which almost overhangs the railway, and this portion of the line needs to be very carefully watched in the future - especially after rain and frost. The cutting between 2 miles 45 chains and 3 miles also requires to be watched. The banks at the Merstone end were made some years ago, and they appear to be standing well. There are the following works:
>
> *Overbridges,* four: two have steel lattice girders, and are only for use as footpaths; the other two, 15 ft span, carrying roads over the railway, are constructed with brick arches on concrete or masonry abutments. It should be added that the girders of the footbridge at 4 miles 59 chains are not yet in position.
>
> *Underbridges,* 12: Two of these have brick arch tops, on concrete abutments, faced with brickwork, the span in each case being only 12 feet; the remainder have steel superstructure, on similar abutments (except in one instance where masonry has been made use of), with spans varying from 8 feet to 25 feet. The longer spans have plate main girders and trough floor, the shorter spans trough flooring only. The whole gave moderate deflections under test, with the exception of the trough floor of the bridge at 2 miles 37 chains; this bridge should be examined, in order to ascertain the cause of the unusual deflection, and it will be necessary to test it again later on. There are cracks in the abutments of the bridge at 1 mile 72 chains (apparently old), which also need attention.
>
> *Culvert,* one, 6 feet diameter, of brick.
>
> *Tunnel,* 620 yards in length provided with refuges for platelayers 1 chain apart. Only 90 yards of this tunnel is provided with 18 in. lining, and considerably more than half the length has only 9 in. lining. The latter can only be considered as a skin, to prevent the fall of small quantities of loose stuff, and the responsibility for dispensing with lining of full thickness must rest with the Engineer of the Company - it being impossible for me to say whether the 9 in. lining will suffice - not having seen the work while in progress.

He highlighted a number of minor deficiencies, including the need for more ballast that justified a return visit but nothing that would prevent the immediate opening of the railway. A special press run was made over the line on Saturday 17th July, 1897; at Merstone Messrs Conacher and Westwood joined the train and took the opportunity of extolling the line's potential to their captive audience - the return trip from St Lawrence to Newport was accomplished in just 15 minutes. The formal opening on Monday 19th July duly received extensive publicity. The *Isle of Wight Herald* reported:

The opening of the NGStL in 1897 was marked by the running of a special train consisting of locomotive No. 6 and a set of elderly LBSC four-wheel carriages. They are seen standing at Newport with, *reading left to right*, J. Seymour (in bowler hat), C. Conacher (in top hat), J. Pierce (driver), S. Lovett (clerk). W. Matthews (guard), W. Bell (carriage examiner). In the cab is F. Young (fireman); the figure in the background is unknown. *R. Silsbury Collection*

A special train from Waterloo brought the London contingent, and the local contingent joined the train both at Ryde, Newport and Merstone Junction. The engine was gaily decorated with flags and evergreens, and bore the appropriate device:

'SUCCESS TO THE NEWPORT, GODSHILL AND ST LAWRENCE RAILWAY'

The several coaches also sported Union Jacks, and as the train steamed through the stations, the Manager had arranged for an explosion of fog signals. The terminus was reached about 1.40 on Monday afternoon, and it was found that the station was gay with bunting, and as the guests detrained there was a round of cheering. A halt was made for the purpose of enabling Mrs Percy Mortimer to drive the bolt which was done under the superintendence of the Contractor, Mr Westwood. The luncheon was provided in a spacious marquee, and the tables were tastefully decorated with a profusion of roses, geraniums and ferns. Entertainment was provided by an excellent string band, which discoursed a programme of the latest music, whilst the guests were taking of a splendid repast. Messrs Bush & Judd of the Royal Marine Hotel were the caterers.

The luncheon took place in the grounds of Elm Dene, the residence of the contractor Charles Westwood. Thomas Lee, editor of the *County Press*, paid tribute to 'the enterprise which had so happily compassed the new railway undertaking'. One newspaper quoted Thomas Bolton as saying that 'It was his honest belief that the Isle of Wight owed its prosperity to the railways and to nothing else. Might they flourish root and branch till time and memory be no more'. The Ventnor extension, then already begun was hoped to be completed 'in about six months' and the 'new station at town level would be a great boon to Ventnor', much more so than 'the other monopolist railway with a terminus half way up the downs'. It was confidently expected that the NGStL would earn £54 per mile per week on its railway, after paying the IWC its share for working the line, which left £9,400 a year to pay interest on the capital expended.

Public services to St Lawrence began the following day with nine trains each way, a frequency that proved ample. Somewhat misleadingly, the destination was described as Ventnor (St Lawrence). Although the stations were painted in IWC colours, the separate ownership of the railway was emphasised by the issue of tickets bearing the title 'Newport, Godshill and St Lawrence Ry'. This did not stop the IWC nominating three Directors to attend a meeting of the NGStL Board on 4th August, 1897 and subsequent meetings thereafter. Despite the hopes of residents, fares were the same as those over the 'monopolist' IWR. An additional 6d. was demanded for travel from St Lawrence to Ventnor town centre on a bus provided by F. Baker of Pier Street, Ventnor, in whose offices a ticket office began operation shortly after the railway was opened; just 24 people availed themselves of the service on the first day. Other road conveyances met trains at Whitwell ready to convey passengers to Niton and Blackgang. Amongst the first travellers over the line was Princess Henry of Battenburg who travelled by a special non-stop train from Newport to St Lawrence on 31st July to lay the foundation stone of a new wing of the National Chest Hospital at Ventnor.

In November 1897 the Board of Trade Inspector made a return visit to check that the deficiencies mentioned in his report had been complied with - not all had been. By then the company lacked a contractor because Charles Westwood had declared himself bankrupt; the opening of the railway to St Lawrence had done nothing to improve the saleability of the NGStL shares he had received. It was not until a third visit on 16th April, 1898 that the Board of Trade Inspector pronounced himself satisfied with the line.

Meanwhile, the company had been embroiled in a High Court case over its attempts to acquire land through Steephill Estate. In 1898 Steephill Castle was purchased by Charles Mortimer who was a brother of Percy, an IWC Director and a nominee to the NGStL Board; Charles Mortimer was a LSWR Director for many years. He resold the necessary land to the NGStL including the estate's stables, the site of which became Ventnor station. Criticism of the division of the estate was met with the response 'we must not let aesthetic ruins stand in the way'. It was hoped 'construction would start again shortly' but this had to wait until J.T. Firbank was engaged as contractor.

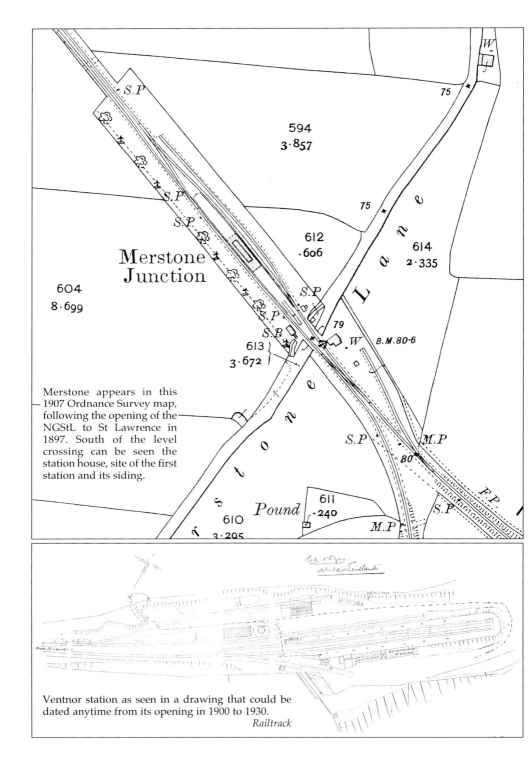

S.P 594 3·857

75

75

L a n e

612 ·606

614 2·335

Merstone Junction

604 8·699

S.P

S.P

S.P

S.P

S.P

79

W B.M.80·6

613 3·672

Merstone appears in this 1907 Ordnance Survey map, following the opening of the NGStL to St Lawrence in 1897. South of the level crossing can be seen the station house, site of the first station and its siding.

S t o n e

S.P M.P 80

Pound

611 ·240

610 3·205

M.P

S.P

F.P

Ventnor station as seen in a drawing that could be dated anytime from its opening in 1900 to 1930.

Railtrack

In April 1900 the *Isle of Wight Herald* reported that the first passenger train had successfully run over the extension carrying 'chief officials of the London and South Western Railway and others interested in the development of the new route' including Sam Fay, superintendent of the line. Lt Col P.G. Von Donop made an inspection on behalf of the Board of Trade and wrote a report of what he found on 21st May, 1900. He had the following to say about the station at Ventnor:

There are two platforms connected by a passage behind the buffer stops, each platform being signalled both for arrival and departure. The platforms are 350 ft long and 2 ft 8 ins in height above rail level and 12 ft in width. The station buildings are on the South side of the line, and include the usual accommodation for all classes. There is a carriage dock on the South side of the line and some sidings on the North side . . .

The station was described as Ventnor Town, not because of its proximity to the town centre but for the reason that it was at town level near the entrance to Ventnor Park. 'In eight or nine minutes passengers can walk to the centre of the town' - clearly they had to be unencumbered with luggage to achieve that! The two-storey station building was built by Cowes builders, J. Ball & Sons, in local stone; the platforms were said to have been capable of accommodating 20 carriages (four-wheelers, of course), there was a cattle dock and goods shed. The latter was a rarity on the IWC but since the IWR had one, the Central had to have its own! The Board of Trade Inspector also commented on the steep gradients and recommended that trains stop at the home signal before entering the terminus. None of the deficiencies was considered sufficiently serious to present a danger to the public and subject to another inspection (carried out in January 1901) he sanctioned the opening of the extension despite the incomplete state of the goods facilities.

Public services began with the departure of a train from Ventnor at 8.30 am on 1st June, 1900. There had been a press run the previous day when the special train took less than 20 minutes to run from Newport to Ventnor, the return being accomplished in 18 minutes; the local press went so far as to list national newspapers that sent representatives: *The Times, Telegraph, Daily Chronicle, Morning Post, Referee, Lloyds* and *Daily Express*. However, publicity could be double edged as the correspondent from the *Daily Telegraph* was moved to write:

The new line to Ventnor opened yesterday, the proceedings being marred by the constant rain. The original terminus was at St Lawrence - called Ventnor (St Lawrence) until the extension to Ventnor Town was opened. This, for the traveller to the English Madeira, could be taken at best as a pious fraud and less charitably as a joke in bad taste. The woods in the grounds of Steephill Castle have been much spoiled by the construction of the new line.

In addition to the press run, a Directors' special train was run on opening day. The *Isle of Wight Mercury* reported that the train, gaily decorated with flags and carrying a board proclaiming 'Success to the Ventnor, Godshill & Newport Railway', entered Ventnor station shortly before 2.0 pm to the accompaniment of loud bangs from fog detonators laid on the line. At the subsequent junketing Percy Mortimer, Chairman of the NGStL, stated that the railway needed to be extended further into Ventnor to make it really successful and ensure that debenture holders got their interest. If built, the line would have passed behind the Royal Hotel and across Alpine Road to a terminus near The Grove in what in recent years became a car park. The high cost of compensation for the necessary land meant that it remained no more than an idea.

A timetable issued in October 1898 listed a service to St Lawrence of five passenger trains, six in the opposite direction (the odd number being balanced by goods workings), an additional two each way on Saturdays and three return trips on Sundays; virtually all ran to and from Cowes and gave connections to the mainland. By January 1901 an identical service was provided but each train ran to Ventnor Town. Trains called at Godshill and St Lawrence by signal; the crossing loop at Whitwell was rarely needed. The Directors wrote in their six-monthly report to shareholders: 'The traffic receipts on the extension to Ventnor Town, which was opened on the 1st June, have been satisfactory, and it is believed will naturally increase the receipts of the Company.' Publicity was aimed at generating considerable traffic from the

Isle of Wight Central Railway
Timetable for January 1901, and until further notice.

WEEK DAYS

Cowes — Mill Hill — Newport

Station		G									SO	
Cowes	Dep.	8.45	10.0	11.45	12.40	2.43	3.40	5.5	5.31	7.28	8.30	9.15
Mill Hill	Dep.	8.47	10.2	A	12.42	2.45	3.42	C	5.33	7.30	8.32	9.17
Newport	Arr.	8.58	10.15	11.58	12.55	2.58	3.55	5.15	5.43	7.40	8.44	9.30

Newport — Shide — Blackwater — Merstone Junction — Horringford — Newchurch — Alverstone — Sandown Junction

Station										SO	
Newport	Dep.	7.50	9.2	10.18	12.0	1.0	3.0	5.17	7.45	8.55	9.17
Shide	Dep.	A	A	A	A	A	A	A	A	A	A
Blackwater	Dep.	A	A	A	A	A	A	A	A	A	A
Merstone Junction	Dep.	8.2	9.14	10.29	12.11	1.13	3.13	5.29	7.59	9.9	9.29
Horringford	Dep.	A	A	A	A	A	A	A	A	A	A
Newchurch	Dep.	A	A	A	A	A	A	A	A	A	A
Alverstone	Dep.	A	A	A	A	A	A	A	A	A	A
Sandown Junction	Arr.	8.17	9.30	10.43	12.25	1.28	3.28	5.43	8.15	9.23	9.44

Merstone Junction — Godshill — Whitwell — St Lawrence — Ventnor Town

Station								SO
Merstone Junction	Dep.	9.13	12.10	1.12	3.12	5.28	7.58	9.8
Godshill	Dep.	A	A	A	A	A	A	A
Whitwell	Dep.	9.22	12.19	1.22	3.22	5.37	8.7	9.17
St Lawrence	Dep.	A	A	A	A	A	A	A
Ventnor Town	Arr.	9.30	12.27	1.30	3.30	5.45	8.15	9.25

Newport — Whippingham — Wootton — Haven Street — Ashey — Ryde

Newport	Dep.	7.25	9.25	10.25	1.10	3.0	5.0	5.45	7.45	8.55
Whippingham	Dep.	A	A	A	A	A	A	-	A	A
Wootton	Dep.	7.35	9.34	10.34	1.18	3.8	5.8	5.52	7.53	9.4
Haven Street	Dep.	7.40	A	A	1.24	A	5.12	C	7.58	9.9
Ashey	Dep.	A	A	A	A	A	A	C	A	A
Ryde (St Johns Road)	Arr.	7.54	9.49	10.51	1.34	3.23	5.23	6.5	8.8	9.20
Ryde (Esplanade)	Arr.	7.57	9.52	10.53	1.37	3.27	5.27	6.8	8.13	
Ryde (Pier Head)	Arr.	8.0	9.55	10.55	1.40	3.30	5.30	6.10	8.16	

SUNDAYS

Cowes — Mill Hill — Newport

Cowes	Dep.	10.0	12.40	2.20	4.5	8.0	9.55
Mill Hill	Dep.	10.2	12.42	2.22	4.7	8.2	9.57
Newport	Arr.	10.13	12.53	2.34	4.20	8.13	10.10

Newport — Shide — Blackwater — Merstone Junction — Horringford — Newchurch — Alverstone — Sandown Junction

Newport	Dep.	12.55	2.47	8.16
Shide	Dep.	A	A	A
Blackwater	Dep.	A	A	A
Merstone Junction	Dep.	1.9	3.0	8.29
Horringford	Dep.	A	A	A
Newchurch	Dep.	A	A	A
Alverstone	Dep.	A	A	A
Sandown Junction	Arr.	1.25	3.17	8.40

Merstone Junction — Godshill — Whitwell — St Lawrence — Ventnor Town

Merstone Junction	Dep.	9.28	8.28
Godshill	Dep.	A	A
Whitwell	Dep.	9.37	8.37
St Lawrence	Dep.	A	A
Ventnor Town	Arr.	9.45	8.45

Newport — Whippingham — Wootton — Haven Street — Ashey — Ryde

Newport	Dep.	10.15	2.37	4.22	8.15
Whippingham	Dep.	A	A	A	A
Wootton	Dep.	10.23	2.44	4.31	8.24
Haven Street	Dep.	10.28	A	A	8.30
Ashey	Dep.	A	A	A	A
Ryde (St Johns Road)	Arr.	10.40	2.57	4.49	8.42
Ryde (Esplanade)	Arr.	10.43	3.0	4.53	8.46
Ryde (Pier Head)	Arr.	10.45	3.2	4.56	8.49

A = Stops by signal to take up or set down passengers. SO = Saturdays only.

The first trains of the day carried first, second and third class passengers, subsequent trains carried only first and second class.

G = Government between Cowes and Newport, Cowes and Freshwater line and Cowes, Sandown, Ventnor, etc.

WEEK DAYS

Ryde (Pier Head) – Newport

Station		G							SO
Ryde (Pier Head)	Dep.	8.25	10.30	12.23	2.25	3.35	5.42	8.5	
Ryde (Esplanade)	Dep.	8.27	10.32	12.25	2.27	3.37	5.44	8.7	
Ryde (St Johns Road)	Dep.	8.33	10.37	12.30	2.32	3.42	5.50	8.12	9.30
Ashey	Dep.	A	A	A	A	A	A	A	A
Haven Street	Dep.	8.43	A	12.40	A	A	6.2	8.22	A
Wootton	Dep.	8.48	10.53	12.45	2.47	3.57	6.7	8.26	A
Whippingham	Dep.	A	A	A	A	A	A	A	A
Newport	Arr.	8.57	11.1	12.55	2.55	4.7	6.15	8.35	9.55

Ventnor Town – Merstone Junction

Station									SO
Ventnor Town	Dep.	8.30	10.50	12.32	2.30	3.40	5.50	8.20	9.30
St Lawrence	Dep.	A	A	A	A	A	A	A	A
Whitwell	Dep.	8.38	10.59	12.40	2.39	3.49	5.59	8.29	9.39
Godshill	Dep.	A	A	A	A	A	A	A	A
Merstone Junction	Arr.	8.45	11.6	12.47	2.46	3.56	6.6	8.36	9.46

Sandown Junction – Newport

Station		G								SO
Sandown Junction	Dep.	8.27	9.45	10.50	12.30	2.30	3.40	5.50	8.20	9.30
Alverstone	Dep.	A	–	A	A	A	A	A	A	A
Newchurch	Dep.	A	–	A	A	A	A	A	A	A
Horringford	Dep.	A	–	A	A	A	A	A	A	A
Merstone	Dep.	8.30	10.0	11.7	12.32	2.47	3.57	6.8	8.37	9.47
Blackwater	Dep.	8.46	–	A	A	A	A	A	A	A
Shide	Dep.	A	–	A	A	A	A	A	A	A
Newport	Arr.	8.57	10.15	11.17	12.59	2.59	4.8	6.20	8.50	10.0

Newport – Cowes

Newport	Dep.	8.15	9.5	11.19	1.4	3.4	4.12	5.15	6.24	7.42	8.55
Mill Hill	Dep.	8.28	9.18	11.30	1.16	3.16	4.25	5.26	6.35	7.52	9.8
Cowes	Arr.	8.30	9.20	11.32	1.18	3.18	4.27	5.28	6.37	7.54	9.10

SUNDAYS

Ryde (Pier Head) – Newport

Ryde (Pier Head)	Dep.	10.50	1.15	3.5	6.20	8.55
Ryde (Esplanade)	Dep.	10.52	1.17	3.7	6.22	8.57
Ryde (St Johns Road)	Dep.	10.57	1.22	3.10	6.28	9.5
Ashey	Dep.	A	A	A	A	A
Haven Street	Dep.	A	A	A	A	9.12
Wootton	Dep.	11.12	1.37	3.25	6.43	9.17
Whippingham	Dep.	A	A	A	A	A
Newport	Arr.	11.20	1.45	3.35	6.53	9.26

Ventnor Town – Merstone Junction

Ventnor Town	Dep.	10.35	9.0
St Lawrence	Dep.	A	A
Whitwell	Dep.	10.44	9.9
Godshill	Dep.	A	A
Merstone Junction	Arr.	10.52	9.16

Sandown Junction – Newport

Sandown Junction	Dep.	10.35	2.13	4.40	8.59
Alverstone	Dep.	A	A	A	A
Newchurch	Dep.	A	A	A	A
Horringford	Dep.	A	A	A	A
Merstone	Dep.	10.54	2.26	4.57	9.17
Blackwater	Dep.	A	A	A	A
Shide	Dep.	A	A	A	A
Newport	Arr.	11.5	2.36	5.8	9.28

Newport – Cowes

Newport	Dep.	9.35	11.22	2.0	3.37	5.10	9.30
Mill Hill	Dep.	9.48	11.33	2.11	3.50	5.23	9.43
Cowes	Arr.	9.50	11.35	2.13	3.52	5.25	9.45

A = Stops by signal to take up or set down passengers. SO= Saturdays only.
The first trains of the day carried first, second and third class passengers, subsequent trains carried only first and second class.
G = Government between Ryde and Newport and Ryde to Cowes, Ventnor and Freshwater lines.

mainland, either brought to Southampton by the MSWJ from the Midlands or from London; there were hints that the route via Southampton, if not quicker, might be more comfortable than that via Portsmouth. The running of through trains from Cowes avoided a change of carriage at Merstone and passengers were reminded that the new line was six miles less than via Sandown and thus cheaper. Passengers were also spared 'the most terrific climb' to the IWR terminus at Ventnor 'half-way up a mountain'!

In June 1901 Charles Conacher invited members of the press to an inaugural journey of an express service. The *Isle of Wight Herald* carried a lengthy article, part of which read:

A NEW EXPRESS SERVICE

Owing to the unwearying exertions, extending over a long period, of Mr C.L. Conacher the Manager of the Isle of Wight Central and its combined railways, a new express service was inaugurated on Saturday last between Waterloo and the Isle of Wight, which, although intended primarily to serve Ventnor and the surrounding district, must inevitably improve the facilities which Cowes and its neighbourhood possess. The down service leaves Waterloo at 11.10, and does not stop until it reaches Winchester. The next stop is at Eastleigh. At Southampton the passengers are conveyed to the Royal pier, practically by the side of the boat, which at once leaves for Cowes, where it is timed to arrive at 3.10. To allow ample margin, the train from Cowes is at 3.30, and this is an express of which the inhabitants of Cowes, as well as passengers from London to Ventnor, will be able to take advantage. It is timed to arrive at Ventnor at 4.10, or four-and-a-half hours [*sic*] only from the time of departure from Waterloo.

The up service is even quicker. The time of departure from Ventnor is 12.32, whilst Cowes will be left by steamer at 1.30. At Southampton, one of the great advantages — to Cowes people as well as to others — will be apparent. Hitherto, people who wished to use the express service, had to walk or take a cab from the pier, conveying their luggage as best they could, to the West station, even then running a chance of losing their connection. Now Mr Conacher informs us, a train is to run from the Southampton pier carrying through passengers from thence to the West End in time to catch the drawing room car express from Bournemouth to London. Once inside this, the only stop is at Vauxhall, Waterloo being reached at 4.47, or 4¼ hours from Ventnor. A further noticeable fact is that these extra facilities are afforded without any increase in the fare . . .

The express service did not bring the expected bonanza the Central desired. The publicity generated little additional income as few Ventnor travellers patronised the Southampton to Cowes route and some custom was probably lost because passengers to Sandown were forced to change at Merstone.

After several years of losses, the IWC Board discussed the matter in August 1903. The Directors wanted to divide trains at Merstone so that both the Ventnor and Sandown lines had through carriages. They were told this was impractical and after much heart-searching it was decided that through trains would run to Sandown from 1st October on a trial basis, with those on the Ventnor line operating to and from Newport or giving connection with Sandown trains at Merstone. Inevitably this change was followed by complaints from the NGStL and local authorities along the Ventnor line. Ventnor Urban District Council wrote in 1904 asking for the reinstatement of through trains, but Mr Conacher demonstrated that most traffic was to and from Sandown so the trial working arrangements were continued through the summer months. The introduction of road buses in the Island in 1905 prompted a fresh look at arrangements. The Manager suggested running through trains to Ventnor in the months of July, August and September; the Board still wanted to divide trains at Merstone and in the end the existing services were left unaltered. During the winter of 1908-1909 there were eight up and seven down trains, an extra working on Saturdays and two each way on Sundays, all of which ran to and from Newport. Goods traffic was mainly coal to the merchants at Ventnor station and the town's gasworks.

After years of procrastination, in 1907 free passes were issued to leading hotel keepers at Ventnor in the hope that they would encourage travel over the line. A year later the route via Southampton was still being advertised by the LSWR and IWC but the expected traffic from the Midlands had not materialised.

Chapter Thirteen
The Years 1905 to 1910

In the early years of the 20th century a number of railway companies sought ways of reducing operating costs on their more lightly loaded branch lines by employing steam or petrol-engined railcars. A small locomotive permanently joined to a carriage was claimed to be cheaper to run than a conventional locomotive and carriages, and additional savings could be made in staffing the stations. On the IWC, the Ventnor line barely earned enough during winter months to cover its costs and was a prime candidate for such economies. At a meeting of the Board on 23rd December, 1903 Mr Conacher was instructed to make enquiries concerning the use of motor carriages. A few weeks later correspondence was read with Avonside Engine Company, builders of steam railmotors for the Taff Vale Railway, and H.F. Stephens, who was experimenting with a small four-wheel steam railcar on the Kent & East Sussex Railway. R.Y. Pickering & Co. offered to supply a car similar to the latter for £400 but the Board deferred a decision pending more enquiries and an inspection of the railcar. Apart from its limited seating capacity, the railcar would have been quite incapable of managing the steep gradients on the Ventnor line so it was fortunate for the IWC that no purchase was made.

In November 1904 the IWC Directors heard that the Isle of Wight Express Motor Syndicate had published a Prospectus announcing the intention to operate motor omnibuses. Services began on 13th April, 1905 on routes that in most cases paralleled railway lines. Fortunately for the railways, the omnibuses proved to be somewhat unreliable and had difficulties in coping with the hills. However, the IWC Board could not ignore the threat and on 28th June, 1905 reduced the third class return fare between Ryde and Newport from 1s. 9d. to 1s. 6d. to match that by omnibus. They also made fares to Ventnor via Sandown the same as those charged via St Lawrence and increased the number of Parliamentary trains to four a day. Within a month third class return fares to Ventnor were reduced in response to reductions in IWR fares. Letters from the local authorities demanding third class fares on all trains were fended off but it was decided to continue issuing cheap summer fares through the winter, an unusual event for a company that regularly withdrew concessionary fares at the end of each summer. The omnibus service was discontinued during the winter and although it was reintroduced in 1906, the omnibus company made a loss and was wound up a year later.

Whilst Mr Conacher's efforts were recognised by a pay increase from 1st January, 1905 to £450 per annum, the Minutes pointedly omitted to mention J.H. Seymour, the locomotive superintendent. On 3rd July, 1905 Charles Conacher wrote that Mr Seymour had obtained an appointment abroad - perhaps he disapproved of the Board's mean-minded attitude to maintenance whilst favouring the purchase of an expensive railmotor. Applications from six individuals were put before the Board on 26th July when it was decided that the Chairman and Col Harrison would interview two; neither proved acceptable. Charles Conacher attended the next Board meeting on 30th August when the appointment was considered of Robert Guest, a young man who had experience of the LSWR railmotors and was already working for the company on loan from the LSWR. Mr Guest was interviewed and accepted an offer of the post of locomotive superintendent at a salary of £4 a week.

In May 1905 fresh tenders were sought for between one and three steam motor cars seating six (instead of 12) first and 40 third class passengers from Hurst, Nelson & Co., Birmingham Railway Carriage & Wagon Co., Metropolitan Amalgamated Railway Carriage & Wagon Co.* and Kitson & Co. The Board discussed the matter in August and September but repeatedly put off a decision, first by asking for an opinion from Mr Guest as to the most suitable railmotor to select and then from Mr Conacher giving details of how he intended working the traffic assuming the company purchased 1, 2, 3 or 4 railcars - how they might be financed was never made clear. On 25th October, 1905 the Board ordered a railmotor from Hurst, Nelson & Co. for £1,450; they wanted it by 1st March, 1906 but the maker's refused to promise delivery before June and the vehicle did not actually arrive until October.

Isle of Wight Central Railway.

The lines of this Company and its allies embrace the whole of the Island, and by a service of well-appointed Trains connect with all the principal resorts. The trains are in DIRECT CONNECTION with the Boats at **Ryde, Cowes,** and **Yarmouth.**

Decide to Spend your Summer Holidays In the Isle of Wight—the Garden of England.

Unrivalled Golfing facilities. Nine Golf Links within a radius of 9 miles, all in close railway communication.

Magnificent Scenery, Fashionable Watering Places, combined with quiet Seaside Resorts.

☞ SUMMER SEASON ARRANGEMENTS, 1905.

IMPROVED COMMUNICATION between **London, the Midlands and West of England, and Ventnor** (the British Madeira) *via* **Southampton and Cowes** by the **Direct Line** from **Cowes to Ventnor. Express Service** from **Waterloo** every Week-day, at **11.40 a.m.,** due **Ventnor (Town Station)** at **4.10 p.m.**

This is the **only direct** rail route to the far-famed Undercliff District, embracing Niton, Chale, Blackgang and St. Lawrence. **Return Express leaves Ventnor (Town Station)** 12.32 p.m., due London **(Waterloo)** **4.47 p.m. each week-day.**

Fast Express Route to Freshwater, *via* **Ryde and Newport; Four Hours Service** from **London (Victoria)** daily at **11.35 a.m.;** two changes only—Portsmouth and Ryde.

OSBORNE, the King's Gift to the Nation. Open every Tuesday and Friday. Cheap Bookings in connection.

☞ 500 MILES TRAVELLING FOR 10s. 6d. ☜

WEEKLY SEASON TICKETS for Tourists, available to alight at any station, by any train, and as often as desired, are issued daily until September 30th, affording continuous travel for seven days over the whole of the Company's system, at the following rates :—

1st Class, 13s. ; 2nd Class, 10s. 6d. Children, Half-Price. No deposit required.

These Tickets have been specially arranged for Tourists, who will find them the most effectual and cheapest means of getting about the Island within the time stimulated.

They embrace the following popular resorts : Cowes, for Royal Naval College and Osborne, Newport, Carisbrooke (for Castle), Yarmouth Freshwater, (for Totland Bay, Alum Bay, and the Needles), Whippingham (for Osborne), Ryde, Sandown, and Ventnor.

Boat, Coach, and Rail Excursions daily, to all parts of the Island. Cheap Golfers', Yachtmen's, Family, Pleasure Trip, etc., Tickets, Official Time book and Excursion Programme free on application.

Cheap Friday and Saturday to Tuesday, and other Period Excursion Tickets, issued from London, Waterloo, London Bridge, Victoria, etc., Stations, to any Island Station, throughout the season.

General Offices :
NEWPORT, I.W.,
August, 1905.

CHAS. L. CONACHER,
General Manager.

The purchase of the railmotor was given generous publicity both locally and nationally - steam railmotors were not just unique to the Island but unusual on a railway of such a small size as the IWC. The local newspapers published the following description:

> The vehicle arrived on the Isle of Wight on 4th October, 1906. It is 61 feet long overall, and is painted bright maroon and cream, with gold lettering. The windows are of plate glass affording good views of the passing countryside.
>
> When running in reverse, it is driven by remote control from the leading end. The driver is 'in electric communication' with the leading fireman on the footplate. There are three men in charge - the driver, fireman and conductor/guard. All wheels are fitted with Westinghouse brakes, and emergency handbrakes are also installed.
>
> The first class accommodation is for six persons, who are provided with longitudinal spring seats next to the engine. The seats are upholstered in blue cloth and separated by lifting armrests. The sides of the first class saloon are panelled with light oak, and there is a lincrusta ceiling picked out in gold. The floor is of linoleum, covered with coconut matting. The entrance is also picked out in maroon and gold, and is between the two passenger compartments. Folding steps, operated by levers within the vehicle, are provided to enable passengers to board or alight at places where regular stations do not exist. The second class portion is arranged with 44 transverse seats in polished pine, back to back with a central corridor. Ventilation is by hinged ventilators running the entire length of the car. The locomotive portion of the car was constructed by Messrs Hawthorn, Leslie & Co., Newcastle-upon-Tyne, and the carriage portion by Messrs Hurst, Nelson & Co. of Motherwell. The total cost of the car was about £1,500. The car was run on its own wheels from Motherwell to Southampton Docks, where it was run over a specially constructed line direct onto the barge on which it was conveyed. It was towed by two tugs to St Helens where it was unloaded in the same manner, and ran directly under its own power to Newport.

---

* A company created in 1902 by an amalgamation of Metropolitan with the Ashbury, Lancaster, Brown Marshalls and Oldbury companies.

A trial run was carried out the next day when the railmotor was posed for photographs in various parts of the Island railway system. It was housed at Newport in a wooden shed built by Messrs Barton for £64 10s. An ability to work return journeys without wasting time running round at the terminus led to an assumption that it could be worked more intensively than conventional trains. The railmotor was placed in service on the Ventnor line but within a month had to be laid aside with an overheating axle; it took two years to cure the problem. By then management had identified other problems inherent in steam railmotors. They suffered from excessive vibration, dirt from the motor unit entering the passenger compartments, insufficient power to pull an additional load and a consequent lack of flexibility in service. The Central's railmotor suffered from vibration and oscillation that was transmitted from the short locomotive wheelbase to the carriage - the hard seats in the second class compartment did not help!

Meanwhile, Cowes Week in 1905 had been a very grand affair and, being arranged to coincide with a visit of the French Fleet, the crowds were the largest ever seen at Cowes. Unfortunately, the Central's transport arrangements managed to incur some adverse publicity:

After the fireworks, the various 9.00 pm (last departures) from Newport all ran, and then returned from their respective destinations to Cowes. Although two trains were already at Cowes, it was not possible to dispatch these trains to Newport to clear the large crowd assembled at Cowes because of the various empty trains coming up from Newport. It was not anticipated that anyone would wish to leave Cowes between 9.15 pm and 11.00 pm, and it was only a sudden fall of rain a little after 9.00 pm that induced people to proceed to the railway station. The first full special left at 11.20 pm, and four more were soon after dispatched within the space of 25 minutes. The number of passengers which could be accommodated on any one train were admitted to the station as the accommodation became available, three of the five specials were worked by two engines. The fifth special left Cowes at 11.45 pm. After the 11.45 pm special reached Newport, an empty train was dispatched to Cowes to clear the 300 or so passengers still remaining, and this sixth special left Cowes at 12.30 am. [*Isle of Wight County Press* 12th August, 1905]

Despite regular complaints about the poor condition of Medina Jetty, it was not until the summer of 1906 that repairs were put in hand; they proved more expensive than expected and 22 additional piles had to be purchased. The electricity company was finally allowed to install four electric lights for which they charged £4 a year. In the absence of a water supply to the jetty, supplies for the steam cranes were transported by tank wagon from Newport. The Ward estate refused to grant a wayleave for water pipes over its land and, when the cost of laying them solely over railway property proved excessive, the water tank wagons were kept in use - an additional steam crane was purchased for £37.

In May 1906 Charles Conacher informed the Board that Messrs Saunders would supply four single line instruments for the Cowes to Newport line at £5 per annum plus £4 a year maintenance. The Tyer's No. 5 electric tablets came into use as replacements for the Staff and Ticket system on 14th October, 1906. By creating two single line sections, Cowes - Medina Wharf and Medina Wharf - Newport North, a train could be disposed of at Medina Wharf without the need to return the staff to Newport to clear the instruments. Surprisingly, there was no interlocking between the two instruments so it was possible for trains to approach Medina Wharf from opposite directions and unless one could be locked into the wharf sidings they were bound to meet! Just as deficient were the instructions that the Newport-Wharf tablet applied throughout the line to Cowes on Sundays.

In February 1906 the RSPCA won a prosecution for overcrowding pigs during a journey over the railway; the company was fined £30 3s. including costs whilst the drover who loaded them was also fined. The Board decided to demote one of the staff involved and Conacher had the task of seeking more cattle wagons. In November 1905 a claim for compensation was received for an accident, presumably fatal, to a Mr Gustar's bullock - after lengthy negotiation, settlement was reached at £14 10s. This was not the only fatal accident to livestock at this time as in June 1906 a cow was killed on the line near Wootton.

In view of the expense of the railmotor and other works, the Board decreed in November 1906 that renewals of the permanent way be postponed and only essential repairs be put in hand. Conacher was very concerned at this and gained approval to have the permanent way inspected by Mr Elliott Cooper; he pointed out that numerous curves needed relaying and many iron rails were overdue for removal. Fresh purchases of sleepers and new and second-hand rails then ensued.

On 14th February, 1906 the death was reported of one of the Directors, David Gibson, and after a decent interval Major John G. Gibson was appointed in his place. In December 1906 Thomas Bolton died barely a month after he chaired a meeting of the Board; the new Chairman was Percy Mortimer, a man who was more inclined to take the advice of the Manager. In January 1907 Samuel Peto, who had been an auditor of the company's accounts, offered himself as a Director and was voted onto the Board. He was followed in June 1909 by Edward J. Martin, a nephew of Henry Martin, who had returned to Britain after spending some years in India as a tea planter. Mr Conacher's salary rose to £500 per year from 1st March, 1907 whilst Mr Guest was awarded £228 a year from 1st September, 1907.

Accidents to passengers included one to a Mrs Blake in December 1906 who put her foot through the floor of Newport waiting room! Later that month the company had to find £50 to compensate a boy who fell whilst swinging on the gates at Smithard's crossing; new gates were put in place later in 1907 and the crossing widened the following year. A Mrs Ballard fell when alighting from a train at Newport for which she received £75.

The railmotor returned to traffic in January 1907. Soon afterwards Charles Conacher conducted trials to compare running costs of the railmotor and an ordinary steam-hauled train - the railmotor was said to have been marginally more economical. Railmotor No. 1 was tried on the Freshwater line during the summer of 1907 and also on a short-lived through service put on to and from Ryde. In order to make the best possible use of the company's investment, Charles Conacher proposed in March 1907 to create a second railmotor by pairing 0-4-2T No. 3 with a new carriage. Tenders were sought for a suitable carriage but all proved far too expensive and instead a Midland Railway bogie carriage was purchased.

Despite protestations of poverty, the IWC found sufficient money during 1907 to construct a house for the station master at Wootton and brick in an arch in the adjoining road overbridge for use as a booking office. A fresh agreement was drawn up with Mr Pittis, owner of the siding at Horringford, for permission to construct cattle pens at the station. An expense that did not fall to the IWC was the construction at Cowes of Granville Road bridge on the site of a wooden footbridge demolished several years earlier. Local newspapers reported the holding of a ceremony at 3.0 pm on Wednesday 27th March when Mrs Snellgrove, wife of the Chairman of Cowes Council, cut a white ribbon to open the bridge decorated with flags for the occasion. It was described as having a width of 24 ft, a span of 28 ft and a height of 14 ft 6 in. above the railway; built by James Ball & Son mainly in brick, the steel girder that formed the main span had to be slid into position one night by the light of flares. The total cost to the local council was about £1,500.

On 20th September, 1907 Lt Col Von Donop from the Board of Trade inspected a siding to serve a small stone quarry owned by Percy Mortimer near the Ventnor terminus. The line was on a gradient at this point so he naturally asked that it be shunted with the locomotive at the lower (Ventnor) end of the train.

Matters discussed by the Board in 1908 differed little from previous years: more relaying of the permanent way was required, a defect occurred in the weighbridge at Medina Wharf and improved sanitation had to be provided at Wootton, Alverstone, Newchurch and Blackwater. In April 1908 it was decided to save money by introducing short time working in certain departments at Newport workshops - a short sighted decision that delayed repairs already affected by the time devoted to the railmotors. Railmotor 1 was still working intermittently, but Mr Guest had been unable to progress the conversion of locomotive No. 3 and its carriage because of urgent repairs to other locomotives.

In November 1908 Mr Conacher wrote to the Board enclosing a list of complaints from the County Council including:

1. Poor connections between IWR and IWC trains at Sandown [Conacher said he was talking to the IWR about this].

2. The desirability of covering the footbridge at Newport [Mr Elliott Cooper had already prepared the necessary plans].
3. The need to keep the platform at Newport free of livestock. [Conacher pointed out this was not possible when merchandise and livestock were conveyed by passenger train. If photographs are anything to go by, a cattle truck attached to the rear of a passenger train was a common occurrence.]

On 23rd December, 1908 a fatal accident took place at Newport. At about 10.30 pm a locomotive was coupled to 11 wagons which stood in the dock siding at Newport station and then drawn forward. The signalman heard a noise and saw all four wheels of the last wagon had derailed. It appears that the shunter had slipped and fallen across the rails so that the wagon became derailed when the wheels passed over his body, death was attributed to misadventure. Both the line and wagons were examined and found to be in 'perfect condition.'

At the beginning of 1909 the IWC decided to become a member of the Railway Clearing House; Charles Conacher was appointed to the RCH General Managers' and Superintendents' Conferences and certain staff were signed up to the Clearing House superannuation scheme. Minor alterations were made to the Manager's office and another typewriter was bought. Work to install the Electric Tablet system between Newport and Merstone reached completion; this allowed a train to be put away at Shide. In June a man trespassing on the railway at Cowes suffered an accident that resulted in the amputation of a leg; the company denied liability but later gave seven guineas towards an artificial replacement.

The service provided by the IWC was not to the liking of the members of Ventnor Urban District Council. They hoped that the existence of two railways in the town would lead to some competition but found that IWC passenger and goods rates were as high as its competitor. The Council vainly asked the Isle of Wight County Council to purchase the Island railways. Although the local authorities were not prepared to help find the necessary finance, the County Council did not give up hope that others might take the ideas forward. In 1909 an engineer, William Upton Marshall, reported that the railways could be bought and electrified for £1,200,000; this included £310,000 for electrification of the existing lines on the single phase high tension AC system fed via overhead wires as used by the LBSCR. In addition to numerous halts he claimed that it would be possible to build extensions including a connection between the two stations at Ventnor and a line between St Lawrence and Freshwater. Towards the end of 1909 a Mr James Gray approached the IWC with electrification proposals and had a lengthy meeting with Charles Conacher. He was told the Directors were not prepared to recommend the shareholders incur the necessary expenditure: '. . . the island traffic was very small, and no service of trains, however frequent, would make the people travel upon the Railway much more than they now did; and there was great road competition with Goods traffic'.

In October a train collided with a horse and cart at the Cement Mills level crossing, one of several such occurrences over the years; the Manager was authorised to employ his brother Mr H. Conacher for a fee of five guineas in the subsequent court action. Warning boards were subsequently erected, enginemen warned to sound the whistle and the cement company issued with padlocks and keys to the gates - not that this solved the problem.

Also in October 1909, Charles Conacher secured the contract for carrying the night mails from Ryde to Newport, Cowes and Freshwater. The *Isle of Wight County Press* commented: 'Thus the old mail coach has passed out of existence in the Island except for two or three rural routes not served by the railways. The new service will be a great advantage to the public, as it will allow a later posting time at Newport and Cowes, and a considerably accelerated early morning delivery at the west end of the Island'.

A mail train would be worked to Ryde Pier Head each evening and left to await the arrival of the early morning mail boat from Portsmouth. The train was timed to leave Ryde Pier Head at 3.35 am, arriving at Newport at 4.0 and Freshwater at 5.40. Revised instructions issued in 1911 warned the crew of the wharf shunter charged with hauling the mail van to Cowes not to abandon it *en route* in order to shunt at Medina Wharf! In September 1910 Percy Mortimer reported that the contract had brought in an additional £252 in the previous half-year.

During the winter of 1909-1910, services were disrupted by flooding at Whitwell and in Ryde tunnel on the LSWR/LBSCR Joint Committee's line. Negotiations began with Mew Langton & Co. for an exchange of land at Newport and the diversion of a footpath to permit

Isle of Wight Central Railway.

WORKING TIME TABLE

FOR

October, 1909, and until further notice.

PRIVATE

For the information of the Company's Servants only.

General Offices, Newport, I.W.

CHAS. L. CONACHER, General Manager.

RYDE LINE.

UP. WEEK-DAYS.

Miles			1 Mail En a.m. (Mondays only)	2 Mail En a.m. (Mondays excepted)	3 Mixed a.m.	4 Pass a.m.	5 Mixed a.m.	6 Lt. En noon	7 Mxd p.m.	8 Pass p.m.	9 Pass p.m.	10 Pass p.m.	11 LtEn. p.m.	12 Mixed p.m.	13 Mail p.m.	14 Pass p.m. (Satdys only)
	NEWPORT	dep	2 30		7 25	9 25	10 25	—	1 10	3 10	5 0	5 45		8 0	8 45	9 15
2¼	Whippingham	A			7 30	9 31	10 31	–	1 15	3 15	5 5	5ps49		8 6	8ps49	9 20
3	Wootton	dep	pass.		7 33	9 34	10 34	-	1 18	3 18	5 8	5 52		8 10	8A51	9 24
4½	Haven Street	A			7 38	9 40	10 39	-	1 24	3 22	5 12	5ps55		8 16	8ps54	9 28
6	Ashey	A	2 45		7 43	9 43	10B44	–	1 28	3 26	5 16	5ps58		8E22	8ps57	9 33
8¼	Ryde (St. John's Rd)	arr	—		7 48	9 48	10 50	—	1 33	3 32	5 22	6 C 3		8 29	9 3	9 40
8¼	Ryde (St. John's Rd.)	dep	2 55	2 30	7 50	9 49	10 51	12 10	1 34	3 33	5 23	6 5	7 55	8 30	9 4	
9	Ryde (Esplanade)	dep	2 58	2 33	7 54	9 52	10 53	12 13	1 37	3 37	5 27	6 8	7 58	8 32	9 7	—
9¼	RYDE (Pier Head)	arr	3 0	2 35	7 56	9 55	10 55	12 15	1 40	3 40	5 30	6 10	8 0	8 35	9 10	—

UP. SUNDAYS.

Miles			1 Mail En a.m.	2 Pass a.m.	3 Goods noon	4 Pass p.m.	5 Mixed p.m.	6 Pass p.m.
	NEWPORT	dep		10 15	12 0	2 40	4 25	8 20
2¼	Whippingham	A		10 20	12 7	2 45	4 30	8 25
3	Wootton	dep		10 23	12 10	2 48	4 33	8 27
4½	Haven Street	A		10 28	12 16	2 51	4 39	8 32
6	Ashey	A		10 32	12 22	2 54	4 44	8 37
8¼	Ryde (St. John's Rd)	arr		10 39	12 30	2 59	4 50	8 43
8¼	Ryde (St. John's Rd.)	dep	2 30	10 40	12 45	3 1	4 51	8 45
9	Ryde (Esplanade)	dep	2 33	10 43	12 48	3 3	4 53	8 47
9¼	RYDE (Pier Head)	arr	2 35	1045	12 50	3 5	4 55	8 50

A Calls by Signal. B Cross No. 3 Down. C Cross No. 8 Down. E Cross No. 10 Down.

NOTES. Week-days.—No. 3 Must run to time to prevent delay to London Services.
Nos. 5, 7 & 12 Not more than one spring buffered wagon, with screw coupling, must be attached to these Trains without special authority. No intermediate Sidings to be worked unless ordered.
No. 14 Cross No. 11 Down at Ashey.

Ryde Goods Trains to run as per notice between 6 a.m. and 7 a.m.

ELECTRIC BLOCK. Newport, Wootton, Ashey. TELEPHONE. Newport, Whippingham, Wootton, Haven Street, Ashey, Ryde.

NOTES—Sundays—

No. 6 to convey Mails, Vans to be left at Pier Head.

DOWN. WEEK-DAYS.

Miles			1 Mail a.m.	2 Pass a.m.	3 Pass. a.m.	4 Lt.En a.m.	5 Mixed noon	6 Pass p.m.	7 Pass. p.m.	8 Pass. p.m.	9 Lt. En p.m.	10 Pass p.m.	11 Emp. p.m.	12 Mail En p.m.	13 Pass. p.m. (Saturdays only)
	RYDE (Pier Head)	dep	3 25	8 20	10 30	11 5	12 20	2 35	3 50	6 0	6 25	8 5	8 35	9 20	
½	Ryde (Esplanade)	dep	3 30	8 22	10 32	11 7	12 22	2 37	3 52	6 2	6 27	8 7	8 37	9 22	
1¼	Ryde (St. John's Rd)	arr	3 33	8 24	10 34	11 10	12 24	2 39	3 54	6 5	6 30	8 9	8 40	9 25	
													Goods		
1¼	Ryde (St. John's Rd.)	dep	3D35	8 30	10 37	Shunt Ryde Yard.	12 30	2 44	3 59	6C10	Shunt Ryde Yard	8 14	9 30		9 45
3¼	Ashey	A	3E43	8 38	10B44		12 38	2 50	4 5	6 18		8G22	9 40		9 52
5	Haven Street	A	pass	8 42	10 48		12 42	2 54	4 9	6 22		8 26	9 45		9 56
6½	Wootton	dep	pass	8 46	10 53		12 47	2 58	4 13	6 27		8 31	9 55		10A1
7½	Whippingham	A	3F55	8 49	10 55		12 50	3 0	4 15	6 30		8 34	10 0		10 4
9¼	NEWPORT	arr	4 0	8 55	11 0		12 55	3 5	4 20	6 35		8 40	10 10		10 10

DOWN. SUNDAYS.

Miles			1 Mail a.m.	2 Pass a.m.	3 Mixed p.m.	4 Pass. p.m.	5 Mixed p.m.	6 Pass. p.m.
	RYDE (Pier Head)	dep	3 25	10 50	1 15	3 10	6 20	8 55
½	Ryde (Esplanade)	dep	3 30	10 52	1 17	3 12	6 22	8 57
1¼	Ryde (St. John's Rd)	arr	3 33	10 54	1 19	3 14	6 25	8 59
1¼	Ryde (St. John's Rd.)	dep	3D35	10 57	1 22	3 18	6 28	9 5
3¼	Ashey	A	3E43	11 4	1 29	3 24	6 35	9 12
5	Haven Street	A	pass	11 7	1 33	3 28	6 38	9 15
6½	Wootton	dep	pass	11 12	1 38	3 32	6 44	9 20
7½	Whippingham	A	3F55	11 14	1 40	3 34	6 47	9 23
9¼	NEWPORT	arr	4 0	11 20	1 45	3 39	6 53	9 28

A. Calls by Signal. B. Cross No 5 Up unless late. C. Cross No. 10 Up at St. John's Road. G. Cross No. 12 Up.

NOTES.—Week-days.

No. 11 cross No. 14 Up at Ashey.
No. 1 D—Arrive on I.W.R. Road, cross over and pick up Tablet. E—Tablet and Staff. F—Stop for Bridge Test.

STAFF SECTION. Newport to Ashey. ELECTRIC TABLET. Ashey to Ryde (St. John's Road).

NOTES. Sundays

No. 3. Train Coaches of No. 12 Up, Saturdays, to be left at St. John's Road for this working, and cleaned there

VENTNOR LINE.

DOWN.

Miles			1 Goods a.m.	2 Mixed a.m.	3 Pass. a.m.	4 Pass noon	5 Pass. p.m.	6 Exprs p.m.	7 Pass p.m.	8 Mixed p.m.	9 Pass p.m. (Saturdays)	Sundays 1 Mixed a.m.	Sundays 2 Pass p.m.
	MERSTONE Jct.	dep	7 0	9 18	10 32	12 10	1 20	pass	5 35	8 15	9 24	9 30	8 34
1½	Godshill A	dep	7 15	9 22	10 36	12 13	1 25	4 4	5 39	8 19	9 28	9 35	8 39
4	Whitwell	,,	7 45	9 29	10 41	12 18	1 31	4 A9	5 45	8 24	9 33	9 40	8 45
5½	St. Lawrence A	,,	7 55	9 35	10 45	12 22	1 35	4 A12	5 50	8 31	9 37	9 45	8 50
6¾	VENTNOR Town	arr	8 5	9 40	10 50	12 25	1 40	4 15	5 55	8 35	9 40	9 50	8 55

A. Stops by Signal.

N.B. All Passenger Trains must stop momentarily outside Ventnor Home Signals—Goods Trains to stop dead.

NOTES. Week-days.

No. 1 Take all Ventnor Line Wagons Must work to time. Shunt Ventnor Yard on arrival. Load Sand when required. No. 3, 4, 6. & 8 Through Trains Cowes to Ventnor Town.

N.B.—See Main Line Sheet for Branch Engine Working.

ELECTRIC BLOCK. Merstone Junction, Godshill, Whitwell, Ventnor Town

TELEPHONE. Same, including St. Lawrence.

UP.

Miles			1 Mixed a.m.	2 Pass a.m.	3 Pass. a.m.	4 Pass noon	5 Mixed p.m.	6 Pass. p.m.	7 Pass p.m.	8 Pass p.m.	9 Pass p.m. (Sats. only)	Sundays 1 Mixed a.m.	Sundays 2 Pass p.m.
	VENTNOR Town	dep	8 25	9 45	10 55	12 30	2 35	4 45	6 0	8 40	9 45	10 35	9 0
1¼	St. Lawrence	A	8 30	9 50	10 59	12 34	2 39	4 49	6 4	8 44	9 49	10 39	9 4
2¾	Whitwell	dep.	8 35	9 55	11 3	12 38	2 43	4 53	6 8	8 48	9 53	10 44	9 8
5¼	Godshill	A	8 40	9 59	11 7	12 42	2 47	4 57	6 12	8 52	9 57	10 48	9 12
6¾	MERSTONE Jct.	arr.	8 45	10 2	11 10	12 46	2 50	4 59	6 15	8 55	10 0	10 52	9 15

NOTES.—Week-days. A Calls by Signal.

No. 1 to bring all Ventnor Line Wagons Heavy Engine. Must run to time.
No. 3 4, & 6 Must run to time. Through Trains to Cowes.
STAFF SECTION. Merstone Junction to Whitwell. Whitwell to Ventnor Town.

N.B.—Every effort must be made to work the Branch Trains to time, so that delay may not result to the Main Line Trains.

Working timetable for October 1909.

SANDOWN LINE.

DOWN. — WEEK-DAYS.

Miles		1 Goods a.m.	2 Goods a.m.	3 Mxd a.m.	4 Mxd a.m.	5 Goods a.m.	6 Pass a.m.	7 Pas	8 Goods	9 Pas	10 Exp p.m.	11 Pass p.m.	12 Mxd p.m.	13	14	15 Goods p.m.	16 Pass p.m.
NEWPORT	dep.	6 30	6 45	7 40	9 5	10 20	12 0	1 5		3 10	3 50	5 15	5 20	8 0		8 30	9 10
Pan Lane Siding	pass																
Shide	dep		7 0	7A44	9A 8	10A23		1A 9								9 14	
Blackwater	A			7 47	9 12	10 26		1 12	3 17	pass	5 23	5 28	8 4			9 18	
MERSTONE Junct.	arr	6 50		7 51	9 16	10 30		42	9 1 17	3 21	4ps0	5 25	5 30	6 12	8 45	9 22	
MERSTONE Junct	dep			7 53	9 18	10 32	11 15	12 10	1 20	3 23		5 28	5 35	6 15	9 15	9 25	
Horringford	A			7 57	9 22	10 36	11 20	12 14	1 24	3 27		5 36	6 19			9 28	
Newchurch	A			8 1	9 26	10 40		12 18	1 28	3 31		5 40	6 22			9 31	
Alverstone	A			8 5	9 30	10 44		12 21	1 30	3 34		5 44	6 25			9 36	
SANDOWN	arr.			8 10	9 35	10 48		12 25	1 35	3 38		5 48	6 30	9 45		9 40	

A Stops by Signal. **N.B. Engines must not run coupled between Newport and Merstone Junction.** **N.B.—The maintenance of connection with I.W.R. Trains is of first importance.**

NOTES Week-days. B.—Branch Engine work Horringford Pit if necessary. Shunt Ventnor Yard.
No.1 Take all Ventnor Line Wagons.
No. 2 Engine of 7·25 Newport to Ryde. Work Pan and Shide to relieve Ventnor Goods.
No. 3. Convey Mew's and Crouchers Sandown Traffic. No. 7 must run to time. Work through to Ventnor.

SUNDAYS.
No. 1 take empty Vectis Wagons to Shide Pit.
No. 5 leave on arrival of No. 1 Up. Worked by 3·45 p.m. Freshwater Engine.

ELECTRIC TABLET—Newport, Shide, and Merstone. ELECTRIC BLOCK—Merstone, Newchurch and Sandown.
TELEPHONE—All Stations.

UP. — WEEK-DAYS.

Miles		1 Goods a.m.	2 Pass a.m.	3 Mixed a.m.	4 Pass a.m.	5 Goods a.m.	6 Pass a.m.	7 Mxd p.m.	8 Pass p.m.	9 Eng. p.m.	10 Pass p.m.	11 Pass p.m.	12	13	14	15	16 Goods p.m.
SANDOWN	dep.		8 30	9 45	10 55		12 30	2 35	3 45		6 0	9 45					10 0
Alverstone	A		8 34		10 59		12 34	2 39	4 48		6 4	9 49					10 4
Newchurch	A		8 37		11 2		12 37	2 42	4 4		6 7	9 52					10 7
Horringford	A		8 41		11 5		12 40	2 45	4 6		6 12	9 55					10 11
MERSTONE Junct.	arr		8 45	10 3	11 9		12 44	2 50	4 6		6 17	9 55				10 13	10 15
MERSTONE Junct.	dep		8 47	10 5	11 12		12 47	2 53	4 12		6 19	9 58					10 18
Blackwater	A		8 51	pass	11 16		12 52	2 57	4 17		6 23	10 2					10 22
Shide	dep		8A54	pass	11A20		12 55	3 A1	4 21		3 A7	10 6			A		10A12
NEWPORT	arr	7 15	8 58	10 15	11 24	1 0	1 0	3 5	4 25	5 10	6 30	10 10	10 15			10 45	10 30

A Stops by Signal. **N.B.—Engines must not run coupled between Newport and Merstone Junction.**
NOTES Week-days No. 3 Must run to time. Attach Wagons of No. 1 Up Branch at Merstone. No. 5 ex Horringford Pit
if necessary. No. 6 must not be held at Sandown after 12·45 p.m. and work to Sandown only.
No. 14 Return of 8·30 p.m. Goods from Newport.

SUNDAYS.
No. 2 To clear out Shide and take up working of 12·0 noon Ryde Goods.
No. 5 Engine to work No. 2 Down Branch.

TABLET SECTIONS. Newport, Shide, and Merstone. STAFF SECTION. Merstone Junction to Sandown.

COWES LINE.

DOWN. — WEEK-DAYS.

Miles		1 Mail a.m.	2 Mixed a.m.	3 Pass. a.m.	4 Pass. a.m.	5 Pass. p.m.	6 Pass. p.m.	7 Pass. p.m.	8 Pass. p.m.	9 Pass. p.m.	10 Pass. p.m.	11 Pass p.m.	12 Pass. p.m.
NEWPORT	dep.	5 10	5 13	9 5	11 5	11 26	1 5	4 30	5 15	6 40	9 0	9 5	
Cement Mills			8 19	9 9		11 29		3 14	4 34	6 44		9 9	
Medina Wharf	pass	5 19	8 23	9 13	11 11	11 33	1 13	3 17	4 39	6 49		9 13	
Mill Hill	dep		8 28	9 18		11 38	1 18	3 22	4 43	5 26	6 53	9 12	9 27
COWES	arr.	5 25	8 30	9 20	11 15	11 40	1 20	3 25	4 45	5 28	8 15	9 15	9 30

Wharf Engine to work as required. N.B.—No Trains must cross at Medina Wharf in either direction. No. 1 to be worked by Wharf Engine.
by 5·30 a.m. No. 5, 6, & 9 Week-days, must run to time. No. 6 can call at Mills.
ELECTRIC TABLET. Newport, Medina Wharf, Cowes. TELEPHONE. Newport, Cement Mills, Wharf box, Medina Wharf, Mill Hill, Cowes.

UP. — WEEK-DAYS.

Miles		1 Pass. a.m.	2 Pass. a.m.	3 Pass. a.m.	4 Pass. p.m.	5 Pass. p.m.	6 Exprs p.m.	7 Pass. p.m.	8 Pass. p.m.	9 Pass. p.m.	10 Goods p.m.	11 Mixed p.m.	12 Mail p.m.	13 Pass. p.m.
COWES	dep.	8 45	10 0	11 45	12 40	2 50	3 35	5 2	5 33		7 42	8 38		10 0
Mill Hill	dep	8 48	10 3	11 47	12 42	2 52	3 37	5A7	5 33		7 45	8 41		10 2
Medina Wharf	pass	8 51	10 7	11 49	12 47	2 57	3 41	5 10	5 36		7 49	8 45		10 7
Cement Mills			10 3					3 47	5 15	5 43	5 40	6 1	9 56	10 11
NEWPORT	arr	8 58	10 15	11 56	12 51	3 0	3 47	5 15	5 43		7 55	8 42	9 56	10 15

No. 4, must run to time.
clear Mills. B. Calls by signal.
A. Saturdays only and other days at Station Master's discretion. No. 9. shunting Engine from Wharf.
N.B. — No Trains must cross at Medina Wharf in either direction.
No. 13 must connect with Southampton Boat.

N.B. Wharf Engine to work as required.

FRESHWATER LINE.

DOWN. — WEEK-DAYS.

Miles		1 Mail & Goods a.m.	2 Pass. a.m.	3 Mixed a.m.	4 Pass p.m.	5 Pass p.m.	6 Mixed p.m.	7 Pass p.m.	8 Pass p.m.
NEWPORT	dep.	4 30	9 2	11 30	1 17	3 15	4 40	9 15	
Carisbrooke	dep		9 9	11A37	1 22	3A22	4 48	6 47	9A22
Watchingwell	A		9 14	11 42		4 55	6 52	9 28	
Calbourne	dep	4 50	9 19	11A47	1A27	3A32	4 58	6A56	9 38
Ningwood	dep	5 5	9 23	11A52	1A32	3A37	5 4	7A1	9 37
Yarmouth	dep	5 30	9 30	12 0	1 40	3 45	5 10	7 5	9 40
FRESHWATER	arr.	5 40	9 37	12 5	1 45	3 50	5 15	7 10	9 45

A Calls by signal.

NOTES.—Weekdays No. 5·45 a.m. Take forward all Goods traffic. Unload Mails and shunt at Yarmouth as required.
Must reach Freshwater by No. 3. Shunt at Freshwater and return with 8·15 a.m. train. No. 2 must reach
to time. No. 3. To convey none but urgent Wagons. No. 5 must work to time. Stop at Watchingwell for Freshwater
Tenants only. No. 6 Cross No. 5 Up at Carisbrooke. Train to be left at Freshwater for 8·15 a.m. working with No. 1 Up.

SUNDAYS.
No. 1 convey Mails only. Return with No. 1 Up.

ELECTRIC BLOCK. Carisbrooke, Calbourne, Ningwood, Yarmouth and Freshwater. TELEPHONE. Same

UP. — WEEK-DAYS.

Miles		1 Mixed a.m.	2 Pass a.m.	3 Mixed a.m.	4 Pass p.m.	5 Goods p.m.	6 Pass p.m.	7 Pass p.m.	8 Pass p.m.	9 Mixed p.m.
FRESHWATER	dep	8 15	9 42	12 20	2 25		4 20	6 15		
Yarmouth	dep	8 20	9 47	12 25	2 30	4 55	5 40	7 25		
Ningwood	dep	8A30	9 55	12 33	2 38	6 5	7 33	10A14		
Calbourne	dep	8A35	10 0	12 38	2 43	6 20	7 A33	10A14		
Watchingwell	A	8A41	10 5	12 44		6 35	7A38	10A22		
Carisbrooke	dep	8 50	10 10	12 48	2A53	4 48	6A27	10A29		
NEWPORT	arr	8 55	10 17	12 55	3 0	4 55	6 33	7 55	10 35	

A Calls by signal.

NOTES. Weekdays
No. 2 must run to time.
No. 6 Goods Train except Saturdays. Cross No. 7 Down at Carisbrooke when work requires.

STAFF SECTIONS. Newport to Carisbrooke. Carisbrooke to Ningwood. Ningwood to Freshwater.

General Note. — The times of Goods Trains are fixed to give the latest running allowed. Earlier running is not prohibited if line clear.

SUNDAYS.
No. 2 Engine to work Sandown Goods.

Working timetable for October 1909.

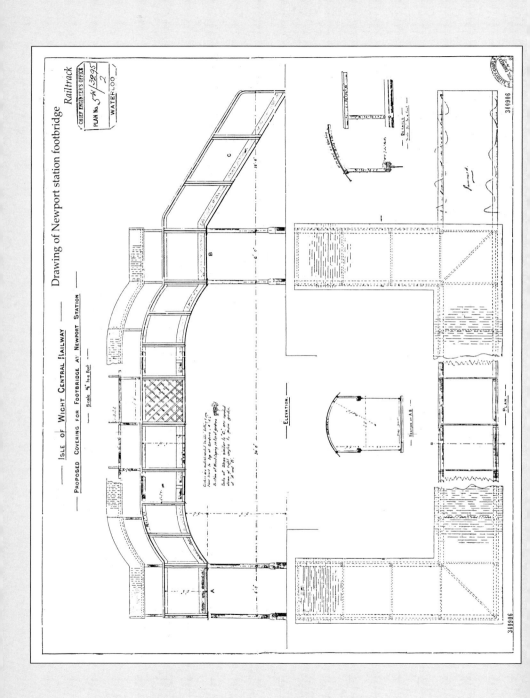

Drawing of Newport station footbridge

Railtrack

ISLE OF WIGHT CENTRAL RAILWAY

PROPOSED COVERING FOR FOOTBRIDGE AT NEWPORT STATION

Scale ¼" to a foot

CHIEF ENGINEER'S OFFICE
PLAN No. 5 W/3295
2
WATERLOO

ELEVATION

SECTION AT A B

PLAN

DETAILS

310906

310906

an enlargement of the goods yard. J. Ball & Son extended the motor shed and roofed the footbridge between the platforms for £73 17s. 6d.; the footbridge alone cost £35.

In an attempt to save money, purchases of permanent way materials had been reduced, much to the concern of Mr Conacher. He again persuaded the Board to have the railway inspected by Mr Elliott Cooper who found several lengths that urgently needed complete replacement. Although the Board agreed to the renewal of the Redway section (on the Sandown line), the manager had a fright when he was instructed not to run the newly purchased locomotive No. 2 on the line. The decision was subsequently reversed but '. . . the Secretary was instructed to tell Mr Conacher to be very careful in using the engine over the Redway section'. Renewal of signalling equipment at Newport station was carried out and a few months later £60 had to be expended on the replacement of an underbridge at Alverstone.

In 1908 Charles Conacher claimed that the numbers of passengers carried by the IWC had risen by 200,000 over the previous 10 years; this was not a constant figure as the increase varied between 150,000 and 250,000 depending on the years compared. There had been a decline in those travelling first and second class but this was matched by an increase in third class passengers, despite the restriction of Parliamentary fares to a handful of trains. Changes in the fare structure came into force in June 1909 and were given wide publicity; they followed an experiment in February of issuing uniform third class tickets on Mondays. The multitude of excursion fares were swept away, third class fares were raised by about 10 per cent but became available on most trains, second class return fares were abolished, single fares reduced roughly 10per cent and all first class fares by about 20 per cent. The changes were later said to have greatly increased the numbers of third class passengers and receipts, but Board of Trade returns show this was more than offset by a fall in those travelling second class.

In March 1910 Charles Conacher resigned and was replaced on a temporary basis by George Henley, the company's accountant. He presided over a poor year for the railway. The death of King Edward VII on 6th May, 1910 received only passing mention; George Henley seemed more concerned about the loss of income following the cancellation of Ashey Races and reduced receipts at Whitsun. One of the first motor cars in the Island collided with the level crossing gates at Merstone on 8th August, 1910; the lady occupants attempted to claim for injuries and repairs to the vehicle but the Board refused to accept liability. The latter half of that year was no better because there were no fireworks during Cowes week - it was an exceptionally wet and rough time for the Island. The railway carried more goods and mineral traffic but an increase in working expenses wiped out much of the extra income; as a result profits for 1910 had shown no improvement over those 10 years previously. The goods traffic was not constant; a reduction in 1907 was attributed to a depression in the Island building trade after years of steady growth whilst a drop in coal traffic mainly to stations on the IWR was sufficient to give concern. The Ventnor line had proved a great disappointment.

Year ending 31 Dec.	Passenger traffic Numbers carried			Goods traffic		Gross receipts		Working expenses	% of expenditure in relation to receipts
	First	Second	Third	Minerals Tons	General Tons	Pass. £	Goods £	£	
1905	41,651	208,488	721,239	133,637	62,140	31,813	16,710	31,264	65
1910	35,225	108,991	779,935	126,995	59,575	31,990	16,754	32,907	68

To finish the chapter, we should try to sum up Charles Conacher's period as Manager. All the investment in replacing the iron rails, locomotives and rolling stock seems to have cut little ice with the public. The writer of a guide book had the following to say about the Island railways and the IWC in particular:

The railway system of the Isle of Wight can hardly be said to have reached mature development. The trains run at infrequent intervals and at a low rate of speed, although the fares are, by comparison with those of other railways, very expensive. The construction of the carriages points pretty obviously to an early period, and the accommodation afforded by the railway stations leaves much to be desired. It is only fair to the officials, however, to say that passengers receive every attention that can be expected.

This photograph of Newport Station staff may have been taken to mark the departure of Charles Conacher in 1910 and included George W. Ranger, traffic inspector (*second from left*), Harry Hill, Cowes station master (*seventh from left*) and Albert (Bert) Beasley, personal assistant to the General Manager (*ninth from left, wearing the cloth cap*). Locomotive 0-4-4T No. 2 stands in the platform, the platform covering looks resplendent in its two tone paint finish and a gas light can just be glimpsed as can the profusion of posters.

T. Cooper Collection

Chapter Fourteen

The Willmott take-over
1911 to 1913

The failure of the NGStL to attract a significant income left the Central with a financial burden that had not been anticipated. The IWC Board never anticipated that they would have to pay the £2,000 a year guarantee to the Godshill company but the reverse proved to be the case and it became a regular feature in the accounts. This was resented by preference shareholders who might otherwise have expected a modest dividend. Matters were made worse when, following the death of Thomas Bolton in 1906, Percy Mortimer became Chairman of the IWC. Mr Mortimer held most of the NGStL shares and about half the debentures, having put up £60,000 to complete the line. He was hardly likely to favour an alteration of the guarantee that might worsen his own position. After Samuel Peto, a preference shareholder, joined the Board in 1907 he took the opportunity privately to press his case but to no effect.

Charles Conacher hinted on several occasions that the company was within 'a measurable distance' of paying a dividend to preference shareholders. This was in the expectation that the troublesome railmotors would bring some economies. Instead, so much workshop time was devoted to the railmotors that overhauls of the locomotives fell behind, whilst the purchase of an additional locomotive in 1909 merely added to the problems. At a meeting of the IWC Board on 23rd March, 1910 it was reported that Mr Conacher had submitted his resignation after having been appointed Manager of the Cambrian Railways. He had invited applications for the vacancy but the Board deferred a decision and promoted the accountant George Henley to Manager on a temporary basis. In addition to a modest pay rise for Mr Henley, Mr Conacher's departure prompted a round of increases for the chief clerk, traffic inspector and permanent way inspector. However, Mr Conacher's recommendation that an Engineer be asked to visit the Island once a month was ignored and the Board seems to have relied on Mr Henley's limited experience interspersed with the occasional Director's visit. Relations with the IWR had improved to such an extent that Horace F. Tahourdin was appointed a Director and, in a reciprocal move, Percy Mortimer joined the IWR Board. Percy Mortimer soon discovered he had more in common with the Directors and management of the IWR than with his own company.

An unscheduled meeting of the Board took place on 18th January, 1911. The minutes baldly stated that '. . . the position of the Chairman was considered' and went on to record a resolution put forward by Mr Peto that a general meeting of shareholders be held for the purpose of terminating the agreement with the NGStL; clearly there had previously been discussions but they were not minuted. Mr Peto could not find any support amongst his fellow Directors so the resolution was lost and the meeting ended. On 22nd February the Board, in the absence of Mr Peto, heard that Samuel Peto and Sidney Herbert had issued a circular to shareholders on 11th February in which they opined that the different classes of shareholder should elect individual Directors so that their interests would be represented on the Board. It was decided that the other Directors would issue their own circular, but Mr Peto's point seems to have been conceded as all the Directors made themselves available for re-election at the next meeting.

A half-yearly meeting of shareholders took place on 1st March, 1911; instead of the usual ill-attended meeting the Directors were joined by 22 shareholders including Harry Willmott and Sidney Herbert with proxies from another 118. Several members of the Mortimer and Gibson families were present plus at least five Directors and employees of the IWR; many IWR shareholders held shares in the IWC and vice versa. The meeting is known to have been stormy but the official record failed to give any hint of what took place beyond a summary of the votes taken. Once the preliminaries had been concluded ordinary shareholders elected Messrs Mortimer, Gibson and Martin as Directors. Col Harrison was rejected by preference

Expenditure on the Capital Account
1911 to 1912

The following summary is made up from numerous lists of expenditure on the capital account as recorded in the Minutes. It is by no means a complete record of the company's expenditure at that time.

			£
Stations	Cowes	raising loading dock, extra barriers, station buildings, urinals	40
	Mill Hill	improving WC	2
	Medina Wharf	new office, sidings and piles	705
		land filling in viaduct, etc.	525
	Newport	improvements to office and station accommodation, refreshment rooms, urinals, footbridge, additional sidings, roadway, coal wharf, cattle dock, shunting signals, additional fire appliances, extra hydrant, fire hose, etc.	1,275
		raising locomotive water tank, new umbrella water tanks	295
		water supply	550
		platform extensions	11
		locomotive footpath and new sand house	62
		new carriage siding	75
		additional machinery, drill & tools	250
	Whippingham	crossing loop, platform, etc.	350
		additional signals, etc.	120
	Haven Street	extension to signal box, waiting shed, etc.	16
		additional point locks, etc.	33
	Ashey	additional shelter on up platform, etc.	36
	Shide	extending platform	11
	Blackwater	station house, lengthening platform, improving coal depot	55
	Merstone	water supply, new engine & pump	61
		platform lighting - acetylene installation	15
		new siding	180
	Horringford	station house, lengthening platform, etc.	35
	Newchurch	station, raising platform and additional oil store	77
		additional siding and cost of land	150
	Alverstone	new station house	125
	Sandown	new brickfield siding	150
General Offices		new safes	50
		new strong room	50
		additional typewriter	12
		legal costs and salaries of additional temporary office staff, etc.	650
Traffic department		additional watches	25
		cabin lamps, platform lamps	70
		additional clock, furniture, etc.	10
Permanent Way		half the cost of permanent way renewals in various places	500
		switches & crossings, point levers, etc.	177
		inspection trolley	12
		improvements to signalling	210
Rolling stock		fitting gas lighting in coaches	450
		other improvements to carriages and wagons	200
		1 goods brake, 7 coaches, 6 box trucks, 3 timber trucks	920
		2 double bolster (batten) wagons	125
		additional wagon sheets	50
		converting 6 open wagons into box vans	300
		scraping and varnishing carriages bought from Great Eastern Railway	60
		conversion of dumb buffered wagons to spring buffers	70
		new travelling crane	220
		carriage gas holders	100

shareholders and withdrew; the next vote appointed Harry Willmott. Horace Tahourdin tactfully chose not to offer himself for re-election and preference shareholders went on to appoint Sidney Herbert to the vacant seat. Messrs Willmott and Herbert were destined to change the course of the company for all time.

Harry Willmott was an experienced railwayman and in a career that began with the Great Eastern Railway in 1865, he passed through the ranks to become goods manager for the London district. In 1895 he became General Manager of the newly opened Lancashire, Derbyshire and East Coast Railway (LD&EC) but when the railway was taken over by the Great Central Railway in 1906 Harry Willmott found himself appointed Sheffield District Agent, the equivalent of an area manager; he saw this as a demotion by the General Manager Sam Fay. Within 12 months Harry Willmott left to become Chairman of the East & West Junction Railway, a poverty-stricken concern that amalgamated in 1908 with two other bankrupt companies to form the Stratford-upon-Avon & Midland Junction Railway (SMJ) - he was appointed Chairman of the new undertaking. Harry Willmott was joined by his eldest son, Russell, who had worked for the LD&EC when his father was General Manager, articled to a Sheffield firm of engineers, then worked for the Great Northern Railway and as resident Engineer to two London underground railways before returning to the LD&EC as district engineer. In 1908 Russell was appointed traffic manager and Engineer of the SMJ. By sheer hard work the Willmotts reversed the fortunes of the railway so that by the end of 1911 the company, if not particularly profitable, was able to pay a small dividend to its shareholders. The Deputy Chairman was Sidney Herbert, JP, a rather shadowy individual who ran his own firm of stockbrokers; in 1912 he was a Director of the SMJ, Didcot, Newbury & Southampton Railway, the Mold & Denbigh Railway and, by then, the IWC.

Following the eventful half-yearly meeting, the IWC Board met in London on 29th March, 1911. The first item on the agenda was the election of Chairman and Percy Mortimer proposed Harry Willmott in deference to his greater expertise in railway management. The meeting then continued normally until a discussion took place about the manner in which the Directors fees were distributed; Mr Willmott was voted £250 a year with the other five sharing the £250 balance.

The next meeting of the Board took place one month later. Mr Willmott used his casting vote to close the London office from 1st October, 1911, dispense with the services of the Secretary Francis Beard, and transfer the company's papers to Newport. Mr Beard was an employee of W.B. Peat & Co., the railway's auditors, and the offices used by the IWC were rented from them. Thereafter the Board met at the Great Eastern Hotel in Liverpool Street, London, a location much favoured by Harry Willmott as the SMJ Board also met there. The workings of the Finance committee were reorganised so that it consisted of two Directors, including the Chairman, and was authorised to pass accounts, sign cheques, etc. that had previously been done by the Board. George Henley was formally appointed as Manager and Accountant at a salary of £400; he was expected to attend all meetings of the Board. Engineering matters, including supervision of the locomotive and permanent way department, were entrusted to H.F. Stephens on a salary of £100 per annum plus expenses. An independent report was commissioned into the condition of the locomotive stock, but such was its tone that the resignation in July of Robert Guest, the locomotive superintendent, was a formality.

Even though the Directors' fees had apparently been settled at the March Board meeting, the matter was raised again in May when the Board resolved that shareholders be asked to increase Directors' fees to £1,250 per annum backdated to 1st April plus £1,000 a year to Mr Willmott '. . . in consideration of his large Railway experience'. Harry Willmott was good at publicising the activities of the Board and when the shareholders met on 11th August, 1911 forecast that within 12 months they would be able to pay a dividend on the 5 per cent first preference stock and in 18 months might pay a dividend to second preference stockholders. He added that stocks that had previously stood at £5 per £100 first and £3 per £100 of second preference stock were now selling at £50 and £20 respectively. It was planned to issue more debenture stock so this statement was clearly aimed at encouraging their sale. Mr Willmott got his pay rise and, vindicated by the shareholders, gained the election of Sidney Herbert as Deputy Chairman at the next Board meeting - previously, a decision had been deferred obviously because Harry Willmott was unwilling to allow Percy Mortimer into that seat! Mr Mortimer resigned in disgust as a Director on 2nd November; the most he had ever taken in fees had been £150 per annum. He was quickly replaced by Lord Willoughby de Broke, a long-serving SMJ Director who also held some IWC ordinary shares. The change in the balance of power in the Board and the appointment of different men in positions of authority was accomplished in a little over six months.

Meanwhile, there had been a further round of changes in management as the Board sought to bring in fresh blood. In September Mr Henley found himself appointed Secretary in addition to his existing duties whilst William J. Sawkins was appointed Assistant Secretary and George R. Newcombe replaced S.H. Burgess as the Manager's chief clerk - both had been SMJ employees. This apparently proved too much for Mr Henley so on 21st November he asked to be relieved of his duties, he had been ill in July when Mr Guest departed the scene. H.F. Stephens found he was unable to visit the railway as frequently as necessary and also resigned; he already had responsibility for numerous impoverished railways in various parts of England. The way was clear for the appointment of Russell Willmott, the Chairman's eldest son, as Secretary, General Manager and Engineer; the contract was for five years from 1st January, 1912 with an annual salary of £600 in the first year, £700 in the second and £750 during the third and later years. The IWC paid his removal costs and agreed that he remain Engineer of the SMJ and carry out inspections of that company's line and rolling stock occupying no more than four days a month. In practice, Mr Sawkins more or less ran the office at Newport whilst Russell Willmott concentrated on engineering matters. They were assisted by Harry Young, a Midland Railway man, who joined the IWC on 15th January, 1912 as station master at Newport and effectively became superintendent of the line. To supervise a hefty programme of capital expenditure Mr Booth, the SMJ permanent way inspector was persuaded to transfer to the Island, his removal costs from Stratford-upon-Avon being paid by the IWC.

Immediately he was appointed Chairman, Harry Willmott began to tighten his grip on the company's finances. The manner in which virtually every item of expenditure had to be sanctioned by the Board or Finance committee was swept away, a renewal fund was established and most routine matters ceased to be discussed. On 26th April, 1911 the Board resolved to borrow £10,000 from bankers using £30,000 of unissued debenture stock as security. The Central's bankers refused to co-operate so Sidney Herbert secured an agreement with another bank - he even managed to increase the loan to £15,000 to pay debenture interest due at the end of the year. The raising of a loan repeated a practice of previous years when borrowings during the winter were repaid from summer traffic receipts; the Board resorted to this arrangement in 1912, 1913 and 1914 when up to £5,000 was borrowed using unissued debentures as security. Much of the £15,000 loan was to be repaid following issue of the debentures, but delays in gaining sanction of shareholders meant that it was 7th December, 1911 before the Board could authorise G.S. Herbert & Sons (the Deputy Chairman's firm) to handle the issue of £20,000 'B' debenture stock. It was fortunate that the whole amount sold quickly; the loan to the bank was paid off at the beginning of January and all the stock sold by 14th February, 1912; a further £3,000 4½ per cent 'B' debenture stock was issued in June.

The capital was needed to pay for an extensive programme of expenditure covering virtually every aspect of the company's activities. Harry Willmott warned the Board in May 1911 that the permanent way needed to be replaced with stronger chaired track. Quantities of new and second-hand bull head rail and chairs were purchased for a renewal of the running lines from Ryde to Newport and Cowes. Redundant materials were used to provide additional sidings at Newport, Medina Wharf, Newchurch, Merstone and Sandown. The siding at Newchurch was on land owned by Edward Carter who agreed to take a somewhat larger plot at Rowlands near Ashey in exchange, including sporting rights over the railway.

At Newport a coal siding was laid partly on land rented from the FYN and following an exchange of property with Mew & Co. One of Mr Henley's achievements during his period in office was in securing Board of Trade permission to allow the propelling of Freshwater line trains into Newport station up and down platforms subject to a 5 mph speed restriction. There were numerous other alterations to the offices and station.

During 1911 and 1912 the Minute book contained lists of purchases and alterations charged to the capital account. Most stations received some improvement, however small, but most expenditure was incurred at Newport, Alverstone and Whippingham where a crossing loop was provided. At Alverstone the station house had been condemned by the Isle of Wight Rural District Council and the previous administration had reluctantly concluded that it was more economic to build a replacement rather than waste a hefty sum on repairs; a quote of £280 was received from H. Livingston on 28th June, 1911 and work began soon afterwards.

Amongst the smaller purchases were station and office furniture, a strong room and typewriter, an inspection trolley, bridge plates, signal box names and loading boards; numerous metal notices were manufactured for the IWC to the same patterns as had been used on the SMJ. Such was the length of the lists that it must be asked how the railway had managed without them for so many years!

On Saturday 15th April, 1912 Tyer's No. 7 automatic single line tablet instruments were introduced between Newport and Cowes with an intermediate instrument at Medina Wharf. As the instruments could be worked by train crews, the signal box at Medina Wharf was abolished saving £60 a year in the signalman's wages. The next day saw the commissioning of the crossing loop at Whippingham and Tyer's 'absolute automatic' tablet instruments controlling the Ashey - Whippingham and Whippingham - Newport sections. Later, Tyer's No. 5 instruments were substituted, probably those previously used on the Newport - Cowes section; the Tyer's No. 7a type remained in use on the Ashey - Ryde section. None of these changes added to staff costs as the station masters at Ashey and Whippingham worked the lever frames. Special arrangements were issued covering the operation of the early morning Ryde to Cowes mail train. At each crossing point the train stopped short of the loop whilst the guard walked forward to unlock the signal box before operating the points and signals. He also exchanged the tablet for that applying to the next section that the signalman had left locked in a special box before going off duty the previous night.

Most of the capital expenditure was aimed at reducing operating costs. During 1913 conversion of the lighting at Newport from gas to electricity reduced supply costs from £33 7s. a year to £14 18s.; 12 months later, £60 was spent on a motor to power the machinery in Newport workshops with equal success and at the beginning of 1916 £120 was set aside for additional motors. In order to obtain an independent supply of water, at Newport a bore hole was drilled to a depth of 175 ft, but the supply was insufficient and boring continued to 560 ft before plentiful water was located. Although the cost had risen to £900 it was considered a good investment as supply costs fell from £158 a year to £30.

When the Willmotts took charge of IWC affairs they inherited a number of long-standing agreements with other railways in the Isle of Wight. The IWR held the whip hand by its charging of 'onerous' rents for the use of the stations at Ryde and Sandown; even Harry Willmott was unable to reduce this burden. On 8th November, 1911 the Board earnestly discussed the discovery that the RNR 1872 Act granted running powers to the IWR between Ryde and Newport, a consequence of the IWR's agreement to running powers from Smallbrook to Ryde. Presumably Harry Willmott feared that the IWR might suddenly commence operating its own trains over the IWC to Newport, they already ran trains to Ashey on race days. Although the discussion died without any tangible result, it emphasised that the Central was in a position of weakness in its dealings with the IWR - no such problems existed with other railway companies in the Island.

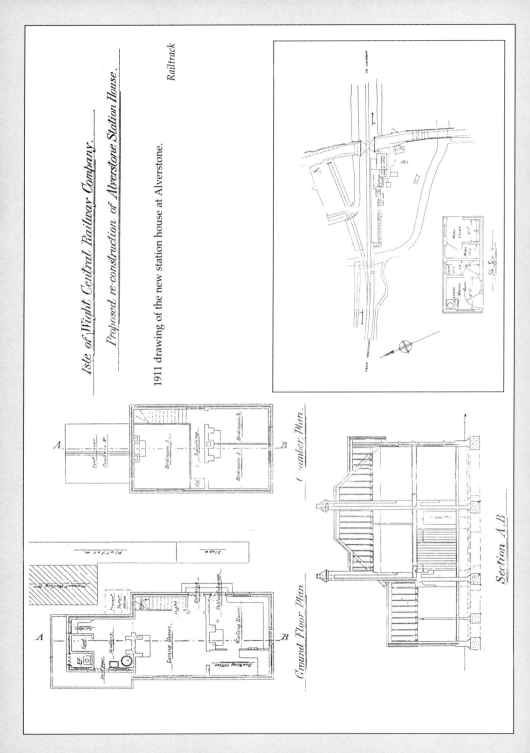

Isle of Wight Central Railway Company.

Proposed re-construction of Alverstone Station House.

1911 drawing of the new station house at Alverstone.

Railtrack

Chamber Plan.

Ground Floor Plan

Section A.B

Apart from additional trains for the workmen, winter passenger train services seem not to have differed to any great extent from those provided in previous years. Holiday traffic suffered in 1915 when the Government suspended all excursion trains throughout Britain at Easter and Whitsun, people being encouraged to spend their holidays at home. Even so, a few extra trains operated during the summer of 1915. A reduction in the ferry service to the Island at the start of the winter timetable on 1st October, 1915 led to changes in the timing of some evening trains to give better connections.

On 28th/29th March, 1916 a violent gale swept across the Island causing widespread damage. Russell Willmott claimed that the '. . . telegraph and telephone wires remained intact, and no delay of any kind was caused to the train services'. On 9th August at about 4.0 pm, part of the roof to Newport locomotive running shed collapsed due to the strain caused by the gale and '. . . excessive warping from severe heat of the sun' - it cost £120 to repair.

By the end of August 1914 25 men were serving in various branches of the army; their wives and families received an allowance funded by the government to bring army pay up to 80 per cent of the men's normal wage. Out of over 200 staff, 37 men had enlisted by May 1916 and another nine had just been released to join the Royal Engineers, Railway and Canal Troops. Those that remained no longer had to negotiate with management for improved wages and working conditions because the creation of the REC had removed this responsibility from the railway companies. Trade unions negotiated direct with the Government and since inflation was quite high they gained the payment of a war bonus funded by the latter; in February 1915 the first of numerous increases for railway employees was notified by the REC.

The 1916 summer train service came into operation on 1st July with somewhat fewer trains than the previous year. Whit Monday and August Bank Holidays had been cancelled by Royal Proclamation reducing the flow of visitors to the Island; a similar reduction in local trippers occurred on Coronation holiday for the same reason. Goods traffic fell because of the erratic arrival of vessels at Medina Wharf and a stagnation in the building trade. Apart from the cancellation of an evening train from Newport to Ventnor the winter service that began on 1st October was largely unaltered. More heavy rain during November and December resulted in another slip that blocked the Ventnor line near St Lawrence.

Income for the first three years of the war actually grew because of an increase in workmen travelling to and from Cowes. The following summary shows how receipts rose during 1915 and 1916.

Year ending 31 Dec.	Gross receipts			Capital expenditure			Renewals expenditure		
	£	s.	d.	£	s.	d.	£	s.	d.
1913	44,529	0	0	36,061	18	0	26,901	0	0
1914	43,072	15	0	8,712	16	3	26,867	4	2
1915	53,887	9	0	769	10	3	37,180	17	3
1916	55,546	5	10	636	1	8	38,913	11	7

As the figures show, some expenditure on the capital account continued up and to beyond the outbreak of war. Unfortunately, attempts to sell £2,000 'B' debenture stock in June 1913 to balance the capital account met with an apathetic response because of the state of the money market; it was April 1914 before the company sold the first £800 and even then it was at a discount of 87 per cent. The issue of £3,650 'C' stock authorised by the Godshill Act met with an equally poor response and much remained unsold when war broke out. On 16th February, 1915 the Board was informed that the Chairman's family had taken up £1,550 'C' stock at a discount of 68 per cent leaving £10,000 'C' stock that the Board proposed to convert to 'B' stock to make it more attractive to buyers. On 26th February, 1915 shareholders gave their approval for the change but by then dealings in railway shares had been frozen and the company was forced to obtain Treasury approval for their issue. Although the debentures were subsequently offered for sale, by August 1916 only £5,200 had been disposed of at a discount of 85 per cent.

During the period of Government control, railways were instructed to keep expenditure to a minimum. Accounts were examined as a matter of routine to ensure that they complied with this requirement, the figures for 1913 being used as the yardstick. In the Central's case, the figures for 1913 were artificially low because of the high level of expenditure in the previous two years. As a consequence, Russell Willmott was called upon to explain why maintenance costs during 1915 were over £5,000 higher than 1913. Other expenditure included £80 on the construction of a larder and bedroom for the refreshment room at Newport and £20 on the tea room at Ventnor. When Newport Corporation asked that the swing bridge to Newport Quay be altered to take heavier vehicles negotiations resulted in the payment of £75 to the Corporation to release the IWC from its liability to maintain the bridge. In 1916 £100 was spent on enlarging Newport station booking hall, and staff renewed a number of piles at Medina Wharf at a cost in materials of approximately £450. A quarry near Ventnor station owned by Percy Mortimer was purchased for £250 (the land alone originally cost £580) to provide a suitable supply of ballast - the IWC had previously been paying 3s. 6d. a ton.

From 1st January, 1917 train services were reduced in response to a Government instruction that virtually tabooed travel except for the strictest 'business and health purposes'. To encourage compliance, all cheap fares were withdrawn and ordinary fares increased by 50 per cent - tourist traffic collapsed and effectively ceased to exist. Even so, the railway carried 100,000 more passengers in 1916 than in the previous 12 months and this rise continued into 1917; Russell Willmott reported on 30th October, 1917:

Our estimated proportion of traffic receipts for week ended 11th August (Bank Holiday week and also holiday week for Cowes Munition Workers) was £1,840 which is easily a record for any week's earnings in history of the Company. Our estimated proportion of receipts to date for this year (excluding Military and Naval passengers and traffic carried free) is £42,210 which is an increase of £6,300 on corresponding period of last year and of £7,520 on 1913, after eliminating Freshwater line traffic.

These increases are practically wholly due to passenger traffic, the profit however goes to the Government.

. . . there had been a considerable increase in workmen's tickets issued to Cowes necessitating additional trains and that further increases were expected which might require further additional trains which would be run as and when required. Arrangements had been made to borrow 8 carriages from I. W. Railway Coy. Also that the Ministry of Munitions were requesting that the 5 am train Ryde to Newport and Cowes should be accelerated in order to leave later. This would necessitate 'switching out' instruments at Ashey and Whippingham and through tablet working Ryde (St Johns Road) and Newport at night time and early morning.

There ensued an exchange of letters with the Board of Trade and Messrs Tyer concerning the switching out of Ashey and Whippingham but contrary to advice from the makers, new tablet instruments were not purchased and the existing arrangements were retained. The company took back responsibility for maintenance of the telegraph and telephone instruments from Messrs Saunders who, despite having the contract for many years, were charging £200 a year - a price Russell Willmott thought excessive. Continued supplies of permanent way materials were obtained and laid down, £200 was spent on repointing brickwork in Mill Hill tunnel and the berth at Medina Wharf dredged at a cost of £270. A proposal to buy a steam fire engine for use at Newport was dropped when it was found that the price had risen alarmingly; some chemical extinguishers were obtained for Medina Wharf and Cowes.

During the winter of 1917-1918, Sunday services were reduced and for the first time the Ventnor line was closed. This frequency continued through the following summer apart from a change in timings of certain trains. Despite this, Russell Willmott told the Board on 13th June, 1918:

To the end of May this year our estimated proportion of traffic receipts, excluding military and naval traffic carried free is £24,100 against £18,400 for the corresponding period of last year. For the year 1913 after eliminating earnings through working the Freshwater Railway the receipts to end of May were £16,000. These increases are due to passenger traffic and of course the Government reap the benefit.

The Passenger Traffic on Whit Monday last (May 20th) constituted a record amounting to £550 for the day which compares with £250 last year. Our previous record day was August Bank Holiday 1917 - £480.

The total passenger Receipts for the Whit Week this year were £1,300.

On 13th June, 1918, with the end of the war in sight, the Board authorised a thorough upgrading of the telephone circuits ostensibly because special military trains might have to be run at short notice and station masters' houses needed to be connected to the telephone circuit, a continuous circuit that allowed anyone on the line to listen into a conversation! About £450 was spent on additional wires, poles and instruments although this was offset by saving £28 a year in Post Office charges for using their poles. At the same meeting the Board sanctioned extensive alterations at Cowes:

The General Manager reported that the heavy munition workers' traffic between Ryde, Newport and Cowes rendered it imperative that the accommodation at Cowes Station should be improved.

At present neither platform was long enough to take the trains now running into and out of the Station which necessitated passengers of ingoing trains being moved into the front of the train at Mill Hill, the circulating area and exit were too restricted for the large crowds which use the Station, and there was not sufficient Siding accommodation to store coaches which work down on the early morning trains and were not required to return until the evening.

It was therefore proposed to alter the exit, increase the circulating area by filling in between the platforms at the buffer stop end for the length of about one coach, lengthen the 'up' platform by about three coach lengths, slew the 'up' sidings and lay in an additional siding on the 'up' side between the Co-operative Society Store and the 'up' platform. As there was no accommodation for dealing with the increased Cattle traffic it was also proposed to build a Cattle Dock on the 'down' side to accommodate three trucks. This traffic at present had to be dealt with on the Passenger platform.

Mr Willmott did not mention that he would also move the signal box from its existing location at the end of the down platform so that it too could be lengthened. The box was extended and placed on a brick base at the Newport end of the station adjacent to the road overbridge.

The alterations at Cowes were an excellent example of the way improvements were financed during the period of Government control. The Board ordered that £350 of the estimated £1,000 cost be charged to the capital account with the remainder borne out of revenue. During the war there was a decline in capital expenditure whilst maintenance costs rose, only part of which can be attributed to inflation during the war. The manner in which the Government paid for maintenance was most attractive, particularly as receipts exceeded 1913 levels: 'For the year 1918 we were a 'surplus' Company, that is after paying War wages and War Bonus and increased prices and all other exceptional charges at the present time, we have to PAY the Government £576 for the year, to reduce our Net Revenue for 1918 to the same as 1913'.

The reduction in capital expenditure was partly a consequence of the company's inability to raise money by the sale of debentures. Fortunately, the capital account received a useful injection during 1917 and 1918 following the sale of three locomotives and a boiler for a total of £2,750. In 1919 more money came from the sale of land opposite the station in Carvel Lane, Cowes that had been bought in the 1870s for an extension of the station; for some reason previous Boards had repeatedly refused to sell it. Russell Willmott was given a bonus of £150 and the balance in the capital account was sufficient to see the company through until 1923.

Chapter Sixteen

The Last Years of the Company
1918 to 1923

After the Great War came to an end in November 1918 Britain's railways remained under Government control for a further year pending a decision upon whether they should be nationalised. Although some politicians were committed to Nationalisation their attempts merely created a Ministry of Transport - it assumed the responsibilities of the Board of Trade in relation to railways, canals, etc. on 23rd September, 1919. The companies were freed of Government control when the REC was wound up in December 1919.

Meanwhile, on the IWC economy was the watchword. The passenger service during the winter of 1918-1919 was reduced so that one locomotive could work the whole system on Sundays; both the Sandown and Ventnor lines were closed. Early in 1919 heavy rain caused a number of slips mainly on the Ryde line; one of the worst was at Round House curve at Fairlee where the embankment subsided several feet and moved towards the main road - half an acre of land had to be bought at this point. The price of locomotive coal had fallen back to 30s. a ton during the war, but inflation was again on the increase, and in 1919 it had risen to 41s. 3d. a ton.

The introduction of an eight-hour-day for railway employees was the culmination of years of activity on the part of the trade unions. Russell Willmott explained the effects to the IWC Board on 12th February, 1919. Several employees were about to be demobbed, so there was no question of actually taking on more men, but he estimated they would need four men for the locomotive running department, five men in the permanent way department and for the traffic department five signalmen, two guards and two porters.

On 12th May, 1919 a minor rearrangement of the signalling at Newport came into use when a new large bracket signal outside the North box was commissioned. Russell Willmott subsequently informed his Directors:

The Board of Trade having agreed certain suggested alterations in the Signalling at Newport for the purpose of running long Passenger trains from Cowes into the Down (Town) side at Newport Station, the work has recently been carried out by the Railway Signal Company at a cost of about £250, which will be chargeable to Revenue. This alteration enables the large number of Workmen to leave the platform expeditiously by the several exits instead of having to come over the footbridge which formerly caused considerable delay and inconvenience to passengers requiring to go over the Bridge in the opposite direction to join the trains. The alternative would have been a supplementary Footbridge.

For the first time in years the summer timetable from 1st June, 1919 contained several additional trains. Two return trips were timetabled along the Ventnor line on Sundays. This largesse did not continue and the following winter service lacked several late weekday trains; again only one locomotive was in use on Sundays when the Sandown and Ventnor lines were closed. Journey times had been reduced somewhat, a consequence of the relaying of the permanent way and Willmott's dislike of mixed passenger and goods trains. Between Newport and Cowes they averaged 10 minutes, Sandown was reached in 26 minutes but a journey to Ryde Pier Head still took 30 minutes; Ventnor was 20 minutes from Merstone.

At midnight on 26th September, 1919 a national railway strike began without warning. The dispute followed attempts by the Government to withdraw part of the war bonus. Most of the Island's railwaymen joined in the strike as the *Isle of Wight County Press* reported:

At midnight on Friday the railwaymen on duty ceased work, the engines having their fires drawn and being left safe by the drivers and firemen both on the I. W. Central and Freshwater lines. With one or two solitary exceptions, the men off duty when the strike commenced did not return to work. Pickets were on duty at the Railway station approach to see that no men returned to work under a misapprehension, but they had little to do . . . Usually one of the busiest places in the Island, the Newport Railway station, was one of the quietest on Saturday, Sunday, Monday and Tuesday, the rows of empty coaches standing in the deserted station, where the bookstall Manager was almost alone except for the station master and a few other officials not involved in the strike. On Tuesday, however, there were signs of returning life and activity, due to the return of a former driver and fireman, both of whom had worked in the war, and volunteered for work. The consequence was that the first train to start since the strike streamed out of the station soon after 2 pm. It consisted of a number of trucks laden with coal for Ryde. The train was greeted with applause by people here and there on the route, and safely reached its destination. The engine brought back from Ryde the coaches left there on Friday as the early morning workmen's train, and proceeded to Cowes to pick up Ryde and Newport workmen leaving the shipyards in the early evening and convey them to their homes. Prior to this the workmen of Ryde and Newport employed at Cowes had been seriously inconvenienced, some not having been able to get to their work, whilst others cycled or were conveyed to and fro in motor lorries and other vehicles. Since Tuesday evening the workers trains have been running regularly, and there has been a fairly frequent passenger service to Cowes and Ryde St Johns Road stations.

The strike ended on Saturday 5th October after the Government reached a compromise with the unions. By then, however, passengers had found that an omnibus could carry them to their destination, farmers began using road transport to carry their milk to market and the same happened with all manner of foodstuffs and other goods. Matters were made worse when in January 1920 the Ministry of Transport ordered companies to increase fares, parcels and goods rates; workmen's tickets rose by 100 per cent over pre-war and this probably lost the IWC all the traffic it had built up during the war. Charges for discharging goods at Medina Wharf rose to 2s. 6d. a ton and to the cement company from 5d. to 6d. a ton. These increases were in consequence of the inflation that was gripping Britain at that time; food prices had risen 130 per cent above 1914 levels prompting more cost of living increases to the company's employees.

On 19th February, 1920 Lord Willoughby de Broke retired from the Board. He was replaced by Sidney Herbert who was immediately appointed Deputy Chairman. Mr Herbert was Chairman of the Association of Minor Railway Companies and '. . . would be of material assistance in any negotiations with the Government &c. which might take place in the near future' - Harry Willmott was also active in the association. By then, Nationalisation had been rejected in favour of regional monopolies formed by the amalgamation of 123 independent companies, but the manner in which those amalgamations were to be carried out remained a subject for discussion.

From 9th May, 1920 an improved passenger train service commenced increasing the number of hours in steam by about 40 a week. A more frequent summer service operated from 12th July to 30th September. On 11th August, 1920 the Board heard that, despite unfavourable weather on the first day, Cowes week was a record and on the evening of the fireworks (6th August) over 5,000 passengers left Cowes station by rail. There had been no congestion in the extended station at Cowes and everything had worked smoothly. Similar comments were expressed following the Ashey races on 13th and 14th October held 'in good weather'.

The greatest blow to befall the railway at this time was the sudden death of Russell Willmott from cancer at the age of only 40 on 25th June, 1920, an event that caused genuine regret amongst IWC staff. The meeting of the Board on 7th July was a sombre affair; sincerest regrets were sent to Ethel Willmott for the loss of her husband with '. . . a special cheque for £2,500 free of tax' - she received a similar sum from the SMJ. Russell Willmott was buried at Carisbrooke when, it is said, mourners from the local Masonic lodge virtually took over the proceedings. In an obituary, the *Railway Gazette* repeated a tribute made when he left the SMJ as being typical of his efforts: 'Through personal attention to every detail of working and determination to make the reorganised system a success have already done marvels for the road, and the shareholders are to be congratulated on having secured a traffic Manager who is not above looking after the smallest details himself'.

Isle of Wight Central Railway
Timetable commencing 3 May 1920

WEEK DAYS

Cowes – Newport

Station					S								NS	NS	S
Cowes Dep.	7.35	8.40		10.2	12.25	12.45	1.25	2.50	3.38	4.50	5.55	7.30	7.40	9.40	10.15
Mill Hill Dep.	–	8.43		10.4	12.28	12.47	1.27	2.52	3.40	4.52	6.0	7.32	–	9.42	10.17
Newport Arr.	7.45	9.53		10.14	12.37	12.57	1.35	3.2	3.48	5.0	6.10	7.42	7.55	9.50	10.20

Newport – Sandown

Station				*						*			NS
Newport Dep.	7.50	9.5	10.25	*	1.5	1.45	3.10	3.53	5.20	*	6.50	8.10	8.22
Shide Dep.	–	9.9	10.29	*	1.9	1.49	3.14	3.57	5.24	*	6.54	8.14	8.26
Blackwater –	–	9.12	10.32	*	1.12	1.52	3.17	4.0	5.27	*	6.57	8.17	8.29
Merstone Junction Dep.	–	–	10.37		1.17	–	3.22	–	5.32		–	8.22	–
Horringford –	–	–	10.41		1.21	–	3.26	–	5.36		–	8.26	–
Newchurch –	–	–	10.44		1.24	–	3.29	–	5.39		–	8.32	–
Alverstone –	–	–	10.47		1.27	–	3.32	–	5.42		–	8.37	–
Sandown Arr.	8.10	–	10.51		1.31	–	3.36	–	5.46		–	8.41	–

Merstone Junction – Ventnor Town

Station		*			*		NS
Merstone Junction Dep.	9.17	*	1.57	4.5	*	7.2	8.34
Godshill –	9.21	*	2.1	4.9	*	7.6	8.38
Whitwell –	9.27	*	2.7	4.15	*	7.9	8.41
St Lawrence –	9.32	*	2.12	4.20	*	7.12	8.44
Ventnor Town Arr.	9.36	*	2.16	4.24	*	7.16	8.48

Newport – Ryde

Station						S					NS	S	
Newport Dep.	6.10	7.47	8.25	10.22	11.43	12.43	1.45	3.10	5.5	6.14	6.35	7.55	8.42
Whippingham Dep.	–	7.53	–	10.28	11.49	12.50	1.51	3.16	–	6.20	6.41	8.1	R
Wootton Dep.	6.17	7.56	8.32	10.31	11.52	12.53	1.54	3.19	5.12	6.23	6.44	8.4	8.50
Haven Street Dep.	–	8.0	–	10.35	11.56	12.57	1.58	3.23	–	6.27	6.48	8.8	R
Ashey (for Nunwell) Dep.	–	8.5	–	10.40	12.01	1.2	2.3	3.28	–	6.32	6.53	8.13	8.57
Ryde (St Johns Road) Arr.	6.29	8.10	8.46	10.45	12.06	1.7	2.8	3.33	5.21	6.37	6.58	8.18	9.2
Ryde (Esplanade) Arr.	–	8.14	8.48	10.49	12.10	1.11	2.12	3.37	5.28	6.41	7.2	8.22	9.6
Ryde (Pier Head) Arr.	6.34	8.16	8.50	10.51	12.12	1.13	2.14	3.39	5.30	6.43	7.4	8.24	9.8

SUNDAYS

Cowes – Newport

Cowes Dep.	10.0	12.0	2.0	4.0	6.40	8.25
Mill Hill Dep.	10.2	12.2	2.2	4.2	6.42	8.27
Newport Arr.	10.12	12.12	2.12	4.12	6.52	8.37

Newport – Sandown (Sandown arrivals via Ryde St Johns Road)

Sandown Arr.	Z 1.39	Z 3.29	Z 8.8

Newport – Ryde

Newport Dep.	10.17	12.17	2.15	4.15	6.57	8.42
Whippingham Dep.	10.23	12.23	2.21	4.21	7.3	8.48
Wootton Dep.	10.26	12.26	2.24	4.24	7.6	8.51
Haven Street Dep.	10.30	12.30	2.28	4.28	7.10	8.55
Ashey (for Nunwell) Dep.	10.35	12.35	2.33	4.33	7.15	9.0
Ryde (St Johns Road) Arr.	10.40	12.40	2.36	4.36	7.20	9.5
Ryde (Esplanade) Arr.	10.44	12.44	2.42	4.42	7.24	9.9
Ryde (Pier Head) Arr.	10.46	12.46	2.44	4.44	7.26	9.11

* = Workmens train. R = Calls to set down upon notice to guard at the previous stop. NS = Saturdays excepted. S = Saturdays only. Z = via Ryde St Johns Road.

WEEK DAYS

Ryde (Pier Head) → Newport

Station					S					NS	S
Ryde (Pier Head) Dep.	6.40	8.25	11.2	12.25	1.24	2.28	4.5	5.55	7.20	8.42	9.20
Ryde (Esplanade) Dep.	-	8.27	11.4	12.27	1.26	2.30	4.7	5.57	7.22	8.44	9.22
Ryde (St Johns Road) Dep.	6.50	8.32	11.9	12.32	1.31	2.35	4.12	6.2	7.27	8.49	9.27
Ashey Dep.	6.57	8.39	-	12.39	1.38	2.42	4.19	6.9	7.34	8.56	9.34
Haven Street Dep.	7.1	8.43	-	12.43	1.42	2.46	4.23	6.13	7.38	9.0	9.38
Wootton Dep.	7.5	8.47	11.22	12.47	1.46	2.50	4.27	6.17	7.42	9.4	9.42
Whippingham Dep.	7.8	8.50	-	12.50	1.50	2.53	4.30	6.20	7.45	9.7	9.45
Newport Arr.	7.13	8.55	11.29	12.55	1.55	2.58	4.35	6.25	7.50	9.12	9.50

Ventnor Town → Merstone Junction

Ventnor Town Dep.	*	9.41	4.29
St Lawrence	*	9.45	4.33
Whitwell	*	9.49	4.37
Godshill	*	9.55	4.43
Merstone Junction Arr.		9.58	4.46

Sandown → Newport

Station							NS
Sandown Dep.	8.20		11.0	1.45	3.50	6.16	7.30
Alverstone Dep.	8.24		11.4	1.49	3.54	6.20	7.36
Newchurch Dep.	8.27		11.7	1.52	3.57	6.23	7.37
Horringford Dep.	8.31		11.11	1.56	4.0	6.27	7.41
Merstone Dep.	8.36	9.59	11.16	2.1	4.5	6.32	7.46
Blackwater Dep.	8.40	10.3	11.20	2.5	4.9	6.36	7.50
Shide Dep.	8.44	10.7	11.24	2.9	4.13	6.40	7.54
Newport Arr.	8.47	10.10	11.27	2.12	4.16	6.43	7.57

Newport → Cowes

Newport Dep.	4.55	7.18	8.10	9.10	11.50	1.5	2.30	4.25	6.50	8.0
Mill Hill Dep.	5.7	7.27	8.22	9.18	12.2	1.15	2.40	4.37	7.2	-
Cowes Arr.	5.10	7.30	8.25	9.20	12.5	1.18	2.43	4.40	7.5	8.10

SUNDAYS

Ryde (Pier Head) → Newport

Station							Z
Ryde (Pier Head) Dep.	10.55	1.10	3.0		4.55	7.32	9.20
Ryde (Esplanade) Dep.	10.57	1.12	3.2		4.57	7.34	9.22
Ryde (St Johns Road) Dep.	11.2	1.17	3.7	4.15	5.2	7.39	9.27
Ashey Dep.	11.9	1.24	3.14	4.25	5.9	7.46	9.34
Haven Street Dep.	11.13	1.28	3.18		5.13	7.50	9.38
Wootton Dep.	11.17	1.32	3.22	4.34	5.17	7.54	9.42
Whippingham Dep.	11.20	1.35	3.25	4.41	5.20	7.57	9.45
Newport Arr.	11.25	1.40	3.30	4.46	5.25	8.2	9.50

Z 8.57

Sandown (Sundays, Z = via Ryde St Johns Road)

Station	Z	Z
Sandown Dep.	2.32	4.27

Newport → Cowes

Newport Dep.	9.35	11.35	1.45	3.35	6.15	8.5
Mill Hill Dep.	9.47	11.47	-	3.45	6.25	8.15
Cowes Arr.	9.50	11.50	1.55	3.48	6.27	8.17

* = Workmens train. NS = Saturdays excepted. S = Saturdays only. Z = via Ryde St Johns Road.

Frank Aman added his own tribute at a meeting of shareholders: 'I knew the late Mr Russell Willmott very well indeed, and I always found him most courteous, polite and attentive to his work. In him we have lost a very good, honest and efficient official of this company . . .'

The death of Russell Willmott resulted in promotion of W.J. Sawkins to the post of Secretary; he had run the office on a day-to-day basis whilst Russell Willmott dealt with engineering matters. G.R. Newcombe was made Manager and Russell Willmott's younger brother, Capt. F.B. (Bernard) Willmott, who already worked on the railway, became assistant manager '. . . particularly to assist in outdoor work'. He was not cut out to be a railwayman and left with a 'golden handshake' in 1923. Within weeks the deaths of Samuel Peto and Major John Gibson were reported - the Board was running out of Directors! William J. Stevens, a Director of the Railway Investment Company Ltd and the Stock Conversion Trust Ltd, was voted onto the Board in place of Mr Peto. Although F.G. Aman wrote asking to be appointed to the Board following the death of Major Gibson, the Chairman replied that it had been agreed several years before that one of the members of the family of the deceased Major Gibson should succeed him - Capt. John G. Gibson duly joined the Board shortly afterwards.

The railway bridge at Coppins Bridge had the largest span of any bridge on the railway. It had been built in the 1870s and although repaired and strengthened in 1902 its condition had deteriorated because of a lack of maintenance in its early life. A.W. Szlumper, Engineer of the LSWR, carried out a thorough inspection of the structure in 1919 and confirmed Russell Willmott's opinion that it should be replaced. A contract was let with Metropolitan Carriage Wagon & Finance Co. of Birmingham for the supply of a steel girder bridge by its subsidiary, the Patent Shaft & Axletree Co. of Wednesbury, Staffs, at a cost of about £5,000. The old structure was never highly regarded as evidenced by the *Isle of Wight County Press* on 16th October, 1920: 'The erection now in progress of a new railway bridge over the road at Coppins Bridge recalls the prejudice which old residents felt, and a few retain it at present, against crossing the old structure in the train when the line between Pan and Newport was completed over 40 years ago.'

As a temporary wooden structure would have been too expensive, the line was closed whilst the bridge was renewed. Steel work was delivered to Newport Quay and partially assembled on land nearby. Demolition of the old structure began on Sunday 24th October. The Central was fortunate that a miners' strike began the following day that lasted until 8th November and on Ministry orders the IWC operated a service reduced by about 25 per cent and saving one engine per day in steam - motor buses maintained a service between Newport and Shide. On Mr Szlumper's advice, the foundations of the bridge abutments were strengthened and four new buttresses built; his staff from the LSWR assisted in the operation for which he was sent a cheque for £50 with the Board's compliments. The *County Press* reported on 6th November:

Yesterday afternoon the second of two massive steel girders, each weighing some 23 tons, was raised into its position as part of the new railway bridge over the highway at Coppins Bridge, the first having been placed *in situ* on Monday. Large crowds witnessed the lifting, by means of a large derrick and winches, one worked by a traction engine, the other by hand windlasses, turned by nearly a dozen men, and have greatly admired the way in which the difficult work has been carried out under the skilled direction of the foreman of the works. The operations involved the closing of the highway from Saturday night until Monday afternoon, and from Thursday morning until this morning, during which time traffic has been diverted over Newport Quay. Now that the most difficult part of the operation has been carried out, there is every prospect of a speedy completion of the work.

On Saturday 13th November four locomotives weighing 112 tons were run over the bridge to test its strength and the line reopened the following Monday. The winter service that began on 4th October, 1920 was roughly the same as that operated the previous year and required the services of five engines in steam, compared with six during the summer.

In 1920 the railway bridge at Coppins bridge was rebuilt. The new steel span for Coppins Bridge is seen following construction at the maker's factory in Wednesbury. Note the builder's descriptive board and the legend on the structure 'Shide end'.   *IWSR Collection*

For a meeting of shareholders on 25th February, 1921, the Directors reported that during 1920 there had been an increase in receipts of £19,000, including £6,400 from passenger traffic despite a drop of 18,000 first class passengers and 100,000 workmen. The increase was explained by higher fares and the carriage of more milk; coal traffic had grown by £11,000, half of which came from increased rates and half from extra traffic.

Receipts had been bolstered by Government compensation. At the beginning of the war the amounts received by the company were relatively small but this changed dramatically after 1918, partly explained by a hefty increase in operating costs - by July 1921 locomotive coal alone cost 54s. 4d. a ton. In November 1920 the *Daily Express* carried articles referring to the relationship between railways and the Government; the IWC was mentioned in one letter and within weeks the Ministry of Transport carried out an inspection of the line. There followed a thorough scrutiny of the 1919 accounts. A matter for disagreement was the level of permanent way renewals made at Government expense, some using new rails. After much discussion the Board agreed to accept a 're-debit' that reduced the amount due from the Government for 1919 by £2,192. The amounts of compensation paid during the years of Government control were:

Year	Amount	Year	Amount	're-debit'
1914	£2,528	1918	-£576	
1915	£4,332	1919	£22,786	-£2,192
1916	£6,482	1920	£20,152	
1917	£4,505	1921	£4,294	

Arguments then ensued over the amounts being spent in 1921 and the Ministry of Transport began deducting sums for 'excessive maintenance'. Naturally, this was challenged but the Ministry delayed discussions until the outcome of a test case against the North British Railway passed through the courts. Although the results of the court case were not recorded, the dispute with the Ministry of Transport was settled in September 1922 by the payment to the Government of £14,000 in settlement of all outstanding claims and counter claims - considering the amounts received during the previous eight years it might be said the IWC escaped lightly.

Whilst the practice of holding a shareholders' meeting every six months had changed to an annual meeting at the beginning of 1914, the Board continued the practice of declaring a half-yearly interim dividend. The war led to a reappraisal of this decision and the Board prudently resolved to wait until the end of each year before declaring a dividend (to the chagrin of shareholders, an interim dividend was never reinstated). The IWC was fortunate that the 1913 season had been good and with Government compensation permitted the payment of a dividend to holders of first preference stock:

	Dividend		Dividend
1913	3½%	1918	3½%
1914	4%	1919	4%
1915	3¾%	1920	4%
1916	3½%	1921	4%
1917	3½%	1922	4%

A serious accident at Abermule on the Cambrian Railways was mentioned to the IWC Board on 11th February, 1921. A Tyer's single line token had been given out for the wrong single line section and in the resulting head-on collision there was considerable loss of life. The Board of Trade Inspector criticised the antiquated practice of placing the single line instruments in the station master's office where anyone had access and recommended their transfer to the signal box. The IWC Board were assured that the single line instruments were already in the signal cabins except at Medina Wharf where the intermediate instrument was operated by the train crew. At smaller stations instruments were kept in the same room as the lever frame.

The difficult economic situation led to a series of strikes in various industries including the coal miners who struck for a second time. From Tuesday 7th April, 1921 the train service was reduced by about 30 per cent followed by more reductions on 5th May. After communicating with the Ministry of Transport, the Ventnor line was closed temporarily; in all the service had been halved since the start of the strike. The *Isle of Wight County Press* for 2nd July recorded when the strike ended:

> With the termination of the coal strike the present emergency service of trains and boats is being superseded by a generous summer service, which according to information available, will come into operation generally about the 10th inst. On the Isle of Wight Central Railway there will be a resumption of the Sunday service, and the line between Merstone, Whitwell and Ventnor Town will be re-opened to traffic.

But the damage had already been done. The Ministry of Transport forced railways to put up fares to compensate for a huge rise in operating costs which, coupled with the disruption caused by the strike, encouraged enterprising Islanders to begin the operation of motor bus services in direct competition with the railways and with each other. This was compounded by motor lorries that creamed off income from the railways. Concerned at the likely effects, a letter written on behalf of the IWC and FYN was sent on 20th April, 1921 to the Ministry asking for freedom to reduce fares and rates in the Island. The Ministry subsequently authorised excursion and other reduced fares if a company was of the opinion that it would increase net income. The IWC duly introduced cheap return fares from 10th July, 1921 for travel on certain trains on specific days of the week at a reduced rate of approximately a single fare plus a third. This coincided with the introduction of the 1921 summer timetable, a repeat of that in 1920. By June 1922 third class excursion fares were on offer for travel from Newport to Cowes for 9*d.*, to Sandown, Ryde St Johns Road and Ventnor Town for 1*s.* 9*d.*, Shanklin for 2*s.* 3*d.*, whilst journeys to Portsmouth or Southampton each cost 3*s.* 9*d.* Despite these changes, the motor bus services persisted and quickly multiplied. One operator, Vectis Buses, began operating in October 1921 and after absorbing numerous competitors, became the largest operator in the Island - in 1929 it was purchased by the Southern Railway and was reconstituted as the Southern Vectis Omnibus Company.

The inflation of the war years continued until 1921 when prices began to fall. For the first time, the economic situation permitted a reduction in the cost of living bonus paid to most employees - their wages were cut by 5*s.* a week from 1st July, 1921. During 1921 net income was roughly the same as in 1920 even though passenger traffic had grown 10 per cent since 1913. Some income came from the carriage of passengers for the Ashey race meeting on 5th and 6th October, 1921 and in recognition of this £50 was contributed towards the purchase of a cup or as a cash prize.

October 1921 proved to be an unhealthy time as both Col Hamilton and Sidney Herbert were too ill to attend a meeting of the Board. The Directors discussed the consequences of decontrol of railways at midnight 15th-16th August. The Central's freedom was short lived as deregulation coincided with the passing of the Railways Act that became law on 19th August, 1921. It provided for the creation of the Southern Railway Company by amalgamation of the LSWR, LBSCR, SECR and smaller companies such as the IWC. Sir Herbert Walker, General Manager of the LSWR, wrote to the company on 14th October, 1921 when he explained that the LSWR would take the lead in purchasing the Island companies. On 20th October he and several members of LSWR staff visited the Island and carried out an inspection preparatory to the start of negotiations.

Whilst the Railways Act put the unions' negotiating rights on a sound footing, other aspects of the Act were not quite so kind to some of their members. In February 1921 the IWC was forced to discharge employees aged 70 and over who were not fit for full duties. Previously they had been given lighter work on reduced pay but recent agreements between the Government and unions no longer made this possible. In October 1921 the Board was told that this rule also applied to men aged 65 in the same situation and several had been discharged before 15th August when the Railways Act became law; despite these retirements, many more employees were made redundant at the end of the summer service. In a number of pension awards, the Board granted an allowance of 20*s.* a week to Mr Williams, station master at Mill Hill, who at age 71 was considered '. . . too old to efficiently carry out his duties' - he had worked on the railway for 51 years.

The winter service from 2nd October reduced the number of engines in steam from six to four. The Ashey races had gone off smoothly, the train service having 'ample accommodation'. The 1922 summer timetable came into operation on 12th June with one or two additional trains; to encourage travel, excursion fares were reintroduced. A renegotiation of the £1,700 rent for the use of the IWR at Ryde eventually resulted in an agreement to divide receipts and expenditure on a mileage basis. Despite unfavourable weather, traffic during the 1922 Cowes Regatta week was very good and about 5,000 people were conveyed from Cowes after the fireworks on the Friday. All records were broken a month later when over 3,000 people travelled to Ventnor Town station for Ventnor Carnival. Five special trains made the return journey from Ventnor during the evening without incident. The winter timetable began on 1st October, 1922 when the number of locomotives in steam was again reduced from six to four. The upheavals in the economy partly accounted for a considerable increase in income and expenditure:

Year ending 31 Dec.	Passenger traffic Numbers carried				Merch. Tons	Goods traffic			Other Receipts £	Gross Expenditure £
	First	Third	Workmen	Season		Coal Tons	Minerals Tons	Livestock No.		
1921	21,128	754,327	97,143	275	5,660	74,647	43,764	4,364	95,815	77,450
1922	20,491	828,343	59,229	325	3,777	107,750	51,202	5,650	82,421	65,550

Traffic to and from IWC stations in 1923

Station	Alverstone	Ashey	Blackwater	Cowes	Godshill	Haven Street	Horringford	Medina Wharf	Merstone	Mill Hill
Population	99	about 30	not stated	16,000	about 300	several thousand	250	-	about 170	11,000
annual receipts:										
Passengers	388.1.6	329.8.4	215.17.0	5,003.19.1	243.10.5	528.6.9	400.12.5	-	268.12.7	3,504.18.10
Parcels	67.2.2	45.11.4	150.17.8	976.7.11½	122.10.5	425.12.0	113.11.7	-	399.18.1	89.19.8
Goods	63.0.10	36.5.4	3.0.3	704.1.7	23.9.3	15.9.2	96.3.4	6,174.0.0	4.14.9	163.2.6
Various	10.18.8	1.8.3	9.5.4	94.8.6	13.14.1	16.5.9	8.12.8	-	15.8.3	50.12.0
General goods tonnage (monthly):										
Forwarded	1	-	10 for year	36	-	4t 10c	-	50t 10c	1t 1c	-
Received	30t 10c	1	9 for year	50t 2c	2	3t 16c	3	9t 2c	15c	-
Coal and coke tonnage (monthly):										
Forwarded	-	-	3t 3c	-	-	-	-	8,183t 6c	-	262 for year
Received	17t 15c	7	6½t 5c	539t 10c	10	-	23t 6c	7t 15c	4t 12c	328 for year
Number of milk churns dealt with daily:										
Forwarded Summer	4	-	4	-	4	16	4 + 5	-	19	-
Forwarded Winter	4	-	3	-	3	15	3 + 4	-	20	-
transferred Summer	-	-	-	-	-	-	-	-	-	-
transferred Winter	-	-	-	-	-	-	-	-	-	-
Received Summer	3	-	-	-	-	-	-	-	-	-
Received Winter	-	-	-	-	-	-	-	-	-	-
Number of regular season ticket holders:	7	1	3 half rate	17	5	3	9	-	4	17
Number of staff employed — Summer	1	1[1]	1	8[2]	1	1	1	3[3]	3	3
Number of staff employed — Winter	1	1[1]	1	8	1	1	1	3[3]	3	2
Monthly number of passengers booked (heaviest month in 1923)	2,958	1,475	832	13,534	1,375	1,987½	1,744	-	724	8,539
Monthly number of tickets collected (heaviest month in 1923)	3,532	2,109	1,038	32,072	1,445	2,594	2,250	-	674	15,336

[1] plus one two days a week. [2] plus one temporary. [3] traffic staff 2, coal gangs 36, cranemen 6. [4] 1 adult and 3 half.
Some of the figures for milk churns clearly quoted the annual totals.

2-4-0T locomotive No. 7 is seen entering Cowes with a train of low roof LSWR carriages. The signal box is in its original position at the end of the main platform and 5-plank open wagon No. 198 stands in the coal road. Going by the locomotive livery and the houses in the background built in 1907, the date not much later than then. *IWSR Collection*

This view of Cowes station shows the longer platforms, bay road, repositioned signal box and new signals that were installed in 1918. Only the LBSCR vans and open wagons betray that this photograph was taken in 1930. *IWSR Collection*

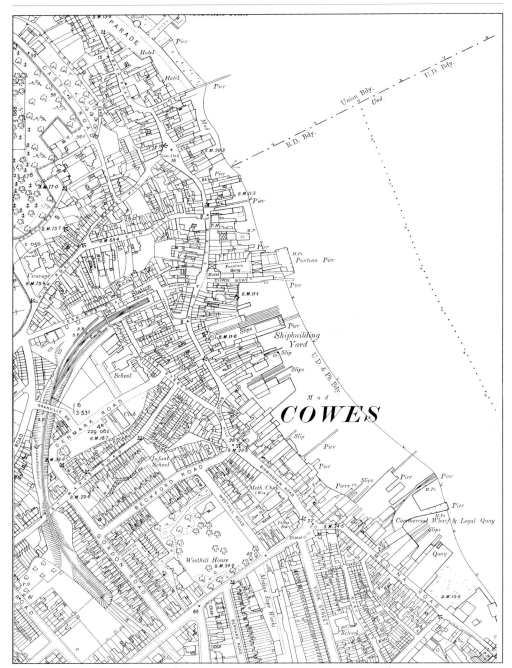

This Ordnance Survey map shows Cowes station as it existed following the extensions made during the 1890s but prior to changes made in 1918.

In 1890 a new bridge was built at Cowes over what became St Mary's Road. On 24th June, 1965 class 'O2' No. 20 *Shanklin* crosses with the 12.24 pm train from Cowes. *T. Cooper*

Mill Hill station seen in 1930 but is unaltered from IWC days save for the laying of chaired track. The barley sugar twist lamps still carry IWC name boards. *G.H. Hunt, IWSR Collection*

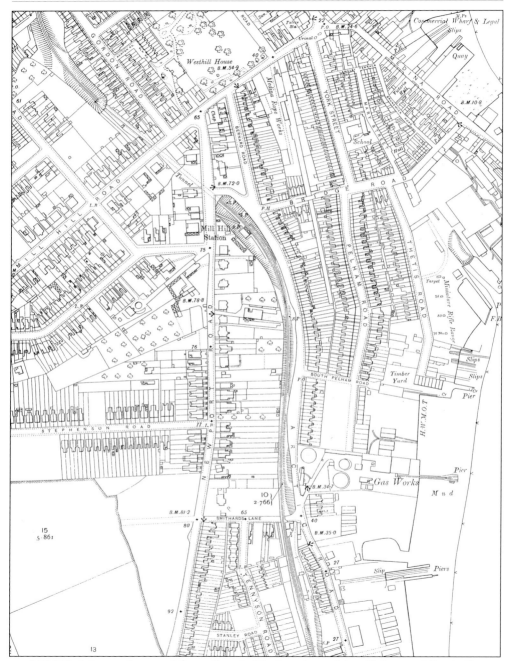

Mill Hill station can be seen at the south end of the tunnel complete with its own siding; to the south of Smithards Lane crossing is Gas House siding.

Cement Mills siding (2 m. 77 ch.) had connections facing down trains and was locked by Annett's key; the siding passed through a gate onto the cement company's land where, by the 20th century, there was a run-round loop and a spur to a wagon repair shed. There followed a short level stretch as the line crossed Cement Mills viaduct, otherwise called Mill Pond bridge (No. 7). Built in timber, the viaduct was rebuilt in 1880 with brick abutments, nine spans of wrought-iron girders and cast-iron piles supporting longitudinal timbers and decking. The line curved closer to the river bank as it passed under Dodnor overbridge (No. 8) carrying a road to Medina cottage. A proposal by the surveyor Mr Bird to provide a station at Dodnor was rejected by the CNR Board in 1862 but a platform existed in 1896 for traffic to and from Parkhurst prison. Then followed a gentle run alongside the river and then a short fall down Hurstake Bank that took the railway to the northern edge of Newport.

Newport station (4 m. 28 ch.) underwent few alterations of any note between the 1890s and the arrival of the Willmotts in 1911, despite repeated complaints about such matters as the condition of the toilets! Double track working began several hundred yards north of the junction with the FYN and continued through the station to the junction of the Ryde and Sandown lines. The booking office, refreshment rooms, etc., were on the down platform, at the north end of which was a short bay road. The two sidings situated between the station and the Freshwater line were quite inadequate for the goods traffic passing through the station. The up platform, reached by a footbridge (bridge No. 9) at the south end, had two faces; at the north end were a handful of sidings including two that led to a carriage shed. Other sidings served a two-road locomotive shed and separate workshops. The station was controlled from a 20-lever wooden signal box at the south end and a newer 35-lever brick built box near the Freshwater junction.

In 1903 the IWC Board sanctioned the demolition of the carriage shed and a rearrangement of sidings on the site; the connections were altered in 1905 to give access solely from the loop - they were simplified again in about 1913. To provide additional power to machinery in the workshop, in 1906 a boiler house was built to house the boiler from CNR locomotive No. 1. Soon afterwards a wooden shed was erected several yards south of the locomotive shed to accommodate railmotor No. 1; during 1909 the length between the two sheds was filled in to accommodate the second railmotor. Also in 1909 a second storey was added between the office building and station building to give the appearance of one continuous building.

In July 1911 the Board authorised the construction of some badly needed coal sidings and a roadway in the goods yard, the cattle dock was later extended and a new 20 ton weighbridge purchased. During 1912 and 1913 there were significant improvements to the station, including the notorious toilets, offices and refreshment rooms. As a first step in upgrading the water supply, balloon type water tanks were installed at the ends of the platforms - by 1913 the up platform was 324 ft long, the down platform 401 ft and the bay 116 ft. To free the sidings at the north end of the station for goods stock, a short carriage siding alongside the up loop line added at the end of 1912 was extended a year later to 450 ft. Parts of the platforms received a tarmac dressing and towards the end of 1914 the approach road was similarly treated.

A few yards beyond the end of the platforms, the railways to Ryde and Sandown separated. The Ryde line crossed the Medina Valley on an opening drawbridge and a brick viaduct (bridges Nos. 10 and 10a) 300 ft. long and 25 ft high before curving sharply to the left as it entered the 73 yds-long Newport tunnel (bridge No. 11), a long overbridge carrying the Ryde road. Negotiating Cross Lanes overbridge (No. 12), later known as Halberry Lane, the line continued to curve towards the north-east until parallel with the river whilst climbing through a steep and rather unstable cutting to Fairlee. After Round House bridge (No. 13), a cattle creep, there followed a level section as the railway curved to the right before heading due east towards Whippingham; en route the line passed under a farm road, over a public road (Pinnock's bridge) and two cattle creeps (bridges Nos. 14 to 17).

Described as 'Whippingham for Osborne', the station (6m. 42 ch. from Cowes) was just over two miles from Osborne House and 1½ miles from the hamlet of Whippingham so saw

Locomotive No. 8 stands at Newport with a train including two North London Railway carriages. Note the short arms on the signal.   *IWSR Collection*

4-4-0T No. 6 is seen in about 1902 standing alongside locomotive No. 9 in Newport station. Note the light flat bottom track used in this, the company's principal station.   *IWSR Collection*

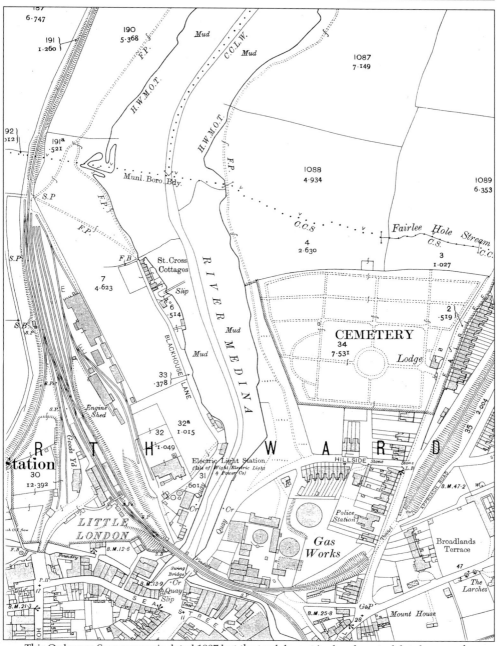

This Ordnance Survey map is dated 1907 but the track layout is already out of date because the connections to the up sidings were rearranged to give access solely from the up loop line following the demolition of the carriage shed in about 1903.

This fascinating photograph of Newport station was taken before 1905 when the sidings in the foreground were rearranged. The original station house and offices are still separate buildings, the footbridge lacks a covering and an attractive two-tone paint finish adorns the platform coverings. The water standpipe on the right predates the erection of balloon tanks. From left to right we see the whitewashed coal, sacks of coal on the trolley, a Medina Wharf water tank wagon in the loop platform and the clutter of luggage and beer barrels on the platforms.

IWSR Collection

A train leaves for Freshwater in this view of Newport looking north. The assortment of vehicles in the sidings includes one of the LBSCR goods brake vans. The whitewashed coal stack looks particularly impressive. The purpose of the tall post on bank to the right is not known as on the original print it was topped by a ball and finial but had no signal arms. There is lighting in the yard so the photograph probably dates from *circa* 1902 to 1905. *IWSR Collection*

Newport looking north from the end of the main platform in September 1920. The changes made by the Willmotts is evidenced by the fine array of signals, whilst one of the balloon tank water cranes can be glimpsed to the left. The FYN siding behind the North signal box contains most of that company's carriages.

IWSR Collection

The RNR and IWNJ crossed the River Medina on an opening drawbridge seen here as it existed during the 1880s. The timbers beyond the bridge belongs to the low level bridge carrying a siding from the railway station on the left to Newport quay.

R. Brinton

This photograph, thought to have been taken in 1913, shows the view along the top of the drawbridge when opened for a sailing barge to pass through. Newport South signal box can be seen on the right.   *J. Mackett*

Immediately after crossing the river the tracks to Ryde (*on the left*) and Sandown separated to curve sharply in opposite directions. The home signals guarding the bridge and entry to Newport station can be seen prominently in this photographed dating from SR days sometime after 1926.   *R. Silsbury Collection*

Class 'O2' locomotive No. 26 and its train crosses the opening bridge shortly before entering Newport station. Note the footings remain for the low level bridge that carried a track from the station on the right to the quay from where the photograph was taken.   *J. Mackett*

A train from Ryde crosses the viaduct as it approaches Newport station in about 1965. The foundations of the pier that supported the low level bridge can be clearly seen.   *T. Cooper*

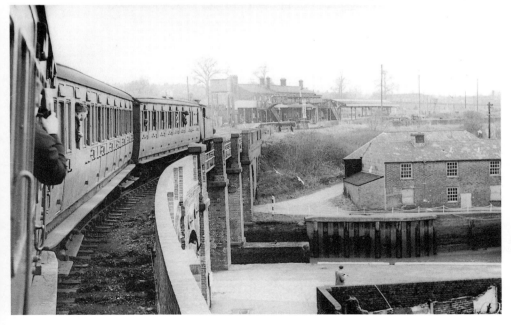

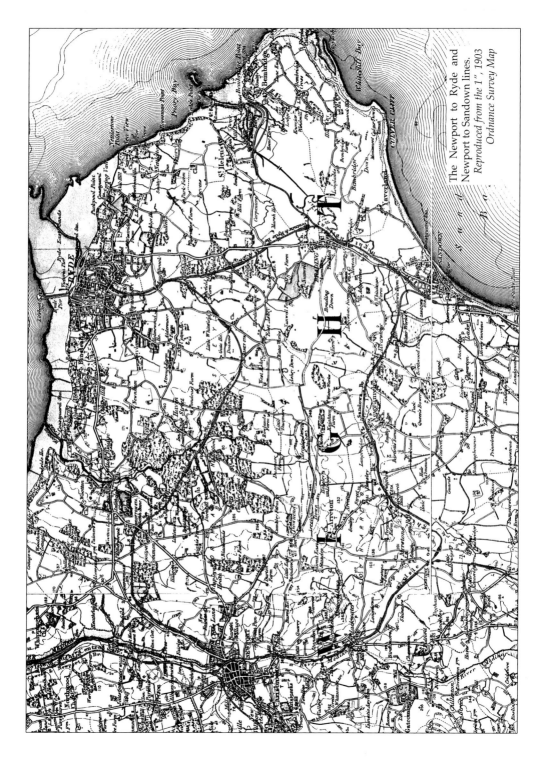

The Newport to Ryde and
Newport to Sandown lines.
Reproduced from the 1″, 1903
Ordnance Survey Map

little traffic. Whippingham had a 235 ft platform on the up side, the length of which was the only concession to its use by royalty. The substantial 'cottage style' red brick building contained living accommodation flanked by toilets for men and women on one side and a booking office on the other; traffic was never sufficient to justify the provision of a covering to the platform. The booking office contained a five-lever frame working signals and points to the 172 ft siding at the Newport end of the station; by 1896 the siding points were also locked with an Annett's key. On 16th June, 1912 a 455 ft crossing loop worked from an 11-lever signal frame was brought into use. There was a new 242 ft 10 in. down platform with a small wooden shelter that was clearly second-hand from elsewhere; it had the appearance of a former signal box and was rumoured to have served in that capacity at Wootton. Shortly after leaving Whippingham, the railway began to climb as it passed under Fatting Park and Fatting Park Farm bridges (Nos. 18 and 19), the former having been rebuilt in 1900-1901; the gradient then steepened as it passed through woodland before a curve to the south-east took it through a cutting to Wootton station.

Sometimes referred to as 'Wootton for Woodside', the station (7 m. 24 ch.) was situated at the summit of the line in a steep cutting immediately to the west of a road overbridge (No. 20) and about a mile south of the village. The bridge spanning the cutting was a substantial three-arch brick structure. A path from the road descended to a platform on the up side where there was a small wooden booking office, waiting room and signal box containing a four-lever frame working home and distant signals. Land for an approach road to a new siding east of the road bridge was purchased in 1898 from the local landowner Mr Chatfield Clarke. The 110 ft-long siding was brought into use on 1st November, 1898, it faced down trains and was worked from a ground frame locked by an Annett's key attached to the train staff. In 1907 a house was built for the station master adjacent to the road and an arch of the road bridge was bricked in for use as a booking office; this was probably when the platform was rebuilt. It is unclear when the signal box and signals were removed but the station remained a block post until the crossing loop at Whippingham came into use in 1912; by then the platform had been extended to 211 ft in length. Leaving Wootton the railway curved to the south-east on a downhill gradient and over Woodhouse Farm and Parkfield bridges (Nos. 21 and 22), both cattle creeps, before passing Woodhouse farm. The railway then dived into Briddlesford Copse, levelled and then under Briddlesford overbridge (No. 23) before emerging briefly between open fields. A further steep fall for about ½ mile took the railway to Haven Street.

Haven Street station (8 m. 73 ch.) was situated immediately west of Haven Street bridge (No. 24), a typical brick structure carrying the line over a road a few hundred yards south of the village. There was a narrow platform 196 ft 3 in. in length on the up side with wooden buildings providing shelter for passengers, a booking office and the same signalling arrangements as at Wootton. In 1886 a siding was built at the same time as a gasworks opposite the station; the points faced up trains and were worked from a fifth lever added to the frame. Although the gasworks closed in about 1920, the siding remained in use for goods traffic - by then it was 144 ft in length. Whereas Wootton was much improved in the early years of the century Haven Street retained its wooden buildings and short platform. The waiting shed, etc. were extended in 1912 at a cost of £16 but this work must have been minor and it was hardly surprising that the Southern Railway swept it all away in a redevelopment of the station in 1926. Leaving Haven Street, the railway climbed on an embankment across open farmland, then followed Blackbridge underbridge (No. 25) and after a stiff climb for half a mile, Rowlands bridge (No. 26) and through Rowlands Wood. The railway gradually curved towards the east through open farmland to reach Ashey station.

Styled 'Ashey for Nunwell' the station (10 m. 33 ch.) was nowhere near any centre of population and generated little traffic. Despite this, Ashey was a block post and for many years the only crossing point on the line between Ryde and Newport; by 1912 the crossing loop was 401 ft in length. The 304 ft 6 in. up platform had a substantial brick building that was a mirror image of that at Whippingham. A 12-lever signal frame controlled points and signals in the station. The 306 ft down platform had a small shelter for passengers. A facing

Whippingham station building is seen complete with the redoubtable Mrs Merewood in the early years of the new century. The unusual light coloured hood on the front of the booking office is a cover to the clock, a feature that was absent at Ashey. *R. Brinton*

Whippingham looking east, seen sometime after the construction of a crossing loop in 1912. The large running-in board is typical of the IWC. Note the extensive use of whitewash to lighten the edging stones, the supports to the lamps and even the telegraph pole. Curiously, the original platform is on the loop with a sharply curved turnout whereas one would expect the opposite arrangement. *IWSR Collection*

level crossing on the up side was a single platform containing a wooden signal box and a red brick single-storey booking office; facing the road was a two-storey house. Originally there had been a run-round loop north of the platform but it was removed when the line opened to Pan Lane. By the 1890s there was a goods siding facing up trains south of a somewhat longer siding facing the opposite direction; off this second siding were kickback sidings to a flour mill and to the chalk quarry on St George's Down. Their provision had been facilitated by powers obtained in the company's 1890 Act that permitted the diversion of a footpath across the railway in the vicinity. By 1896 the Railway Signal Company had replaced the original signal box and frame with a new box containing a nine-lever frame working points to the sidings, signals, and a lock to the level crossing gates. Despite a decision to extend the platform in 1912 it was still only 174 ft 7 in. in length when the line was surveyed. Electric lighting was added a year later. Leaving the station across the level crossing, the railway climbed as it headed south besides the river and continued to do so for the next mile or so interspersed with short level sections as the railway criss-crossed the Medina on Knight's and Marvel bridges (Nos. 33 and 34), here no more than a stream. Some distance to the left on the opposite side of the high road was a rope-worked incline to Ruffin Blake's gravel pit - one of many industrial tramways in the Island.

Blackwater (6 m. 36 ch.) had little more than a proximity to a road to commend it. Hemmed in by a stream (bridge No. 35) and just north of a level crossing was a two-storey red brick house on the down side and a short wooden platform. In 1896 there was an old six-lever frame working signals, a bolt on the level crossing gates and connections to a 173 ft-long siding to the south of the level crossing. The platform was extended to 246 ft 5 in. in 1912 and improvements made to the station house. Leaving Blackwater the railway began to cross gently rolling farmland and downs as it climbed gently to reach Merstone - there was just one bridge on the this length, Stone bridge (No. 36).

Immediately south of another level crossing, Merstone station (8 m. 18 ch.) was about half a mile south of the hamlet of that name and 1½ miles east of Rookley. The house was to the same design as Blackwater but had its frontage stone clad. There was a short platform and a 204 ft 4 in.-long siding with points facing down trains, all being on the up side of the line. There were no facilities north of the level crossing prior to 1895 when a greatly enlarged station was opened in anticipation of the opening of the line to Ventnor. Leaving Merstone, the line bore left before descending the half mile Redway bank; along this section was the only road overbridge on the line, Budbridge bridge (No. 38). There followed a fall for 1¾ miles crossing Redway bridge, Redway culvert and Stickworth bridge (Nos. 39 to 41) in the process.

Horringford (9 m. 62 ch.) was intended to be the first terminus of the railway. The station was immediately west of a crossing of the Newport to Sandown road about a mile from Arreton village; like other stations on the line, it lost most of its passenger traffic to the omnibus. There was a single platform on the down side of the line and a substantial station master's house quite different in design to those at Merstone and the other stations. At the Newport end was a short-lived run-round loop for the abortive attempt to open the line in 1872; it had been replaced by a siding before passenger services began in 1875, a spur from the siding led to a gravel pit about ½ mile away. In 1896 the station possessed a lever frame containing five levers controlling bolts on the gates of the level crossing, home and distant signals; the siding had a separate ground frame locked by an Annett's key. By 1912 the platform was 181 ft long and the siding 319 ft, part of which served a cattle dock. Adjacent to the level crossing, a stream passed under the road (bridge 42). Leaving Horringford was a level stretch and then a fall for about ½ mile crossing two river bridges in the process, Heasley bridge (No. 43) and Veniscombe bridge (No. 44).

Newchurch (10 m. 69 ch.) was half a mile downhill from the village at a point where the road crossed the railway. Next to the level crossing on the down side of the line was a small house approximately half the size of that at Horringford. Alongside was a short wooden platform and in 1886 a siding was added opposite the platform; 10 years later the station was

Apart from the replacement of the permanent way, there is little evidence of any changes made by the SR at Shide by the late 1920s when this photograph is thought to have been taken.

IWSR Collection

Blackwater station building was typical of the station houses at the northern end of the IWNJ. Note the absence of road traffic and, for that matter, any sign of life. *R. Brinton*

Between the station house and track at Blackwater can be seen the wooden platform that served as a station. Although dating from SR days the station has changed little since it was built.

IWSR Collection

Blackwater looking south shortly before closure in 1956 shows how the station had changed over the years. The siding was sited beyond the level crossing.

T. Cooper

Merstone station was enlarged by the construction of a new platform and sidings north of the level crossing ready for the opening of the line to Ventnor. The island platform with its platform shelter was signalled for two way running, the slope to the subway, signal box, water tank and sidings. Not visible is the station master's house on the right of the camera in front of which was the original wooden platform.   *R. Silsbury Collection*

0-6-0T locomotive No. 9 is seen at Merstone with a Newport-bound train of LSWR carriages sometime between 1902 and 1910. The distinctive style of the building and platform furniture is worthy of note.   *IWSR Collection*

Passing the site of the original platform at Merstone, IWC locomotive No. 2 and a train from Sandown approaches the new station in about 1899. The station house differs from those elsewhere by being faced in stone. *Real Photographs*

Merstone seen in 1958 shortly before the removal of the permanent way. The first platform was situated next to the left of the station house and the original goods siding is in the right foreground. The trackbed of the line to Ventnor trails in from the left. The pine trees behind the signal box were planted to act as a windbreak for the station. *T. Cooper*

Horringford was briefly the first terminus of the IWNJ in 1872 and possessed a building approximately twice the size of those at the level crossings at Alverstone and Newchurch. The goods siding is behind the camera to the right.   *IWSR Collection*

Newchurch possessed a platform shelter and booking office from elsewhere. Note the wooden platform and light flat bottom rails, typical of the Sandown line in IWC days.   *IWSR Collection*

a block post. The buildings were a real mixture. According to a writer in the *Southern Railway Magazine*, the office, shelter and storeroom had previously been the station building at Pan Lane whilst the waiting room had been a signal box at Mill Hill. Certainly the latter, which was of some age, had the air of a signal box but it is unlikely to have come from Mill Hill as its box was apparently still *in situ* during SR days. The lever frame was equally odd as it was in two halves - one half had three levers and the other five - one portion was said to have come from Sandown. A kickback road was added to the siding in 1911 and by the following year the platform had been extended to 232 ft, in wood, of course; the original section of siding was 121 ft long and the new section 220 ft 6 in. Leaving Newchurch there was a short straight section followed by a curve to the right, a climb, a fall, a level stretch, then more falls crossing Black Rock bridge (No. 45) *en route* to reach Alverstone.

Apart from the Webster family's tenants Alverstone had no great residential population. The station (12 m. 1 ch. from Cowes) was next to a level crossing across a minor road and had a small house on the down side of the line similar to that at Newchurch. On 15th October, 1878 Major General Hutchinson inspected a siding built opposite to the platform. There was a short wooden platform adjacent to the house and a Saxby & Farmer dwarf lever frame containing six levers controlling points, home and distant signals. By 1896 there was a seventh lever working a bolt locking the level crossing gates. The house was condemned and replaced in 1911 by a more substantial residence and booking office with a rendered upper storey. In early 1914 £15 was spent in providing an 'earth' platform in place of the wooden structure but the length was only 199 ft and nothing was done for passengers who still had to wait in a primitive corrugated iron shelter; gentlemen had the use of a similarly unpleasant privy. Connections to the 126 ft siding were transferred to a separate ground frame locked by an Annett's key on the train staff and a new five-lever frame provided to work the signals and gate bolt. The site was literally surrounded by streams; the main line crossed one (bridge No. 46) and there was even a bridge under part of the siding (No. 47).

This view of Alverstone was taken prior to the replacement of the station building by a new house in 1911-1912. The narrow platform is bare apart from a corrugated iron shelter, name board and a few advertisement signs.
IWSR Collection

Alverstone Railway Station near Sandown

Alverstone with its large new station building and booking office was a great improvement but passengers could still be exiled to the shelter should the station master fail to take pity on them.
IWSR Collection

A healthy number of passengers wait as locomotive No. 11 draws up at Alverstone with a Sandown-bound train in September 1921.   *H.J. Patterson-Rutherford, IWSR Collection*

The station mistress Mrs Young looks out on one of Alverstone's periodic floods - did she really have to use the ladder to get into her home? Beyond the ground frame is the corrugated iron waiting room, the platform is on the right. *R. Brinton Collection*

Locomotive No. 4 with a mixed collection of carriages approaches Sandown station. The first two carriages behind the locomotive are of GER and NLR origin, the remainder are probably ex-LSWR. The permanent way has been renewed using second-hand LSWR materials.

H. Gordon Tidey

Pulling away from Sandown with a Newport train, locomotive No. 4 hauls a train consisting of the two Lancaster bogie carriages and two of the company's assorted four-wheelers.

Lens of Sutton

Leaving Alverstone there followed a few level sections separated by switchback gradients as the line criss-crossed the river on numerous wood bridges: Burnt House, Scotchell's and Waterworks bridges (Nos. 48 to 50). About ¾ mile short of Sandown, a 190 ft siding was built in 1905 to the waterworks of the Isle of Wight Waterworks Company (12 m. 62 ch.). The points faced up trains and were worked by a ground frame locked by the inevitable Annett's key. The line then ascended steeply for about half a mile (the steepest gradient on the IWC) from the valley of the Eastern Yar before curving from east to south to enter the terminus at Sandown (13 m. 35 ch. from Cowes). IWC trains had the use of the west side of the 323 ft island platform and nearby sidings. Sandown line trains were limited by the length of the 344 ft run round; the sidings on the IWC side of the station could accommodate 57 trucks.

Merstone to Ventnor

For the opening of the line to Ventnor a crossing loop and 299 ft island platform was built at Merstone on the Newport side of the level crossing. Despite its quiet location, there were generous facilities for passengers including a lengthy covering to protect passengers, changing trains; this was in direct contrast to other stations on the Sandown line which lacked such luxury. Passengers gained access to the platform from the adjacent level crossing as the subway (bridge No. 37) connecting the platform with each side of the line could rarely, if ever, be used because of persistent flooding. The lengthy crossing loop extended beyond the level crossing which then had the distinction of being the only one in the Island that crossed two running lines. The nearby brick signal box by Ball & Son of Cowes was fitted out by Saxby & Farmer with 28 levers. The signalman had the luxury of a wheel to operate the gates - other Island crossing keepers had to brave the elements to open and close their gates by hand! The signalling was so arranged that trains could arrive and depart from both platforms in either direction, a useful arrangement that permitted Sandown line trains to cross in either platform; Ventnor line trains could only use the down line. On the up side a 378 ft 7 in. siding supplemented the original goods siding on the south side of the road; there was a 34 ft 6 in. refuge siding at the Newport end of the station on the down side from which a 343 ft kickback road was added in 1912.

The line to Ventnor curved away from the Sandown line immediately beyond the level crossing on a sharp right-hand curve before alternately climbing and levelling as it pursued a straight course through open country towards Godshill, *en route* crossing a private road at Kennerley bridge (No. 51); the bridge was typical of those on the line by consisting of wrought-iron troughing on brick abutments. Approaching the outskirts of the village it crossed the main road to Newport at Bow bridge (No. 52) before passing between more fields to reach Godshill station.

Godshill station (9 m. 66 ch.) was about half a mile from the village in the shadow of Bleak Down; the lengthy 300 ft platform was on the up side of the line with a two-storey station master's house and single-storey additions for the booking office, etc., a short canopy fronted the station offices. The substantial building, like those at Whitwell and St Lawrence, was red brick at ground floor level whilst the upper storey was decorated with strips of plain concrete on roughcast to give a half-timbered effect. A double-ended siding (186 ft 6 in. and a 97 ft kickback road) with a loading dock lay just beyond the platform, 'a modest goods yard' according to the company's publicity; it was locked by an Annett's key on the train staff. Distant and home signals were controlled from a separate four-lever ground frame on the platform; the ground frame and signals were removed early, probably in 1900.

Leaving Godshill, the line climbed past more farmland as it bore left on a gentle curve to the south in the direction of Whitwell. After about ¼ mile the line crossed Bridge Court bridge (No. 53), followed closely by Bridge Court Farm bridge (No. 54) and a steep climb for a further ¼ mile took the line over a public road at Nodehill bridge (No. 55). There followed a straight section as the line, still climbing steadily, passed over Roud underbridge (bridge No. 56). The

The lengthy platform at Godshill stands deserted in September 1920. This view looks towards Merstone. *IWSR Collection*

Whitwell is seen facing south soon after the opening of the line in 1897. The surface of the loop platform has not yet been made up to level of coping bricks. *IWSR Collection*

IWNJ in January 1872 although precisely who paid for it is unclear. A couple of trial trips were run along the railway from Horringford to Sandown for invited guests, but after the debacle with the Board of Trade *Brading* dropped out of sight.

To work the IWNJ following its opening, on 2nd May, 1872 the LSWR offered a choice of two locomotives on hire at a rate of £2 a day including engineman and fireman with an option to buy for £1,100. Naturally, the IWNJ preferred to hire and selected a 2-2-2 well tank *Comet* built to the designs of Joseph Beattie at Nine Elms works in June 1852 at a cost of £1,830. *Comet* arrived at Brading Quay during June and travelled over the IWR to Sandown. The locomotive worked trains between Sandown and Horringford on Coronation day 28th June, 1872, but was then stored until the following February when a Mr Pain carried out repairs costing £1 8s. Inevitably the IWNJ failed to pay the hire charges and the LSWR demanded the return of *Comet*; it was sold to the Hoylake Railway in 1875.

Left without a locomotive, George Sheward obtained a replacement from the LNWR, of which he was a Director. The purchase was a 2-2-2 well tank that cost £1,850 when delivered in January 1861 by R. & W. Hawthorn & Co. to the Whitehaven Junction Railway where it was named *Queen Mab*; the locomotive passed into the hands of the Furness Railway and in 1866 to the LNWR. Purchased through the English & Foreign Credit Company, in June 1874, it was shipped to St Helens and then taken over the IWR to Sandown. Named *Newport*, the locomotive resided in the shed at Sandown where the driver did his best to keep it in running order. Whenever his efforts failed, or as in May 1876 when the crank axle broke, *Newport* was taken to Ryde Works. During one such visit a cab was fitted similar to those carried by IWR locomotives with two round spectacles to the front and three to the rear; the livery was said to have been a sandy brown colour. *Newport* worked trains following the opening of the IWNJ in 1875 with assistance from the IWR when required. Despite the all too apparent failings of *Newport*, in June 1875 the IWNJ Board refused an offer of two locomotives at £850 each from Vincent Barton, a dealer in second-hand rolling stock.

Construction of the RNR was also carried out with the assistance of *Brading*. There was no locomotive on the line until about April 1874 but after that date *Dorothy*, as *Brading* was then called, was mentioned on several occasions. If it worked the first public trains on the RNR, as stated by the late D.L. Bradley,* *Dorothy* must have been the fourth engine which Henry Martin owned in December 1875. Martin charged the RNR £199 10s. for the use of a locomotive ballasting the line and working the trains between December 1875 and June 1876, a task for which *Dorothy* would not have been entirely suitable. *Dorothy* then moved to the IWNJ as that company's Minutes mentioned the use of a '4 wheel engine on the line' in December 1878; a sale to the Brading Harbour Improvement & Railway Company took place in 1879 or 1880 where it gained the name *St Helens*.

On the RNR was a second locomotive *Bee*. One of a standard class of tiny 0-4-0 saddle tanks built by Henry Hughes of Loughborough, it was only the third locomotive to be built by that firm when completed in 1875 for the 'Isle of Wight Tramway Company', a firm that has not been traced. The RNR had obtained Parliamentary powers to use a steam locomotive over the Ryde Pier Company's horse tramway from the IWR station at St Johns Road as far as Simeon Street. *Bee* may have been purchased by George Young with that in mind. *Bee* passed into the ownership of Henry Martin and was hired by the Joint Committee for odd shunting and construction work. The Minute book mentioned the existence of a locomotive No. 6 but it was not clear whether this referred to *Bee* or *Dorothy*. Driver Barrett had a story to tell about *Bee*. The locomotive was fitted with a pullout regulator that tended to open too readily; one day at Medina Jetty it started off with only the fireman on board and driver Barrett was fortunate to catch up with and stop the locomotive before it got away. Much too small for general use, *Bee* was sold to R.T. Relf, a contractor of Okehampton, Devon in 1888; departure to the mainland took place from Newport Quay in June that year.

The expectation that the IWR would take on the operation of the RNR delayed consideration of motive power until the line was almost ready for opening. On 17th June, 1875

---

* A *Locomotive History of Railways on the Isle of Wight* by D.L. Bradley (Railway Correspondence & Travel Society 1982).

Drawing of the locomotive *Bee*.

No. 4 may already have been withdrawn from service when photographed outside Ryde Works
in early SR days.   *IWSR Collection*

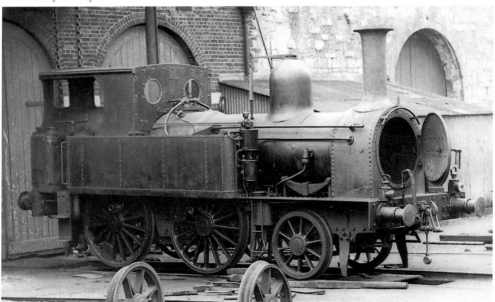

the LSWR Locomotive and Stores committee considered a request from George Young asking to buy two locomotives; Mr Beattie was asked to quote a suitable price. Two antique 2-4-0Ts *Aurora* and *Chaplin* dating from 1856, offered at a price of £785 each, were allegedly refused because their outside cylinders would have fouled the platforms. Desperate for motive power, on 14th July, 1875 the RNR Board decided to place an order with Beyer, Peacock & Co. of Manchester for two 2-4-0Ts at £1,765 each. Ordered in the name of George Young under the title 'Isle of Wight Extensions', Beyer, Peacock's records gave the following information about them:

Progress No.	Tried in steam	Delivered	Notes
1583	16th November, 1875	25th May, 1876	To be numbered 4 with the name COWES
1584	18th November, 1875	25th May, 1876	To be numbered 5 with the name OSBORNE

A great improvement on the CNR pair, they were smaller versions of the IWR 2-4-0Ts. It is not entirely clear what livery they carried when delivered - possibly red - but by 1887 they were certainly dark chocolate. They had the characteristic Beyer, Peacock cabs, copper-capped chimneys, brass safety valve domes, rectangular brass plates on the tank sides, oval maker's plates on the bunker sides and 8 in. brass numbers rivetted to both sides of the chimneys. As with all new purchases from the mainland, the price did not include shipping costs which on this occasion amounted to £85 17s. 4d.

The dates of their steaming and delivery imply that George Young had difficulties in funding their purchase. Henry Martin was eventually prevailed upon to guarantee instalments to Beyer, Peacock spread over a period of five years. At a shareholders' meeting on 31st August, 1876 the Directors guardedly voiced their anger at the refusal of the IWR to work their line saying '. . . large items of locomotive expenses have arisen from temporary arrangements for hire of engines, which the Company were compelled to make in order to carry the traffic'.

Using locomotives hired from Henry Martin plus the two RNR Beyer, Peacock 2-4-0Ts, a Joint Committee of the CNR and RNR took over the operation of their railways in 1876 and three years later of the IWNJ. The unreliable *Newport* was a constant headache but somehow services were maintained through the summer months. This situation could not be allowed to continue and, after rejecting the offer of a locomotive from Messrs Frimin, Hill & Co. in January 1880, Henry Martin made a shopping expedition to the North London Railway's Bow Works. He purchased NLR No. 106 (previously No. 35), a 4-4-0 tank engine that had been built by Slaughter, Gruning & Co. in October 1861 at a cost of £2,650. It was reasonably priced at £750 and proved to be a good investment. The locomotive was resold to the Joint Committee in April 1880 for £800 at the rate of 12 per cent per annum of which 4 per cent was a sinking fund for purchase. The LSWR received £24 19s. 6d. for permitting it to pass over its railway from Kew Bridge to Southampton and the NLR 17s. 6d. for its man's time in taking the locomotive there. The locomotive remained in NLR lined black livery but gained the name of *Whippingham*. It is about *Whippingham* that various stories as to ownership have emerged. According to an IWC driver there was a cast-iron plate affixed to the frame stay saying 'H.D. Martin - Owner'. However, the Joint Committee made instalment payments for three carriages purchased at the same time to a Miss Martin, one of Henry's family, and this probably led to the claim that the locomotive was 'owned by two old ladies' - Henry's sisters.

At 36 tons *Whippingham* was altogether heavier than any of the previous purchases and there were numerous derailments on the IWNJ's less than robust permanent way. It was, however, capable of hauling a reasonable number of carriages and a goodly number of coal wagons. Whenever *Whippingham* was unavailable, such was the poor state of the other motive power that separate passenger and goods trains had to be operated.

If the IWR accounts are to be believed, Ryde Works occasionally carried out work for the Joint Committee and the CNR before it - obviously the practicalities overcame any animosity between the companies! This was in addition to the hire of locomotives to the IWNJ during the period Joseph Bourne was its manager. There were also occasions when IWR locomotive

No. 5 *Osborne* photographed in about 1890 at Freshwater has lost the brass number on the chimney but acquired front footsteps and handrails along the tops of the tanks.

IWSR Collection

No. 5 is seen at the south end of Newport station in about 1919 looking very smart in its lined black livery. Note the Hurst & Wheeler chimney and the deeper cab side sheets. The wicker baskets were used for coaling locomotives.   *R. Silsbury Collection*

crews were hired, probably with their locomotives, on special occasions such as Ashey race days. During Joint Committee days the CNR 2-2-2Ts were each provided with a tapered stovepipe chimney, a square cab and a large circular sandbox on the boiler in place of smaller boxes over the driving wheel splashers - the sandboxes were identical to one carried by *Whippingham*. *Mill Hill* also received a larger square cab in place of its original.

In 1880 the English & Foreign Credit Company was wound up; *Newport* and the rolling stock eventually passed into IWNJ ownership and from 1882 were included in the Joint Committee's returns to the Board of Trade. *Newport* is unlikely to have been greatly used following the arrival of *Whippingham*. In September 1881 Mr Simmons reported that the locomotive had burst its boiler and recommended that it be replaced. He was overruled and *Newport* was not then mentioned until the 1890s by which time it had been out of use for many years.

On 26th October, 1887 the Minute book of the newly formed IWC recorded the issue of debentures to the value of £10,000 to Henry Martin for the purchase of six locomotives and a quantity of rolling stock; a month later a cheque was drawn for £594 6s. 2d., being the balance owed on *Whippingham*. Unfortunately, a valuable source of information in the form of the Central's boiler book has been lost in recent years and it is only from the writings of other authors that we know anything of its contents. The late D.L. Bradley recorded that the locomotives were allocated running numbers, repainted and had their names removed (the RNR pair may also have lost the brass numbers from their chimneys at that time); the dates infer that *Mill Hill* and *Whippingham* had only painted names on the tank sides. *Newport* was probably never repainted nor numbered.

Name	No.	Name removed	Name	No.	Name removed
Pioneer	1	1893	*Cowes*	4	1893
Precursor	2	1895	*Osborne*	5	1892
Mill Hill	3	1888	*Newport*	6	not known
			Whippingham	7	1888

A specification describing the locomotive livery was sent to Beyer, Peacock a few years later:

Smokebox and chimney to be primed over and filled up with best filling and after rubbing down to receive two coats of Griffiths Bros. quick drying Black Enamel and two coats of varnish. Firebox to be treated in similar manner. Remainder of engine to be prepared, and afterwards receive two coats of Red Oxide as ground for Metallic Crimson Lake then two coats Crimson Lake, the surface to be picked out and fine lined to pattern sent by I.W.C. Ry. Co. Two garters also supplied by I.W.C. Ry Co. to be transferred on centre of tank sides the figures to be painted inside the garters in 4 in. black figures with 1 in. black shading and gilded to match garter. Three coats of varnish to be given. The first and second coats to be flattened when dry. Buffer beams painted vermilion with 1 in. black border and ⅝ picking out line 1 in. from inside of border line. A yellow fine line between the black lines equidistant from each, and one outside of black picking out line ½ in. from inside edge. All accessories to be blacked. Top of cab inside, painted white and varnished.

Whilst this may have been the official specification, the IWC seems not to have been quite so scrupulous when repainting its existing locomotives - samples taken from No. 11 show that it carried a dull brick red, cheap paint made from red oxide. The garter came to be applied to locomotives from 1893 when Messrs Tearnes* supplied suitable transfers in two sizes to the company, one measured 12¾ in. wide by 14¾ in. high, the other being 9½ in. wide by 11½ in. high. Carrying the words 'Central Railway' around the edge, the body of the garter was vermilion and the remainder gilt.

On 30th October, 1889 Mr Simmons submitted a list of tenders to his Board for the supply of a brand new locomotive ostensibly for working the FYN. After discussion the Board

---

* *Railway Heraldry* by G. Dow (David & Charles, 1973).

For a locomotive that was broken up in 1906, the first No. 7 appeared in a surprising number of photographs. Seen at Newport in the summer of 1900, it carries the running number on the side tanks inside the IWC garter. On the right is a tank wagon that supplied water to the steam cranes at Medina Wharf.

A.B. MacLeod Collection

decided to accept the tender of £1,845 from Black, Hawthorn for what was essentially an updated version of the NLR 4-4-0T; the large driving wheels were clearly in anticipation of its use on the company's fastest trains. The IWC Board wanted the locomotive delivered by 31st March, 1890 but this proved rather premature as a strike delayed arrival until June 1890; the final cost was £1,913 plus £41 14s. 7d. for conveyance from Southampton to Cowes. IWC No. 6 proved to be the most powerful locomotive in the fleet and rapidly became the Central's pride and joy. The locomotive was the first to be fitted with the Westinghouse brake, but this was no guarantee that the company would soon cease relying on hand brakes and it took until the end of 1893 to equip the remaining passenger locomotives.

There was no mention of any significant expenditure on the company's existing locomotives until April 1892 when Beyer, Peacock received £57 10s. for new cylinders and E. Walker £329 10s. for a new boiler, apparently for No. 1. Other locomotives underwent subtle changes in appearance: the Beyer, Peacock pair gained some additional handrails high above the tanks that were used when a member of the crew had to reach the front of the locomotive whilst it was in motion - the handrails were removed after 1900 when new safety legislation outlawed the practice.

In August 1891 Herbert Simmons reported an approach from the NGStL contractors asking if the company would sell one of its old locomotives. The Board guardedly asked what price they would be prepared to pay but the response was evidently unsatisfactory as nothing more was heard of the matter. Disposal of the IWNJ 2-2-2T *Newport* with other 'scrap' was raised by Mr Simmons in September 1892 but the Board rejected his suggestion and ordered that it be retained as a source of spares for other locomotives. After another request on 24th October, 1894 the Board relented; soon afterwards it was deleted from Board of Trade returns, dismantled and the remains sold - an old boiler disposed of in June 1896 for £15 probably came from *Newport*.

The construction of the NGStL was carried out with the assistance of three locomotives. In September 1893 the contractors purchased *St Helens* for £650, an enormous sum for such a relic. Renamed *St Lawrence*, there is a persistent rumour that it ran in steam along the public highway from one section of the works to another. In November 1896 *St Lawrence* assisted in construction of High Hat tunnel, working down from Merstone in the morning and returning at the end of the day. Desperate for serviceable motive power, the IWC hired the locomotive in 1897 for shunting at Medina Jetty. *St Lawrence* can have been of little use as the boiler pressure was down to 60 psi; driver Barrett described her as 'a real antique'. She was, after all, built in 1841 and by far the oldest locomotive in the Isle of Wight. Dumped at Whitwell, the IWC unsuccessfully offered to buy the locomotive for £10 for conversion to a tar tank wagon and it was broken up in June 1898. According to local legend, the remains were tipped into the formation along the Undercliff, a reasonable act as once stripped of any brass and copper, the remaining non-ferrous metal was virtually worthless.

Mr Westwood also purchased an 0-6-0T from Kerr, Stuart & Co. Named *Godshill*, it had been rebuilt in 1895 from a locomotive said to have been built by Worcester Engineering Company in 1863. On 3rd August, 1898 the IWC Board received a letter from the representative of Charles Westwood, who was then bankrupt, asking about *Godshill* and other plant that the IWC had allegedly removed from the construction site. The IWC responded that they had not taken any materials belonging to Mr Westwood except *Godshill* which was at Newport, having been hired for a total of 45½ days; the £45 10s. rent had been deducted from his debt to the IWC. *Godshill* later passed into the hands of J.T. Firbank who took over the construction of the Ventnor extension. The locomotive left the Island following completion of the construction work and ended its days on the Great Central Railway Marylebone extension works.

Firbank employed a third locomotive on the Ventnor extension. Built in 1888 by Hudswell, Clarke for T.A. Walker, a contractor building the Manchester Ship Canal, *Weaste* was a small 0-4-0T that had a cut down chimney presumably in order to negotiate low structures. It left the Island when construction of the NGStL ended. In 1901 it was being used on the

The second No. 6 seen outside Newport shed in 1900. The burnt smokebox door emphasises its need for an overhaul.   *IWSR Collection*

On 2nd June, 1921 No. 6 stands in the loop platform at Newport. The Westinghouse brake pump has been moved to the right of the boiler, there is a smaller sandbox and a Hurst & Wheeler chimney.   *H.C. Casserley*

The second No. 7 was equally popular with the photographers. It is seen at Cowes soon after arrival painted in the IWCR lined red livery and with a highly polished dome.   *Lens of Sutton*

No. 7 in the lined black livery at Newport ex-works following an overhaul in 1920. Note the Ramsbottom safety valves, painted dome and what appears to be a dent on the bottom left end of the tank side!   *T. Cooper Collection*

Beyer, Peacock painted No. 8 in photographic grey for this picture shortly before delivery in 1898.   *The Museum of Science and Industry of Manchester*

Although this photograph of No. 8 at Ventnor dates from early SR days, we have included it to show the rear section of the cab and coal bunker which has been modified with the addition of a top cover.   *R. Silsbury Collection*

The Isle of Wight Central Railway has just added a powerful new engine to its rolling stock. For the purpose of landing it from a Southampton lighter, a temporary line was constructed across a field to the water's edge, where a platform was erected. The engine was conveyed on the metals off the lighter across the field to the permanent way at Medham, about a mile from Cowes. The plan adopted for the transfer of the engine was simplicity itself, and it worked admirably. A gang of men were employed for a week in making the necessary preparations.

On 17th December, 1902, following the receipt of £3,895 from the sale of £4,100 'A' debenture stock, the Board decided to pay off the Southern Counties Rolling Stock Co. in respect of 25 wagons and locomotives Nos. 8 to 11 at a total cost of £3,852 4s. 10d.

The Minute book during 1903 was peppered with references to the motive power: new cylinders were ordered for No. 7, the wharf engine No. 3 had broken its crank pin and No. 10 needed a new crank axle, tyres and other repairs costing £120. On 24th June, 1903 Mr Conacher gained the Board's approval to seek an additional locomotive. A month later the Board refused to pay £700 for the LBSCR class 'A' locomotive *Wapping* on account of its age (it was built in 1872) but on 26th August agreed to offer the same amount for No. 84 *Crowborough*; it dated from 1884 and was the last of the class to be built - settlement was reached at £725. The *Isle of Wight County Press* reported that IWC No. 12 arrived at the end of November.

Despite Mr Seymour's report in 1901, No. 4 had not received a new boiler and by May 1904 also needed a replacement firebox and cylinders. As on previous occasions, the Board hesitated and considered offers of second-hand locomotives from the LBSCR at £750 and the Midland & South Western Junction Railway at £800 to £1,000. Since Beyer, Peacock was prepared to supply a boiler and cylinders for £445 it was decided to repair No. 4. A decision to break up Nos. 1 and 2 had been delayed because their owners, the Southern Counties Rolling Stock Company, wanted £500 to clear the outstanding debt. Lacking the necessary cash, on 31st August the IWC Board decided to sign over ownership of locomotive No. 12; apart from the retention of the boiler from No. 1 to power workshop machinery, they were dismantled and the remains sold as scrap.

Locomotive No. 7 failed in traffic in July 1906 and whilst repairs costing £55 were authorised, the new locomotive superintendent, Robert Guest, evidently thought they were not worth doing and recommended that it be replaced by a locomotive with similar capabilities. On 28th November the Board approved the purchase of a Beyer, Peacock 2-4-0T from the Midland & South Western Junction Railway for £695 after a previous offer of £650 had been rejected. The new No. 7 was one of a batch of three 2-4-0Ts supplied in 1882 to the Swindon, Marlborough & Andover Railway, a predecessor of the MSWJ. The locomotive was much larger than previous Beyer, Peacock purchases, having a size more akin to the IWR's *Bonchurch*. Its arrival heralded a minor change in livery with the title on the tank sides abbreviated to 'I. W. C. R.' This style gradually spread to the existing locomotives as they passed through works. The 4-4-0T was dismantled and the remains sold for scrap with some old rails for £235 10s.

On 4th October, 1906 steam railmotor No. 1 was delivered to the IWC (*see Chapter Thirteen*). The *Railway Magazine* described it in the following terms:

The engine and boiler are of the ordinary locomotive type, carried on a four wheel bogie. These wheels are coupled and power is transmitted from two high-pressure outside cylinders to the trailing axle. The valve motion is of the Walschaert type, which is particularly adapted to this form of engine. Coal and water are carried in bunkers and side tanks on either side of the boiler, and dry sand is applied to all four wheels of the engine. The boiler is fitted to the frames in the usual manner, and has been fitted with a pair of Crosby's Patent Duplex Safety Valves.

The vehicle is 61 ft long and divided into the following compartments. Engine, luggage-locker, second class, entrance gangway, first class, and driver's compartment for use when travelling in a backward direction. The compartments are furnished and upholstered according to the latest ideas of comfort in travelling, and are well ventilated. The seating accommodates 44 passengers and the luggage compartment has been constructed to hold 20 cwt. Sliding doors separate the various compartments. No smoking accommodation is provided. The outside painting is in the railway's standard colours, with the addition of relief in cream colour on the upper portion of the car body.

Drawing of railmotor No. 1.

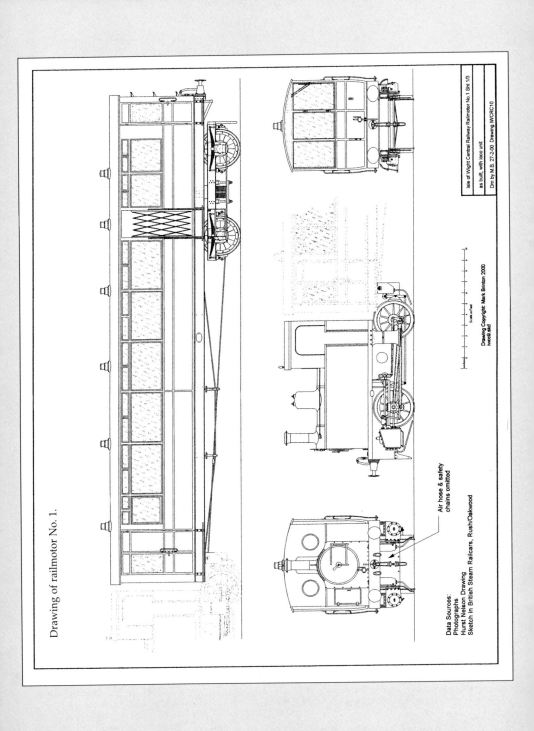

Data Sources:
Photographs
Hurst Nelson Drawing
Sketch in British Steam Railcars, Rush/Oakwood

Air hose & safety
chains omitted

Scale in Feet

Drawing Copyright: Mark Brinton 2000
iwccd.ifdd

Isle of Wight Central Railway Railmotor No.1 Sht 1/3

as built, with loco unit

Drn by M.B. 27-2-00 Drawing IWCRC10

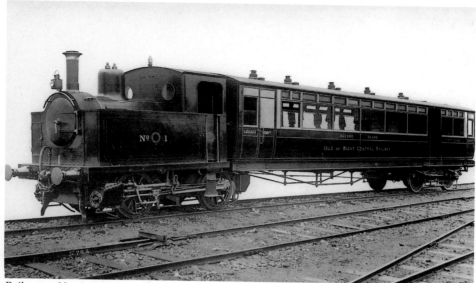

Railmotor No. 1 is seen in the condition in which it was delivered to the IWC in 1906. The photograph cannot do justice to the cream and maroon livery. *R. Silsbury Collection*

The locomotive portion of the railmotor was painted in red oxide lined yellow and black; in the centre of the tank sides was 'No. 1' in 5 in. gilt block lettering placed each side of the garter transfer. Within weeks of delivery the railmotor was laid aside after the locomotive axles overheated and the Board naturally delayed the final payment until the matter was sorted out. Although the railmotor returned to service in January 1907 the locomotive springs were damaged whilst passing over Towngate viaduct on the Freshwater line - it cost £30 to repair. Repeated overheating of the crank axle led to several exchanges of letters with the makers who eventually supplied a replacement axle box; even so it was July 1908 before the railmotor was fully fit for service.

The apparent savings from the employment of railmotor No. 1 prompted a decision to use locomotive No. 3 with a carriage in a similar manner. At first the purchase of a purpose-built carriage was considered and various makers were asked to quote for its construction. Tenders were read out on 29th May, 1907 for a carriage seating eight first and 40 third class passengers:

Bristol Wagon & Carriage Co.	£2,398
Metropolitan Amalgamated Railway Carriage & Wagon Co.	£1,630
Hurst, Nelson & Co.	£1,125

All were considered far too expensive but on 24th September, 1907 Mr Conacher wrote that the Midland Railway had offered a composite bogie coach for sale at £130. Its conversion including the addition of Westinghouse brake, lighting, etc. would add £120 to the cost and the conversion of No. 3 a further £300. According to the accounts, the Midland Railway were actually paid £115 14s. 2d. plus £41 13s. 2d. to get the carriage to the Island. It was one of a batch of 12 built in 1875 by Ashbury Railway Carriage & Wagon Co. of Openshaw, Manchester for the opening of the Midland Railway's extension to Carlisle. The eight-compartment composite carriage measured 54 ft by 8 ft, weighed approximately 22 tons, had six-wheel bogies and a clerestory roof.

This very faded photograph of IWC 0-4-4T No. 2 has been included for its historical interest and shows the locomotive after its weight had been lightened by shortening the side tanks.

M. Barnsley

The black sheep 0-4-4T No. 2 resides minus its cab half out of the locomotive shed at Newport.

IWSR Collection

By May 1908 another crisis in the locomotive department was looming. Such was the time spent on the railmotors that maintenance of other locomotives was falling behind. At that time, overhauls were not swift and a locomotive might spend a year or more in the workshops. Given that more than one would be stopped for repairs, this was probably why an additional locomotive was thought to be essential. Although Mr Guest proposed the purchase of a locomotive from the Metropolitan Railway for £500 the Board were unable to contemplate the expenditure. Mr Guest was pressed to push on with the conversion of No. 3 but work had been delayed by the need to carry out urgent repairs to No. 8. The problem did not go away and at a Board meeting on 12th August, 1908 offers of locomotives were read out from:

LBSCR	£1,000
Great Western Railway	£800
Metropolitan Railway	£480
MSWJ	£800

On 26th August it was decided to ask the Cambrian Railways' Engineer to inspect a 43 ton GWR 2-4-2T No. 1304 *Plynlimmon* and offer £700 if it was found satisfactory. This decision was rescinded when the Board were informed that the engine would not be needed until the new year; when enquiries were recommenced in 1909 the GWR had tired of the process and withdrew it from sale, despite an offer of £800. After rejecting offers of more locomotives from the MSWJ, LBSCR and LSWR, none of which the Board considered suitable, Charles Conacher wrote on 25th May, 1909 recommending the purchase of an 0-4-4T for £875. It had been constructed in 1895 at Seaham harbour for hauling passenger trains on the Londonderry railway; it served the Port of Seaham (Co. Durham) and nearby collieries owned by the Marquis of Londonderry. The railway was taken over by the North Eastern Railway in 1900 and the locomotive placed in store. The Board thought the asking price too high and wanted to offer only £700 but after some argument '. . . as the matter was pressing' paid £750. Of comparable weight to the LSWR class 'O2' 0-4-4Ts sent to the Island by the Southern Railway, IWC No. 2 proved far too heavy for the permanent way. The cab and side tanks were shortened in an attempt to reduce the weight but it still had the unfortunate habit of spreading the track. Even when restricted to the Ryde - Newport - Cowes line, No. 2 was never as powerful nor sure-footed as Nos. 6 or 7.

Mr Guest and his staff spent months in fitting out locomotive No. 3 and the Midland Railway carriage for their new role. Although always referred to as a railmotor, the alterations created more in the way of a pull-push unit as the pair were never permanently joined together. The carriage was fitted with a hand brake, had its oil gas lighting adapted to coal gas by the installation of larger cylinders and was converted from the vacuum brake to the Westinghouse air system. A first/third class composite when on the Midland Railway, the IWC retained the existing seating but relabelled the third class compartments as second. One end compartment was stripped for the driver who was provided with windows in the end to see the track ahead. Control was entrusted to a notoriously unreliable system of wires as used by the LSWR. In the driving compartment was a winding drum from which a pair of wire ropes ran along the roof to the locomotive where they connected with the regulator. The locomotive boiler and tanks received a cladding of steel sheet whilst more was used to give a more modern look to the cab. A repaint in red with a garter on the locomotive enclosing the number 2 finished off the ensemble. It seems to have entered service in about May 1909. Unfortunately, nothing could compensate for that fact that the IWC was employing a weak, worn out old locomotive to push and pull a heavy bogie coach over some of the steepest gradients on the company's system. Valiant efforts were made to make railmotor No. 2 work but it seems to have spent more time in workshops than in use.

Although somewhat more reliable than when first delivered, the life of railmotor No. 1 as a single unit was drawing to a close because, for all the failings of its power unit, passengers had a far more comfortable ride in the Midland Railway carriage than in the purpose-built carriage. The extension of third class accommodation to more trains also put the railmotors at

Photographs of 0-4-4T No. 2 in service are very rare. Here it is seen working a train on the Ventnor branch in 1910. Even after a reduction in the size of the tanks, the locomotive is massive when compared with the LSWR carriages trailing behind.

K. Nunn Collection

a disadvantage as they seated only first and second class. Following a report from Mr Guest, on 29th June, 1910 the Board approved the separation of the locomotive and carriage portions at a cost of £100. When the work was carried out later that year, the locomotive was fitted with an extended frame at its rear, an enlarged coal bunker, buffing and coupling gear. A second bogie was purchased for the carriage; it also received buffers, couplings and other alterations.

The locomotive department came under intense scrutiny following the appointment of Harry Willmott as Chairman of the IWC. Charles Conacher had departed several months earlier but, despite his recommendation, no Engineer had been appointed to keep an eye on matters. Mr Guest prepared a summary of the condition of the locomotives that inferred they were in reasonable condition. However, all was not well and Mr Thom from the LSWR carried out an independent inspection. His report made unpleasant reading:

No. 1 rail motor. The locomotive portion had just returned to service following repairs and alterations lasting six months. The water spaces in the front and back of the boiler had not been cleaned and were full of sediment. About 30 boiler tubes needed replacement.

No. 2 locomotive. The spiral springs to the leading axle boxes caused the locomotive to hunt and roll when running. A new arrangement was suggested and various faults with the boiler needed correcting.

No. 3 had bent its crank axle and broken the left cylinder and crank pin. It was not of much use to the traffic department and was worth repairing only because some expenditure had already been incurred.

No. 4 had not been in works since 1905. The boiler tubes needed replacement and the firebox was in deplorable condition. It was immediately taken out of service for a thorough overhaul.

No. 5 had last been in shops in 1906. The boiler tubes and firebox were little better than No. 4 but temporary repairs were possible so that it could be kept in traffic for a few months.

No. 6 was in workshops for repairs. The firebox copper back plate was so thin that it was quite unable to carry any pressure.

No. 7 had not been in workshops since purchase in 1906. The main frames were broken (a common problem with elderly Beyer, Peacock locomotives), the locomotive was riding badly on its springs and the firebox was in a poor condition - it was still serviceable.

No. 8 had been in shops in 1907. The locomotive was in fair condition except for the boiler tubes that needed renewal.

No. 9 had not been in workshops for *eight* years (when it had cost £121 to repair). Surprisingly, the boiler tubes were in fair condition although due for replacement. The springs and axleboxes and other motion work were worn and needed a thorough overhaul.

No. 10 had returned to service in February 1911 after spending 12 months undergoing repairs. Parts of the copper firebox were rather thin and the manner in which the boiler and firebox had been repaired was said to be most unsatisfactory.

No. 11 had spent the whole of 1909 in workshops but already the axleboxes were badly worn. The firebox, however, was so thin that it was dangerous and quite unfit for use.

No. 12 had never been overhauled since its purchase in 1902! The brakes, springs, axleboxes, boiler tubes and firebox were all in bad condition. Temporary repairs were needed to the firebox and the boiler pressure reduced from 140 lb. to 120 lb. so the engine could be kept at work for a short period. It was mainly employed shunting on Medina Wharf.

Mr Thom's main criticisms were aimed at the condition of the four steam cranes on Medina Wharf. The boilers from crane Nos. 1 and 3 were condemned whilst that from crane No. 4 was filthy and the water spaces encrusted with sediment. The jib of crane No. 2 was broken and needed replacement.

Inevitably Robert Guest was held responsible for the poor state of the motive power and promptly departed from the scene. Although not mentioned in the Minute book, the SMJ provided some assistance in bringing the condition of the locomotives up to an acceptable standard. Russell Willmott took charge in January 1912 and rationalised the passenger service to make more efficient use of the motive power. The troublesome railmotors were early targets for withdrawal as they could only maintain a lightly loaded passenger service, whereas a conventional locomotive could cope with additional carriages or haul a goods train during quiet periods. If not laid aside following service reductions in January 1912, their fate was sealed by a colliers' strike in March and April when more trains were taken off. A reduction in the amount of shunting following the construction of additional sidings at Medina Wharf and Newport led to further economies.

In July 1913 the FYN took over the working of its own line and, in accordance with clauses in the working agreement, purchased some rolling stock from the IWC. Locomotives Nos. 4 and 6 were offered for sale but no price could be agreed and the FYN bought locomotives from the mainland - for the first time the Central was left with a distinct surplus of motive power.

On 13th July, 1914, a few weeks before the onset of the Great War, William Glassey, a former Caledonian Railway driver, was appointed the locomotive foreman at Newport. He assumed responsibility for the day to day management of the motive power and remained at Newport well into SR days. His influence extended to the fitting of mellow Caledonian type hooters so that signalmen at Ryde could distinguish the Central's locomotives from the shrill Beyer, Peacock whistles used on the IWR. Routine expenditure was no longer mentioned in the Minutes; the few exceptions included the ordering of a firebox for 2-4-0T No. 8 in 1914, fitted the following year, plus injectors and brake gear for No. 7.

The LBSCR 0-6-0Ts had become the most useful locomotives on the Central and it was no surprise that the Willmotts lavished some money on them. No. 11 had received coal rails in 1904 but the increased height of coal blocked the view through the lookouts. None of the other 0-6-0Ts received any similar alterations until 20th December, 1912 when the Minutes mentioned the decision to spend £9 extending the length of the bunker on No. 9; eventually all four 0-6-0Ts were so modified. Their lives were not trouble-free as on 31st July, 1913 No. 11 suffered a mechanical failure between Wootton and Haven Street whilst working an evening passenger train from Newport to Ryde. The 30 passengers had to wait 74 minutes until another engine could be sent out to retrieve it and the train's return journey had to be cancelled. The provision of replacement boilers for the LBSCR locomotives had first been mooted by Mr Thom in 1911, but the Minutes pointedly omitted any mention of negotiations with the LBSCR for two new class 'A1X' boilers, probably due to the sensitivity of incurring such a large expenditure during wartime. They were fitted to Nos. 11 and 12 in 1918 and 1916 respectively; the boiler from No. 12 was refurbished at Brighton Works and fitted to No. 9 in 1917. The four received replacement cylinders, cast-iron chimneys supplied by the Newport firm of Hurst & Wheeler (who still trade today under the name of W. Hurst & Son) and had their wooden brake blocks replaced by cast-iron ones. No. 11 again disgraced itself when on 3rd July, 1920 the trailing axle broke as it approached Ryde St Johns Road station on a Saturdays-only train from Pier Head. The locomotive had been overhauled the previous January but a flaw in the axle had not been detected.

At a Board meeting on 8th August, 1917 Russell Willmott reported that locomotive No. 2 had been sold as it stood at Newport to Messrs Armstrong, Whitworth & Co. for £1,200. Although the permanent way had been much improved since its purchase, the locomotive had been out of service for some time and such a modest profit was considered most satisfactory. No. 2 was shipped from Ryde Pier on 17th July, 1917 en route for the Armstrong, Whitworth armaments factory at Elswick; it is understood to have been broken up there in 1921.

The high prices being paid for locomotives led to the decision to sell locomotives Nos. 1 and 3, neither of which had been used for five years, and No. 4, the oldest and weakest of the working stock. On 14th February, 1918 Nos. 1 and 3 were reported sold for £950 and £750 to Holloway Bros Ltd of London, Government contractors. No. 1 became Holloway Brothers' No. 8 and along with No. 3 was used in laying out the yards of the Furness Withy Shipbuilding Co. at Haverton Hill, Middlesborough. Upon completion of the contract No. 1 was sold to William Benson & Sons Ltd of Fourstones Quarry, Hexham where it was later broken up. No. 3 went to Plenmeller Collieries near Haltwhistle and was scrapped there in about 1930. Although No. 4 was not sold, the opportunity was also taken to dispose of the stationary boiler that had been in CNR No. 1 and which had become redundant following the conversion of the machinery in Newport workshops to electricity; it went to a Bournemouth laundry in June 1918 for a reasonable £200.

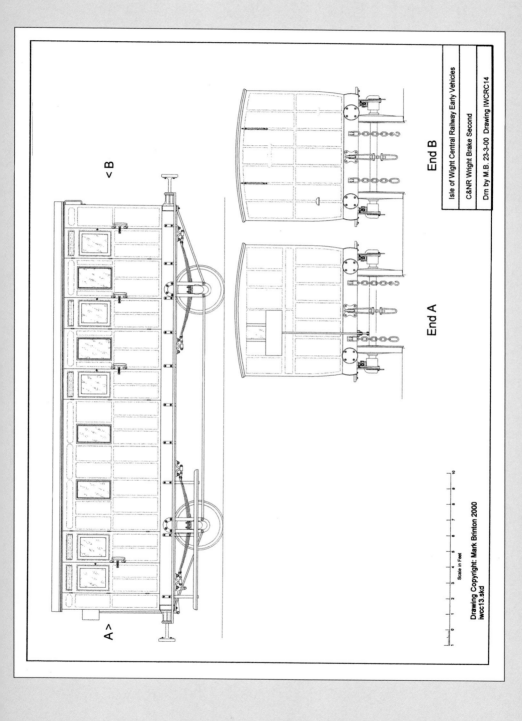

< B

A >

End A

End B

Scale in Feet

0   1   2   3   4   5   6   7   8   9   10

Isle of Wight Central Railway Early Vehicles
C&NR Wright Brake Second
Drn by M.B. 23-3-00 Drawing IWCRC14

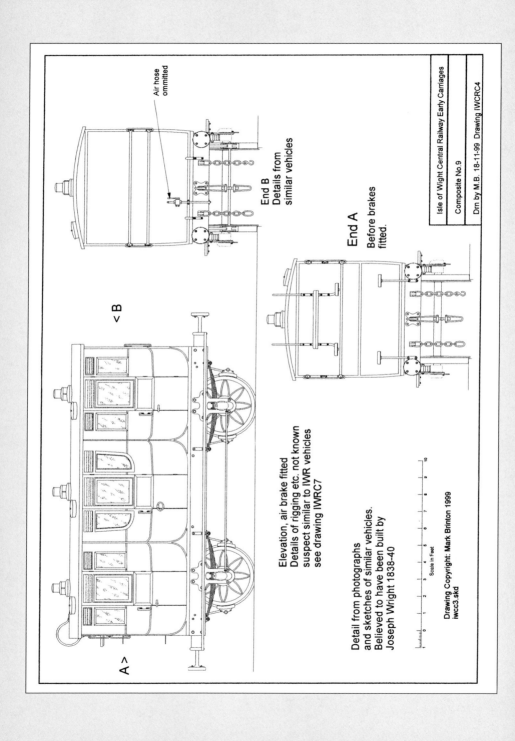

Air hose
ommitted

End B
Details from
similar vehicles

End A
Before brakes
fitted.

< B

A >

Elevation, air brake fitted
Details of rigging etc. not known
suspect similar to IWR vehicles
see drawing IWRC7

Detail from photographs
and sketches of similar vehicles.
Believed to have been built by
Joseph Wright 1838-40

Scale in Feet

Drawing Copyright: Mark Brinton 1999
iwcc3.skd

Isle of Wight Central Railway Early Carriages

Composite No.9

Drn by M.B. 18-11-99 Drawing IWCRC4

1878 the Joint Committee decided to order 20 open, six covered wagons and a goods brake van; the numbers actually rose by 29 that year. An additional 25 coal wagons from the Railway Carriage Co. of Oldbury were ordered in October 1879 - they were in use by the end of that year.

In 1879 the Joint Committee began working the IWNJ and took over that company's rolling stock. Evidently it had been maintained by the IWR in a much better condition than the Joint Committee's stock as the IWNJ Chairman, George Sheward, later complained: 'The rolling stock of this Company was in a most efficient state, but unfortunately that of the Ryde & Newport and Cowes & Newport was not in good condition. The result was that the cost of the repair of rolling stock fell very heavily on this Company'.

During a visit to the NLR works at Bow in January 1880 Henry Martin inspected and purchased three five-compartment carriages which he resold to the Joint Committee for £350 with interest at 8 per cent per annum - payment was made to Miss Martin, a relative. They had the distinction of being fitted with Clark's chain brake, the first vehicles in the Island to possess anything more than hand brakes; to work with them, brake carriage No. 21 was fitted up with a winding drum in the guard's compartment. There were no further purchases of passenger carriages by the Joint Committee but 10 wagons were added to stock in 1883 and another 10 in 1886; this ignores replacements for accident victims of which there must have been a few.

In 1887 Henry Martin's rolling stock was taken over by the IWC. An unofficial list recorded their numbering as:

1-4	CNR Wright & Co. carriages - they ran as a single set, one composite having been converted to a brake second.
5-12	Other Henry Martin carriages and vans.
13-21	RNR LNW carriages.
22-24	NLR carriages - used with brake van No. 21 as one set.
25-27	IWNJ Bristol carriages - also called 'market' carriages, they were added to trains to provide extra accommodation when required.
28-30	IWNJ Metropolitan carriages - worked in one set.
31-33	IWNJ composites.

There had already been one loss as Board of Trade returns show there were actually 32 assorted items of passenger stock and 148 wagons. The passenger stock was a delightful hotchpotch of vehicles that all too easily reflected their mixed origins and hard lives. The carriages fell into two distinct types: Nos. 1-4 and 22-30 were relatively modern with four or five compartments. The remainder were mainly three-compartment vehicles in the autumn of their lives - the IWC could ill afford to dispense with their services, quite the contrary. No list of goods vehicles has survived but it is likely they were numbered in order of date of purchase, newer vehicles being those with higher running numbers - there never seemed to be enough of them. The IWC adopted the practice of re-using numbers to replace accident victims and others withdrawn for rebuilding. By 1923 the wagon stock was a jumbled assortment carrying numbers that bore no relation to their origins.

There was a desperate need for new rolling stock. When Queen Victoria travelled from Whippingham to Ventnor on 11th February, 1888 she used a train supplied by the IWR, apparently because the IWC had nothing considered fit for royalty. After enquiries had been made with several makers, on 27th March, 1889 Herbert Simmons was authorised to order two bogie carriages from Lancaster Carriage & Wagon Co. IWC No. 34 had compartments for first and second class passengers, whilst No. 35 had a guard's and luggage compartment flanked by one first and three second class compartments. Delivered in early 1890 at a cost of £1,113 plus £49 2s. 5d. for their shipment from Southampton, they were usually reserved for the Ryde to Freshwater through trains. The Central could not afford any more new carriages and, following a report from Mr Simmons on the availability of carriages from the LSWR and LBSCR, the Board decided on 30th October, 1889 to purchase four carriages and a van from the LBSCR; they

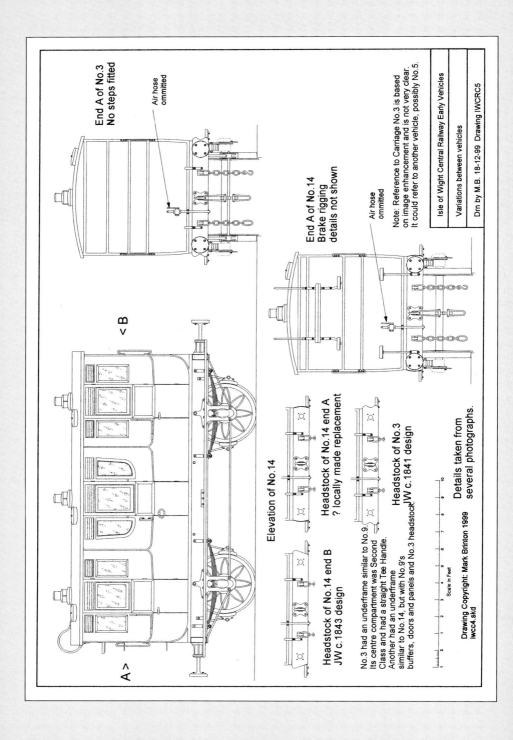

End A of No.3
No steps fitted

Air hose
ommitted

< B

End A of No.14
Brake rigging
details not shown

Air hose
ommitted

Note: Reference to Carriage No.3 is based on image enhancement and is not very clear. It could refer to another vehicle, possibly No.5.

Isle of Wight Central Railway Early Vehicles

Variations between vehicles

Drn by M.B. 18-12-99 Drawing IWCRC5

Elevation of No.14

Headstock of No.14 end A
? locally made replacement

Headstock of No.14 end B
JW c.1843 design

Headstock of No.3
JW c.1841 design

No.3 had an underframe similar to No.9. Its centre compartment was Second Class and had a straight Tee Handle. Another had an underframe similar to No.14, but with No.9's buffers, doors and panels and No.3 headstock

A >

Scale in Feet
0 1 2 3 4 5 6 7 8 9 10

Drawing Copyright: Mark Brinton 1999
iwcc4.skd

Details taken from
several photographs.

were numbered 36-40 and cost £375. The low purchase price reflected their age which probably dated from 1860 or earlier; in external appearance they were little different from the LNWR carriages but the internal furnishings would have been in a better state.

The purchase of the Brighton carriages coincided with discussions about the fitting of continuous brakes to the passenger stock, a requirement of the 1889 Regulation of Railways Act. The stock already carried the Westinghouse brake and when asked if they would pay a little extra to leave it in place, the Directors agreed; in turn, this prompted the adoption of the brake for the rest of the Central's stock.

During 1888 the company bought two batches of 10 new goods wagons costing £450 and £487 8s. 5d. respectively. The second purchase of 8 ton wagons from Gloucester Wagon Co. were painted brown with white shaded black lettering, but that should not be regarded as an indication of the livery carried by other IWC goods wagons at the time. The wagons had oil axleboxes, a brake working wooden brake shoes acting on one side only and safety chains; to save money they had dumb buffers. Despite these purchases the Central remained so short of wagons that some were hired from Henry Jackson who was the contractor maintaining the FYN; he received numerous payments during 1890 and 1891. When Jackson offered 10 ballast wagons for sale at £10 each, the manager was instructed to select the best six. There was at least one goods brake van in use because it was involved in an accident at Cowes; a month later the level crossing gates at Alverstone were demolished '. . . by running away of Goods Brake Van' - clearly its brakes were not what they should have been. In November 1891 the Board considered the purchase of 10 coal wagons and at the next meeting the Secretary read out a lengthy list of tenders for new and second-hand 8 ton wagons - nothing was done. Matters came to a head exactly two years later when, following complaints about a shortage of wagons, Herbert Simmons drew up a specification for 10 new trucks. The line was blocked on 27th October, 1893 for an hour after an axle of a coal wagon broke, one of 30 wagons all a 'good deal worn' that needed replacement; it seems that axles were purchased but no wagons.

On 29th August, 1894 a fresh list of tenders for wagons was read out from 10 makers. This time the Board asked '. . . whether trucks with dead buffers are allowed by the Board of Trade'. Mr Simmons inspected some second-hand wagons offered by Clemens Abell & Co. In October 10 were bought for £200 and in December it was agreed to pay £387 for sixteen 8 and 10 ton wagons (the accounts show that one was actually a van). They were not enough and after considering tenders for brand new 9 ton wagons in December 1896, a quote for 25 from Harrison & Camm Ltd at £56 15s. per wagon was accepted on 24th February, 1897. Delivered during the summer, payment was made through the agency of the Southern Counties Rolling Stock Co. from whom the wagons were hired at £192 10s. per annum for 10 years - they were the last purchases of new wagons.

By then, the cement company had relieved the IWC of the need to transport its chalk from Shide to Cement Mills in the Central's wagons. The chalk wagons were not the only privately owned stock on the IWC. In May 1894 A. Sharpe & Co. put timber trucks on the railway but by 1916 they were no longer required and the IWC bought two. There also existed an 'Ashey Pit Brake Van' because Charles Conacher wrote in January 1898 asking the Board who owned it! After much correspondence and discussion he was told that it belonged to Mr Gibson, owner of the quarry.

The public's poor opinion of the railway naturally included the rolling stock. On 26th May, 1894 the *Isle of Wight County Press* claimed that the company possessed only two or three good carriages and for the greater part of the year first class passengers needed to carry umbrellas when the weather was wet! This was despite the expenditure of £240 on repairs, of which £60 was recouped by the sale of some old carriage wheels. Desperate for some new stock, Charles Conacher inspected carriages built by Metropolitan Railway Carriage & Wagon Co. for the Brecon & Merthyr Railway. He recommended that the Board sanction the purchase of six 4-wheel vehicles of the same type. The Directors thought Metropolitan's quote of £3,092 10s. excessive and after tenders were obtained from other firms they again prevaricated by asking for quotes for six-wheel stock.

It was another four years before the purchase of more passenger carriages was considered and the opening of the NGStL had to be performed using the LBSCR carriages - there was nothing better. At a meeting of the Board on 19th January, 1898 the tenders were updated:

Supplier	Previously £	Updated £	Supplier	Previously £	Updated £
Oldbury Rly C. & W. Co.	3,239	3,239	Metropolitan Rly C. & W. Co.	3,092	3,421
Brown Marshalls & Co.	3,362	3,620	Gloucester Rly Carriage Co.	4,216	4,606
Lancaster Rly C. & W. Co.	3,390	3,614	Ashbury Rly Carriage & Iron Co.	3,342	3,642

Meanwhile, the locomotive superintendent, Mr Seymour, had been to see some second-hand carriages belonging to the LSWR. Tempted by a bargain, it was arranged that Messrs Bolton, Mortimer, Conacher and Seymour would visit Eastleigh to see the stock. After months of correspondence and another visit to inspect stock, on 20th April, 1898 the Board agreed to buy from the LSWR four composite carriages, a passenger guard's van and a saloon, IWC Nos. 41-45 and 19. Quite apart from the £482 2s. 10d. cost, funded by the Southern Counties Rolling Stock Co., the indecision stemmed from attempts to get the LSWR to refurbish them before delivery. The payment included repairs, fitting of spring buffers if required (some were in close-coupled block sets) and Westinghouse brakes - they had been built in the 1860s and 1870s.

More complaints about a lack of wagons resulted in quotes for new and second-hand wagons. A list was read to the Board in February 1898 when orders were given that the cheaper second-hand wagons be inspected. In April 1898 the IWC bought from Bute Works Supply Co., dealers in second-hand rolling stock, two badly needed tar tank wagons for £100 and the best 40 from a batch of 50 eight ton wagons at £17 10s. each. This time the wagons were purchased through North Central Wagon Co., a credit company, by quarterly instalments of £356 13s. 4d. a year for three years. In June six converted wagons were bought from Bute Works Supply Co. at £35 each, including tarpaulins; what they looked like is not known. By the end of 1898 there were over 100 more goods vehicles than six years earlier.

Locomotive No. 6 stands at Sandown with the company's newly purchased bogie carriages and one of the IWNJ Market four-wheelers - the dale is 1890. Note what appears to be the old IWNJ locomotive shed in the left background.   *A.B. MacLeod Collection*

Ever the publicist, Charles Conacher made sure the purchases were known about and on 4th June, 1898 the *Isle of Wight County Press* carried the following:

> The Isle of Wight Central Railway are to be congratulated on the acquisition of the important addition of rolling stock which has just been made in order to keep pace with the requirements of the traffic. The new stock includes a powerful new engine of the most modern type, built at a cost of £2,000 by one of the foremost engineering firms of the country. In addition, six carriages, which are nicely appointed, and are of an improved design have also been purchased, and made their initial journeys on Whit Monday. One of the new vehicles is a second class saloon seating 25, the use of which may be secured for the cost of 12 return fares. A further 40 wagons have been added to the stock for merchandise and mineral traffic, and six new goods wagons, and two tar tanks have also been introduced. The line now possesses 40 carriages and 270 wagons in total, and has a staff of 250 employees.

The second-hand purchases brought their own problems with them. Although the wagons generally complied with Railway Clearing House requirements by having modern oil axleboxes, brakes acting on wheels one side, couplings etc., they were a mixture of well worn 8 and 10 ton wagons with four- and five-plank sides in an assortment of styles. A handful of wagons had end doors for which the IWC had no use and which were removed when they received heavy repairs. Other purchases included 15 replacement wheel sets and 20 urgently needed wagon covers. A lull in further purchases lasted until January 1900 when four merchandise wagons came from Bute Works Supply Co.

Also in January 1900, the IWC Board agreed to buy five carriages that were on offer by the LSWR; in fact six were bought at a price including repairs of £488 14s. 6d. A report of their arrival in the *Isle of Wight Herald* on 27th April, 1900 is interesting for the positive comments about their smooth running and ventilation, features that were lacking in the company's other stock!

> The new rolling stock . . . was landed near Medham on Tuesday night, and put on the rails. On Wednesday, a trial trip was run, and an opportunity was afforded us of inspecting the new train. Of this we availed ourselves, with the result that we are bound to congratulate the Company and its Manager, Mr Conacher.
>
> The train consists of five coaches, including a guard's van, and the whole of the compartments are roomy and comfortable. They are uniform in design, and present an excellent appearance. The upholsterings are good, and a long journey if such were possible in the Isle of Wight, could be undertaken without the least fear of discomfort and inconvenience. The carriages appear to run smoothly, and the arrangements for ventilation are very complete, including overhead air passages on what is known as the torpedo system. Everything is quite up to date, and there are probably no better carriages on the mainland engaged in a similar style of traffic.
>
> The guard's van is of the composite description, having two compartments for passengers, and a very roomy section for the guard's own use, together with the necessary brakes, etc. By the way, the train is fitted with Westinghouse patent brake, which would, if necessary, bring the whole train to a standstill in a very short distance.
>
> . . . the train will probably be kept entirely for the Cowes to Ventnor through service . . .

Mr Seymour's report on the condition of the locomotives in 1901 included a summary of the carriage and wagon stock. The 47 passenger carriages were in reasonable condition but several required minor repairs; 14 elderly carriages were variously 'unsafe to run, worn out' or 'required general repairs' whilst only two were considered in 'good repair'. There were 271 wagons and vans of which about 10 needed rebuilding, and 30 lesser repairs. Work began on fitting spring buffers to the dumb-buffered wagons when they fell due for heavy repairs; ever conscious of the cost, the Board decreed that no more than 20 wagons be converted in any one year. There was also an urgent need to replace the old fashioned 'D' shackle and pin couplings with which most of the company's wagons were equipped; they had been blamed for a serious accident at Yarmouth on 5th February, 1901 when the station master slipped and lost his leg when a wagon ran over it.

The Midland Railway bogie carriage was altered on several occasions during its life.

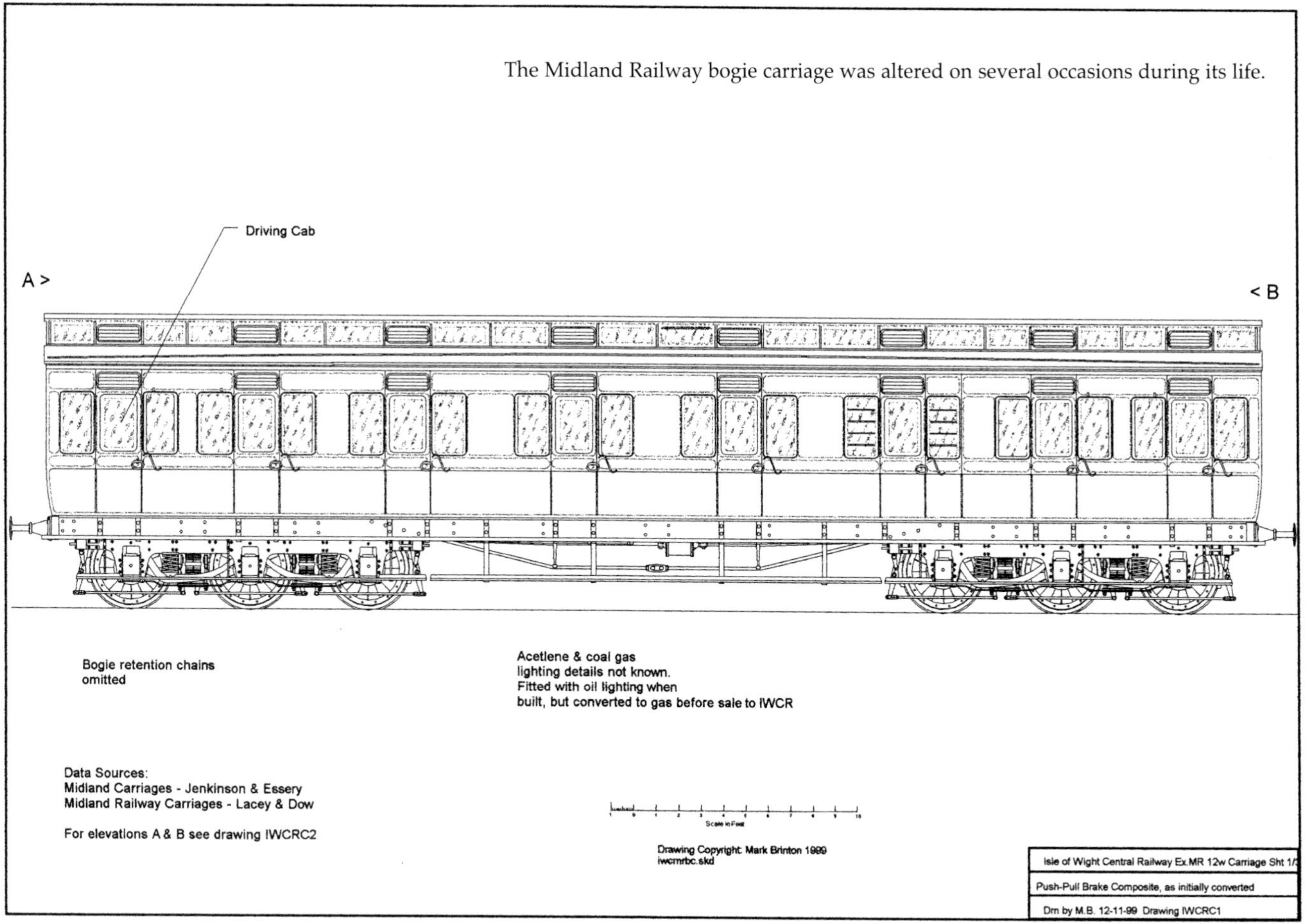

A >

< B

Driving Cab

Bogie retention chains omitted

Acetlene & coal gas
lighting details not known.
Fitted with oil lighting when
built, but converted to gas before sale to IWCR

Data Sources:
Midland Carriages - Jenkinson & Essery
Midland Railway Carriages - Lacey & Dow

For elevations A & B see drawing IWCRC2

Scale of Feet

Drawing Copyright. Mark Brinton 1999
iwcmrbc.skd

Isle of Wight Central Railway Ex MR 12w Carriage Sht 1/2

Push-Pull Brake Composite, as initially converted

Drn by M.B. 12-11-99 Drawing IWCRC1

The Prevention of Accidents Act 1900 was considered at a Board meeting on 23rd April, 1902 and at the next meeting on 4th June Directors authorised the purchase of three goods brake vans at £40 each from the LBSCR, evidently the existing vans were no longer acceptable. Their arrival at St Helens a month later was swiftly followed by a £5 bill from the IWR for hauling them to Sandown.

In August 1903 the IWC Board were informed that some Mersey Railway rolling stock was available for purchase. When this met with no response the Directors had to be reminded that several old carriages required replacement. Although Mr Conacher was instructed to investigate the use of motor carriages, the message had hit home. On 24th February, 1904 the purchase was authorised of five carriages and a van for £65 each but which, including repairs and delivery to Medina Wharf, actually cost £624 16s. 11d.; their arrival permitted the breaking up of six old carriages. On 28th June, 1905 Conacher was given permission to buy two five-compartment seconds, three composites with one first and three second class compartments and a brake carriage with a luggage and two second class compartments; the final bill was £472 18s. After much prompting, on 27th February, 1907 the Board agreed to buy four carriages at £70 each plus £171 14s. 1d. to put them into good repair. A fourth goods brake van was bought a month later from the LBSCR for £40 and accompanied the carriages on a barge from Southampton to Medina Wharf. Their purchase completed the replacement of the LNWR, IWNJ and Brighton carriages, although several lived on as passenger guard's vans and carriage trucks. The overall numbers of vehicles had not increased but the new carriages had a greater seating capacity than those they replaced. There was also railmotor No. 1 and the Midland Railway bogie carriage newly purchased for use in a second railmotor.

In April 1904 an urgent need for cattle wagons spurred the Board to consider tenders for new vehicles from four makers. The prices, varying from £110 to £130 each, were too high and two second-hand cattle vans were bought from Messrs Frazer & Sons, rolling stock dealers, at £22 10s. each, along with 10 covered vans for £25 each and two timber trucks at £30 each. Following complaints about the overcrowding of livestock, the company purchased paid £22 10s. each for two cattle wagons and £50 for a replacement horse box from Messrs Frazer & Sons. Their shipment to St Helens cost £19 and the IWR extracted a modest £2 5s. for taking them to Sandown. A few months later Messrs Frazer charged £26 each for six more covered vans; several additional purchases of vans were made in 1907 and 1908 - most, if not all, were of GER origin.

Passenger comfort may have been improved by the purchase of newer carriages but the lighting was still provided by dim, smelly oil lamps of doubtful reliability. In 1906 Charles Conacher was refused permission to fit acetylene gas lighting, but his persistence paid off in 1909 when it was decided to fit 10 LSWR carriages with acetylene lighting and a second 10 for coal gas. The results of the experiment went unrecorded but the Midland Railway carriage and railmotor No. 1 were both converted to coal gas illumination.

Mr Guest was obliged to prepare a report for Harry Willmott in April 1911 detailing work that had been carried out to the passenger and goods rolling stock between 1st January, 1910 and 31st March, 1911. He explained that his staff had been handicapped by the need to have all passenger stock in use for Ashey races and Cowes week. There were daily checks of vehicles in regular use when they were cleaned but spare stock in Newport yard was only examined just before use. Nine passenger vehicles had gone through the workshops including No. 29, a four-compartment composite that had been converted into a mail and parcels van. Twelve assorted wagons, one goods brake, a cattle truck and a covered van had been heavily repaired with new woodwork whilst over 240 wagons and other vehicles had received attention of some sort.

Despite Mr Guest's positive report, an independent inspection revealed that all was not well. Several older passenger carriages had panels made of paste board, a material that needed regular painting to avoid rapid rotting; those on parcels van No. 28 were badly bulged. This gives the impression that lesser passenger vehicles were not finished in the varnished wood finish that is regarded as the company's accepted livery. Inside the workshops, a second class brake carriage was having its hardwood mouldings renewed in deal, a most unsuitable material. Another carriage was being varnished in close proximity to

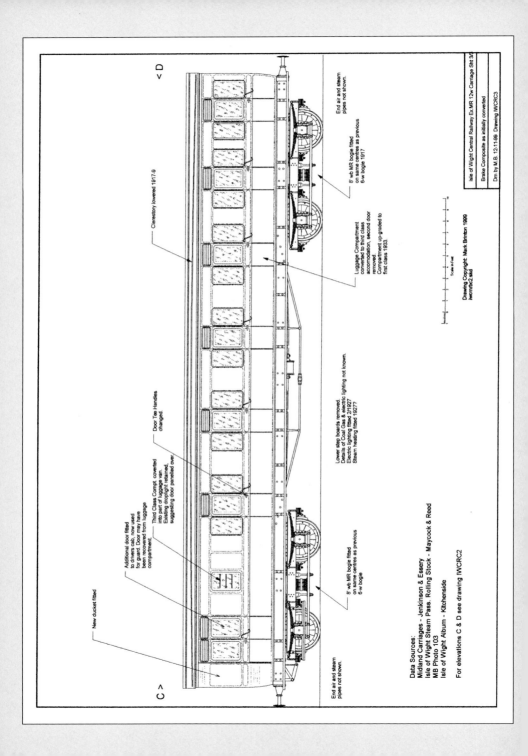

C >

< D

New ducket fitted

Additional door fitted to drivers cab, now used for guard. Door may have been recovered from luggage compartment.

Third Class Compt. converted into part of luggage van. Existing droplight retained, suggesting door panelled over.

Door Tee Handles changed.

Clerestory lowered 1917-9

End air and steam pipes not shown.

8' wb MR bogie fitted on same centres as previous 6-w bogie

End air and steam pipes not shown.

8' wb MR bogie fitted on same centres as previous 6-w bogie 1917

Luggage Compartment converted to third class accomodation, second door removed. Compartment up-graded to first class 1933.

Lower step boards removed. Details of Coal Glass & electric lighting not known. Electric lighting fitted 2/1927 Steam heating fitted 1/6277

Scale in Feet

Data Sources:
Midland Carriages - Jenkinson & Essery
Isle of Wight Steam Pass. Rolling Stock - Maycock & Reed
MB Photo 103
Isle of Wight Album - Kitchenside

For elevations C & D see drawing IWCRC2

Drawing Copyright Mark Brinton 1999
iwcrmfbc2.skd

Isle of Wight Central Railway Ex.MR 12w Carriage Sht 3/3

Brake Composite as initially converted

Drn by M.B. 12-11-99 Drawing IWCRC3

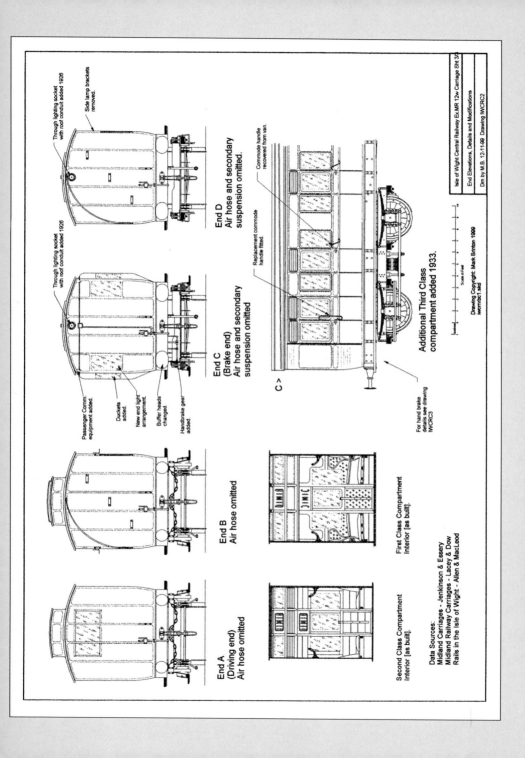

Through lighting socket
with roof conduit added 1926

Side lamp brackets
removed.

Through lighting socket
with roof conduit added 1926

Passenger Comm.
equipment added.

Duckets
added.

New end light
arrangement.

Buffer heads
changed.

Handbrake gear
added.

Commode handle
recovered from van.

Replacement commode
handle fitted.

End A
(Driving end)
Air hose omitted

End B
Air hose omitted

End C
(Brake end)
Air hose and secondary
suspension omitted

End D
Air hose and secondary
suspension omitted

C >

Additional Third Class
compartment added 1933.

For hand brake
details see drawing
IWCRC3

Second Class Compartment
Interior [as built].

First Class Compartment
Interior [as built].

Data Sources:
Midland Carriages - Jenkinson & Essery
Midland Railway Carriages - Lacey & Dow
Rails in the Isle of Wight - Allen & MacLeod

Scale in Feet

Drawing Copyright: Mark Brinton 1999
iwcrmbc1.skd

Isle of Wight Central Railway Ex.MR 12w Carriage Sht 33s

End Elevations, Details and Modifications

Drn by M.B. 12-11-99 Drawing IWCRC2

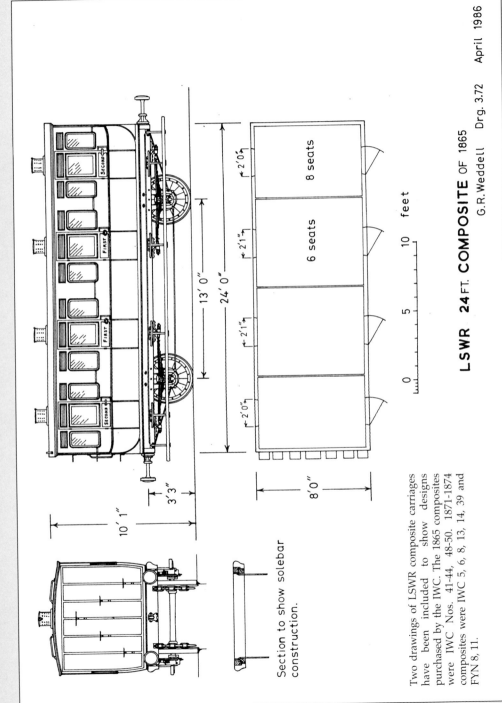

Second First First Second

13' 0"

24' 0"

⊢2'0"⊣ ⊢2'1"⊣ ⊢2'1"⊣ ⊢2'0"⊣

8 seats

6 seats

0   5   10   feet

3' 3"

10' 1"

8' 0"

Section to show solebar construction.

LSWR 24 FT. COMPOSITE OF 1865

G.R.Weddell   Drg. 3.72   April 1986

Two drawings of LSWR composite carriages have been included to show designs purchased by the IWC. The 1865 composites were IWC Nos. 41-44, 48-50. 1871-1874 composites were IWC 5, 6, 8, 13, 14, 39 and FYN 8, 11.

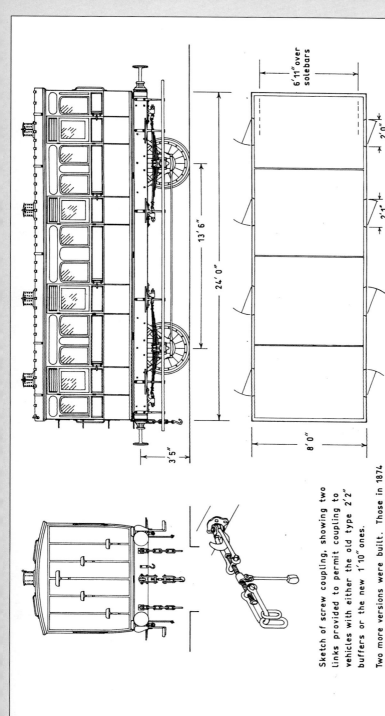

6' 11" over solebars

13' 6"

24' 0"

3' 5"

8' 0"

2' 0"

2' 1"

0   5   10   15 feet

Sketch of screw coupling, showing two
links provided to permit coupling to
vehicles with either the old type 2'2"
buffers or the new 1'10" ones.

Two more versions were built. Those in 1874
had rounded bottom corners to the windows
and panels with the total height increased
to 10'11¼". The 1876 ones were based on
these but are the subject of another drawing.

LSWR 24FT. **COMPOSITE** OF 1871–1874

G.R.Weddell   Drg. 3.99   February 1989

Although the centre of this photograph taken at Newport in 1920 or 1921 is No. 7, the carriage is the more interesting. It is third class No. 50, originally a composite dating from the 1870s and typical of the older LSWR vehicles in the company's fleet.   *Lens of Sutton*

One of the earliest known photographs of IWC rolling stock is this maker's photograph taken in February 1889 of wagon No. 139, one of a batch of 10 dumb-buffered coal wagons supplied by Gloucester Railway Carriage & Wagon Co. The brown livery and shaded lettering was not typical of that carried by other IWC wagons.   *R. Silsbury Collection*

the smithy and was thus being spoilt by dirt in the atmosphere before it had dried. Tons of metal turnings lying in the yard should have been sold and several wagon wheels lay rusting in the open air. Although pre-prepared oak was purchased for use in wagon repairs the carpenters were spending too much time cutting and shaping - it was suggested that components be bought ready for assembly. They were paid £6 15s. for rebuilding a wagon, apparently an excessive sum. Goods brake and transhipment van No. 2 had been rebuilt in 1911 but many more vehicles remained in poor condition. The underframe of a 2 ton crane that had not been used for about two years was rotten and it was recommended that the crane be reused as a station yard crane. Breakdown van No. 33 was used as a store as it was quite unfit to leave Newport yard. It was regular practice to attach cattle wagons to passenger trains, but their wheels and springs needed to be replaced or improved to bring them up to current Board of Trade requirements.

Several vehicles were not considered worth rebuilding and H. F. Stephens decided to replace them with new acquisitions. In 1911 the company purchased six third class carriages from the Great Eastern Railway and some Midland Railway goods vehicles including a handful of open wagons, a mobile crane, an additional brake van, three timber trucks and three ballast wagons. Several old carriages and vans were donated to the permanent way staff for use as cabins and £200 set aside to refurbish the remainder and convert them to coal gas lighting. Six wagons were rebuilt as covered vans and money was made available to complete the fitting of spring buffers. By the end of 1912 the company possessed 36 carriages, 20 other items of passenger stock, 335 wagons and five other vehicles.

It is not clear how much use was made of the railmotor carriages after Russell Willmott took charge. The hardwood seating in 'No. 1 Motor Carriage' was downgraded from second class to a more appropriate third class. The first class compartment became a third class smoking compartment; in April 1913 the Board authorised the expenditure of £10 on making an entrance to the smoking compartment. Soon afterwards, the two Lancaster carriages became redundant when the Ryde to Freshwater through trains ceased running and £30 was set aside for alterations to composite brake carriage No. 35. This was probably when the guard and luggage compartments were moved from the centre to one end of the carriage in order to improve visibility for the guard during shunting at Cowes. Other carriages had recently been redecorated and £40 spent on additional luggage racks and 'Views &c.' In July 1913 the FYN took over the working of its line and in accordance with clauses in the working agreement purchased four composite coaches, 30 wagons and a goods brake van. Russell Willmott evidently distrusted the FYN as he expected 'cash to be paid before delivery' - payment was actually made by cheque just before the stock was handed over!

One accident that did not take place on the IWC was mentioned at a Board meeting in September 1913. A collision on 2nd September at Aisgill on the Settle and Carlisle line of the Midland Railway was made worse by a fire in the gaslit carriages - several passengers died. The General Manager reported that the passenger guard's vans were being fitted with fire extinguishers and tools whilst all the drivers had recently undergone eye tests - conversion of the gas lighting to electricity was not discussed!

Towards the end of 1913 the opportunity was taken to acquire additional second-hand wagons. There had been repeated complaints that a shortage of wagons delayed the unloading of coal barges at Medina Wharf, but in the past the IWC had blamed coal merchants for being tardy in unloading their deliveries. The Willmotts had enlarged some goods yards, particularly at Newport, and on 18th December the General Manager recommended the purchase of 18 eight ton dumb-buffered mineral wagons at a very reasonable £15, plus £3 15s. per wagon for shipment from Southampton. Traffic wagons with dumb buffers were declared illegal after the end of 1913 but this seems not to have been of concern to the IWC and a few dumb-buffered wagons were still in use as late as 1923. The livery of goods stock on the IWC has been described as grey with small white letters and numbers just one plank in height. During the Willmott days, wagons began appearing in black with a much larger 'IWC' in the same style as carried by IWR wagons although many remained in the old livery until SR days.

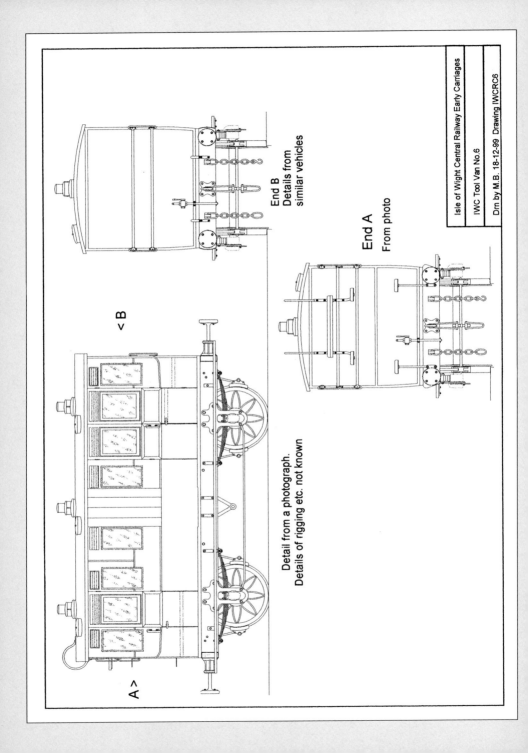

< B

A >

Detail from a photograph.
Details of rigging etc. not known

End B
Details from
similar vehicles

End A
From photo

Isle of Wight Central Railway Early Carriages

IWC Tool Van No.6

Drn by M.B. 18-12-99 Drawing IWCRC6

This picture taken at Sandown in 1919 is well known but is one of the best views of pre-Group Isle of Wight goods rolling stock. Nearest the camera is IWC brake van No. 5, obtained from the Midland Railway in 1911. The three-plank open with rounded ends is an IWR wagon. The goods van is one of the GER vehicles purchased by the IWC in about 1908 and has one side brake lever and grease axleboxes.
G.M. Muskin, T. Cooper Collection

Other GER vehicles included cattle wagon No. 42 seen after repainting in SR livery. Unlike most of the goods stock they were Westinghouse braked.
R. Silsbury Collection

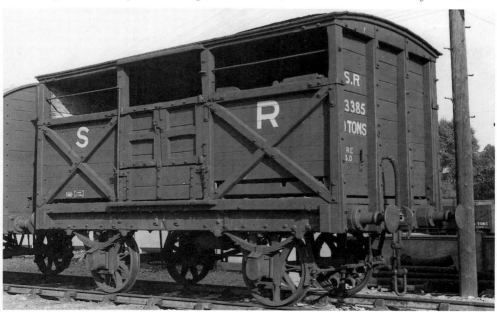

Although the Directors mentioned at a shareholders' meeting in early 1914 that the company proposed to buy three or four more passenger carriages, nothing had been done by the time war broke out. The idea seems to have been dropped in favour of renovating more of the existing carriages, of which there were ample after second class was abolished in 1913. By 1917 there had been a considerable increase in the number of workmen travelling to Cowes to work in Munitions factories and shipyards. Such was the need for stock that eight carriages were borrowed from the IWR. Additional third class seating was created by downgrading first class compartments and every item of passenger stock was pressed into service, including the railmotor carriages. In 1917 the Midland Railway brake composite had its six-wheel bogies replaced by four-wheel bogies purchased from Derby and the clerestory roof removed; this may also have been when the driver's and adjoining compartments were converted into a guard's/luggage compartment.

In 1919 the IWC printed an Appendix to the Working Timetable, apparently the first in the history of the railway. It contained a summary of the passenger and goods rolling stock; several composites had been downgraded to thirds but the total in stock was otherwise unchanged since 1913 - railmotor carriage No. 1 had been renumbered as brake third 52. One writer commented that the stock had got into a bad state during the war years and in 1920 were still being '. . . redecorated and the exterior painted and varnished a standard colour'. It is not clear what was the standard colour at that time but a contemporary photograph fostered the impression that some carriages had been painted as one displayed a bad case of peeling paint work. Once the workmen's traffic faded away a few carriages were surplus to requirements; eight IWC vehicles were deleted from stock lists by the Southern Railway in 1923 and sold or broken up.

The Southern Railway inherited from the IWC 43 passenger, 317 goods and seven other vehicles. Compared with 1919, composites Nos. 44 and 50 had been downgraded to thirds and six 10 ton open wagons had been built as replacements of an assortment of miscellaneous vehicles.

In July 1923 three sets of LSWR bogie carriages arrived from the mainland for use on the Ryde to Cowes and Sandown to Cowes services. They were followed by LBSCR four-wheel and LCDR former six-wheel carriages. The IWC carriages with their inadequate coal gas lighting were withdrawn by the end of 1927. A handful of LSWR and GER four-wheel thirds were fitted with electric lighting, along with a solitary brake third used as a mail van and the four bogie carriages. They were repainted in SR lined green livery and most later received steam heating. In 1931 the last four-wheel thirds were condemned; the mail van lasted until 1933. Of the four IWC bogie carriages, the Midland Railway bogie composite was withdrawn in 1937, the Lancaster pair went in 1938 whilst the railmotor carriage lasted until 1949. All were replaced by LCDR and LBSCR bogie carriages.

A similar programme of replacement was pursued in respect of the goods rolling stock. Quantities of LBSCR open wagons, covered vans, cattle wagons, timber wagons and vehicle trucks were sent over and some LSWR road vans replaced the goods brake vans. Wagons with the smaller and non standard capacities were withdrawn first but a good number of the 10 ton wagons saw out the 1920s. A few IWC vehicles were repainted in SR goods brown livery including the last examples of ordinary goods stock: two open wagons and a cattle wagon were withdrawn in January 1934. A handful of passenger and goods vehicles were converted to departmental stock.

Chapter Twenty

The Southern Railway and afterwards

The story of the IWC lines under Southern Railway and later managements will form part of a separate book in this series. A programme of improvements by the SR taking ten years to complete saw the strengthening of numerous bridges and the complete renewal of the permanent way with bull head chaired track so that heavier standard locomotives and rolling stock could be employed, this inevitably resulted in the withdrawal of the company's non-standard locomotives, carriages and wagons. Medina Wharf was finally rebuilt but relatively little money spent on the company's stations; an exception was Haven Street which received a crossing loop, platform and new buildings so that a more regularly timed service could be operated. The aftermath of the 1939 to 1945 war resurrected changes begun after World War I and hastened the decline of the railways as they lost out to road transport. Nationalisation of Britain's railways on 1st January, 1948 did nothing to improve matters and after being starved of investment the Merstone to Ventnor and Sandown to Newport lines closed during the 1950s; the Cowes-Newport-Ryde line soldiered in until 1966. The Isle of Wight Steam Railway has since re-opened the section of railway between Smallbrook Junction (where there is a station on the Ryde to Shanklin line) to Havenstreet and Wootton.

The IWC today

Despite the efforts of long-dead entrepreneurs who fought so hard to create the railways owned by the IWC and its predecessors, there are few surviving reminders of their existence.

Cowes to Newport and Ryde (closed 21st February, 1966)

At Cowes, a person walking up the hill from Fountain Quay will find no evidence that there ever existed a railway station. After the lifting of the permanent way in 1971 the station was completely demolished and a supermarket and luxury flats built on most of the site. The overbridge at Granville Road vanished in 1990 when the road was widened and from Granville Road to Denmark Road the trackbed was infilled and sold for enlarged gardens or new housing. A linear garden leads to Mill Hill tunnel which has been converted to a rifle range and a store. There is a short length of platform at Mill Hill station but the remainder of the land has been built on. From there to the edge of Cowes more housing occupies the line. Between Arctic Road and the northern edge of Newport the railway has become a cycle track. En route can be seen Medina Wharf which was totally rebuilt by the Southern Railway. Some distance beyond, the derelict buildings of West Medina cement mills can be glimpsed in the undergrowth - they closed in 1944. The mill pond and surrounding area is a nature reserve and can be crossed by the viaduct but the road overbridge at Dodnor has been demolished. Approaching Newport the trackbed disappears under a confusing network of new roads and buildings on the site of the station. The Railway Medina public house in Holyrood Street looks out on what remains of the station approach road; the diligent will discover traces of the drawbridge abutments in the river and a greatly extended quay, but otherwise there is little else to mark the passing of the railway.

At the time of writing, much of the trackbed between Newport and Wootton is being converted into a cycle route. On the east bank of the River Medina, Newport tunnel has become a subway under Fairlee Road but a few yards of the trackbed beyond has been built

Although photographed in BR days not long before closure in February 1966, this view of the concourse at Cowes station changed little since its rebuilding by the IWC in 1918.   *M. Reed*

on. A footpath then follows the railway as far as Mews Lane, Fairlee but the next section has reverted to farmland. Whippingham station building is largely unaltered in its new role as a private residence; the loop platform can also be seen. The cycle route can be used between Whippingham and Wootton passing the site of Fatting Park bridge which was demolished several years ago and under a new brick arch replacement for Park Farm bridge. At Wootton, the road overbridge was filled in years ago but the adjacent station master's house survives in private ownership.

It is still possible to travel by steam train from Wootton to Havenstreet, Ashey and Smallbrook on the Isle of Wight Steam Railway. The Steam Railway commences at a new station constructed to the east of the road that bears no likeness to its predecessor. The station at Havenstreet dates from 1926 when it was rebuilt by the Southern Railway with a crossing loop, island platform and a new station building. The Steam Railway has added a refreshment room, workshops and converted the derelict gasworks' retort house for use as a museum and shop.

At Ashey, the crossing loop and sidings have long since gone. The station building is a private house but steam trains call at the former loop platform on which stands a shelter erected in 1961. As regards the quarry branch, close to the station there are some earthworks but a section beyond has been ploughed over and only a neat hedge remains to show its course. Near the quarry is a cutting, partially filled, and the remains of a kickback siding intended to prevent runaways; the tunnel under the road was filled in during 1999.

Continuing a short distance to Smallbrook, the steam railway terminates at an interchange station with the Ryde to Shanklin electric railway. Opened in July 1991, the station has no road access apart from a footpath to a nearby road overbridge for use in emergencies. The double track thence to Ryde St Johns Road is used by the electric trains.

Newport to Sandown (closed 6th February, 1956)

The permanent way on the line was removed and the railway bridge at Coppins Bridge demolished in 1960; the remaining railway structures in the vicinity disappeared during the 1970s. From Coppins Bridge to Shide the railway has vanished without trace. At Shide, the siding leading to the quarry has gone but the quarry itself is accessible as a nature reserve and the tunnel mouth may still be seen. The trackbed to Blackwater became a cycle track. There, the station house has been sold and extended across the trackbed whilst the goods yard across the road is part of a garage forecourt. An unofficial footpath continues to Merstone.

At Merstone, the island platform remains in a council depot but is devoid of all buildings; the station house and adjoining siding have disappeared under a cul-de-sac of bungalows. Much of the next section of trackbed has been ploughed over although a footpath that followed the line can still be walked to Budbridge Lane overbridge, which still exists. The overgrown railway down Redway Bank can be glimpsed but no path exists before Horringford where the station building has become a private residence. On the opposite side of the road, the trackbed is a bridle way to Newchurch where a bungalow occupies the site of the station. A footpath continues to Alverstone where the station building is a private house; the platform and siding have gone without trace. The peace of the river at this spot belies its past popularity. A cycle track along the trackbed continues to a point just beyond Alverstone waterworks; the railway then climbs out of the Yar valley to Sandown station, the route being marked by a line of SR concrete fence posts. At Sandown the station remains in use to serve the electric trains between Ryde and Shanklin. A disused and rusty length of track behind a fence backing platform three leads to short sidings next to the trackbed of the Newport line.

Merstone to Ventnor (closed 15th September, 1952)

The branch from Merstone to Ventnor has been abandoned for the longest period of time but a surprising amount of the earthworks remain, as do some brick abutments of bridges - lifting of the permanent way began in November 1953. The first section of the railway to Bow bridge on the outskirts of Godshill is overgrown; the bridge was demolished as part of a road widening scheme in 1959. Godshill station has been converted into two residences and the goods yard is occupied by farm buildings. Between Godshill and Whitwell the trackbed has largely disappeared under farm land and only the occasional bridge abutment remains to mark its course. Where the line passed through a cutting near Whitwell a brick overbridge survives as does Whitwell station, a private residence complete with platforms, station building and the up platform shelter. Nature covers the trackbed thence to the Ventnor road. The crossing keeper's house at Dean can be seen next to an access road that follows the trackbed to a mushroom farm in the tunnel. The south end of the tunnel is overgrown but east of St Rhadegund's footpath, the line disappears under housing. St Lawrence station is a private residence and looks quite unaltered, as does the adjacent road overbridge and massive retaining wall. The remaining section to Ventnor has been largely developed for housing but roads and a footpath follow the trackbed to the terminus where Ventnor station building still stands.

Mention has been made of the survival of IWC locomotive No. 11, a LBSCR 0-6-0T and its return to service on the Isle of Wight Steam Railway. A number of carriage and van bodies that belonged to the Central Railway were sold during the 1920s but virtually all have since disappeared due to a combination of age and redevelopment; two van bodies await restoration at Havenstreet where a few small relics can be seen in the Steam Railway museum. Together they are all that remains to portray the Central, the largest of the Island railway companies.

Directors and Chief Officers

The Cowes & Newport Railway Company

Chairman	The Hon. Henry W. Petre	1859-1887

Directors	The Hon. Henry W. Petre	1859-1887
	Henry Pinnock	1859-1866
	William C. Hoffmeister	1859
	George B. Crawley	1859-1860
	Robert J. Jewell	1859-1862
	John Lambert	1859-1864*
	George H. Donaldson	1864-1873
	John S. Burke	1866-1868*
	Henry J. Castle	1868-1887
	Philip W. Colley	1873-1876 and 1877-1887
	Joseph Bourne	1876-1886
	Joseph Groves MD	1886-1887

Secretaries	Charles W. Estcourt	1859-1862
	Edward Lincoln	1862-1878
	John Crick	1878-1887

Solicitors	Charles W. Estcourt	1859-1862
	Merchant & Pead	1862-1887

Engineers	John S. Burke	1859-1866
	Henry D. Martin	1859-1887

Contractor	Henry D. Martin	1862-1876

The CNR Act of 1859 authorised up to five Directors (including the Chairman) but with powers to reduce the number to three. At a shareholders' meeting in August 1862 the number of Directors was reduced to three. This decision was rescinded in 1877.

The Ryde & Newport Railway Company

Chairmen	George Young	1872-1887*
	Henry Pinnock	1887

Directors	George Young	1872-1887*
	Henry Pinnock	1872-1887
	John R. McClean	1872
	Col Thomas C. Lyons	1872-1875
	Capt. Frederick Young	1875-1887
	Henry W. Anderson	1877-1882
	Roderick MacKay	1878-1887
	J.P. Benwell	1882-1887

Secretaries	Edward Lincoln	1872-1878
	Francis L. Beard	1878-1887

* Died in office

1863

Isle of Wight Valley Junction Railway
Essentially the railway followed the route of the 1862 Isle of Wight Railway except at Newport where it followed the east bank of the river to a point north of Coppins Bridge before crossing the river to trail into the CNR facing Cowes. Edward Woods, the Engineer, estimated construction costs at £85,000. The scheme was abandoned before a Bill appeared before Parliament.

Isle of Wight Railway Central Lines
One railway would have left the Isle of Wight (Eastern Section) Railway south of Ryde opposite Smallbrook Farm before heading west to the River Medina about a mile north of Newport, then south to approach the town along the east bank. A branch from the CNR north of its Newport terminus trailed into the line near the gasworks; it would have crossed the river about 440 ft below the existing roadway bridge and quay on a bridge having one 30 ft opening span 15 ft above high water mark (the branch was struck out by Parliament although the CNR obtained an Act for it a year later). A second line ran south past Godshill before climbing steeply to rejoin the Eastern Section railway just beyond Wroxall station. The Engineer, John Fowler, estimated they would cost £180,000 to construct. The Bill became law on 18th July, 1863 as the Isle of Wight Railway (Extensions) Act but the railways were abandoned in 1868.

1865

Brading, Newport & Yarmouth Railway
Commencing a short distance south of Brading, the railway would have followed the valleys of the rivers Yar and Medina to the southern edge of Newport. A second line continued west to Yarmouth and Freshwater. Together they had a total length of 18 miles 29 chains. Branches were proposed to a pier at Sandown - 1 mile 47¼ chains, around the west of Newport to the CNR - 1 mile 28 chains and to the shore at Yarmouth - 2 miles 23¼ chains. The Engineer and promoter, Sir Charles Fox claimed the maximum gradient was 1 in 100. The Bill was thrown out by the House of Lords in May 1865.

1866

Sandown & Newport (Isle of Wight) Railway
A 6 mile 25 chain railway branching from the Isle of Wight Railway near Sandown station along the Yar and Medina valleys to a point about 2¼ miles south of Newport where it would have trailed into the IWR's Newport to Wroxall railway. The Engineer, Richard Saunders claimed that the maximum gradient was 1 in 70 and it would cost £70,000. The Bill was thrown out by the House of Lords in March 1866.

1867

Isle of Wight (Newport Junction) Railway
Railways would have begun at the IWR Brading and Sandown stations before running parallel to the IWR to meet and combine near Morton. Passing along the Yar and Medina valleys, upon reaching Newport at Shide the line ran straight through the town across High Street and Quay Street to form a junction with the CNR just north of its terminus, a total length from Sandown of 9 miles 26½ chains. Cutting across the CNR, a further 2 mile 1.7 chains railway looped around the north of Hunnyhill in an 'S' shape before connecting with the IWR's authorised Western Lines railway to Yarmouth and Freshwater near Gunville. Except for the section beyond Gunville, the promoters wanted the IWR to abandon its Central and Western lines. The Engineer, Richard Saunders estimated the cost of the railways at £120,000. The Bill had made no progress by the time the Parliamentary session ended.

1868

Isle of Wight and Cowes & Newport Junction Railway (Martin's line)

A 7 mile 23½ chain railway commencing at a triangular junction with the IWR between Smallbrook and Brading; the southern spur facing Ventnor left the IWR immediately south of Truckells bridge and the northern spur in Whitefield Woods. The railway would then have headed due west past Green Lane and Ashey before turning to the north-west through Briddlesford Copse to Wootton and then descending on gradients of up to 1 in 100 north of North Fairlee and East Medina Mill to the banks of the River Medina crossed on a 110 yds-long viaduct with a 25 ft opening bridge 12 ft above high water mark. Towards the west bank the railway split in two to form a triangular junction with the CNR nearly a mile north of Newport at Dodnor. The steepest gradient was said to be 1 in 90 but most were more gentle, the easiest being 1 in 282; the sharpest curves were 10 chains on the triangular junctions at Dodnor. The Engineer, Henry D. Martin, estimated the cost at £56,509 including £3,700 for the viaduct. Although not mentioned in the Bill, it was proposed to construct a station at Dodnor linked by a new road to Parkhurst; a station was also envisaged at Truckells. It was claimed that Mr Brassey was willing to build it for £44,209. The Bill was thrown out by the House of Lords in April 1868 in favour of the Bill for the IWNJ.

Isle of Wight Central Railway (Stratton's line)

A railway 7 miles 16 chains in length from Sandown to Newport promoted by a local landowner Mr Stratton. It would have branched from the IWR at its Sandown station, descended at 1 in 70 to cross the valley of the Eastern Yar near Alverstone; south of Lower Knighton it turned west to follow the chalk ridge north of Arreton. Passing through a tunnel it turned to the north at Pan Farm along the east bank of the river; beyond Pan Lane it turned sharply to the west immediately south of Newport gasworks to cross the river on a viaduct with an 25 ft opening span, 30 ft above high water mark. Upon reaching the opposite bank close to the town quay a sharp curve brought it alongside the CNR a few yards north of its terminus with a connection facing Cowes. The Engineer, Alfred Giles, estimated the cost of the railway at £60,000 including £4,550 for the tunnel. The Bill was thrown out by the House of Lords in April 1868 in favour of the Bill for the IWNJ.

Isle of Wight (Newport Junction) Railway (Saunder's line)

The 9 miles 29 chains railway left Sandown station, turned immediately towards the west and descended into the Yar valley before following the valleys of the Yar and Medina to Shide and Pan Lane where it crossed Newport south of the gasworks to join the CNR about 100 yards north of its terminus. The alignment through Newport differed from that proposed in 1867. The intended bridge at Newport had two 40 ft spans and 16 ft high (originally just 5 ft) above high water mark. There was also a branch to a quarry at Shide. The only gradients of note were at Sandown when the line fell at 1 in 52 to the river valley; there were to be six level crossings, one overbridge and numerous culverts. The Engineer and promoter, Richard Saunders, estimated the cost at £71,500 including £9,380 for a 343 yard viaduct at Newport. The Bill became law on 31st July, 1868.

1871

Isle of Wight and Cowes & Newport Junction Railway

The route of the 6 mile 67¾ chain railway was virtually identical to that proposed in 1868 apart from the absence of a northern spur at Dodnor. William Hunt, the Engineer, estimated the railway would cost £51,072 to construct including £3,700 for the viaduct. It was thrown out by the House of Commons in July 1871.

1872

Ryde & Newport Railway

A 7 mile 68.6 chain railway branching from the IWR about a mile south of Ryde before heading west past Ashey, Haven Street, Wootton and Whippingham. It then curved to the south-west to descend through cuttings to emerge on the banks of the River Medina at Newport just south of the gasworks, crossed the river on a viaduct with a bridge containing a single 60 ft fixed span, 15 ft above high water mark, to join the CNR just north of its terminus. It had the advantage over the Isle of Wight and Cowes & Newport Junction proposals by connecting with the CNR at Newport from the south and thus serving both Newport and Cowes whilst avoiding the objectionable viaduct across the river north of the town. The Engineer, Frank Stileman, estimated the cost at £60,809 including £5,500 for the viaduct. The Bill became law on 25th July, 1872.

Signal Diagrams

Although the last significant changes to signalling at IWC stations were made during the 1890s, in the absence of detailed drawings some of the signal diagrams are dated 1924.

The IWC employed a number of lever saving devices including the use of 'economical' point locks worked from the same lever as that operating the points. There were few shunt signals but Stephens' drop flap signals working as point indicators were a common alternative, being linked to the points they also saved on the use of levers.

The 1918 diagram of Cowes shows how the lever frame was enlarged to provide ground signals in compliance with modern practice. Our earliest drawings of Newport prepared for the opening of the FYN in 1889 show the existence of the carriage shed and the siding to Newport Quay. The 1924 drawing omits certain sidings to the workshops and locomotive sheds but does show a northerly extension to the carriage siding alongside the up loop and additional sidings at the south end that were added by the SR. The two 1911 diagrams for Whippingham includes an arrangement that was not adopted.

The diagrams for the Sandown line call for little comment except that for Newchurch with its two lever frames and the 1878 plan of Alverstone which is typical of early signalling on the line. The diagrams for the Ventnor line date from the opening of the line in 1897 except for Ventnor which is from 1900.

A full list of signal boxes is as follows:

Signal box	Built	Supplier	No. of levers	Notes
Cowes	1892	Saxby & Farmer	16	Cabin moved and enlarged to 22 levers in 1918
Mill Hill			4	New ground frame installed by 1896, removed after 1900
Medina Wharf	1878	Easterbrook	11	Replaced by 2-lever ground frame 1912
Newport North	1889	Railway Signal Co.	35	
Newport South	1875	Stevens	20	
Whippingham	1875	Stevens	5	Enlarged to 11 levers 1912
Wootton	1876	Stevens	4	Removed by 1913
Haven Street	1876	Stevens	5	
Ashey	1875	Stevens	12	
Pan Lane	1875			Original replaced by 3-lever frame in 1887
Shide	1875			New Railway Signal Co. 9-lever frame in use by 1896
Blackwater	1883		5	Old frame relocked by 1896 with 6 levers
Merstone	1880			New Saxby & Farmer 28-lever box installed in 1895
Horringford	1875		5	New Railway Signal Co. cabin and frame in use by 1896
Newchurch	1886			Frame enlarged to 8 levers by 1896
Alverstone	1878	Saxby & Farmer	6	7-lever frame by 1896, new 5-lever frame 1914
Sandown	1875	Stevens	3?	Incorporated in new IWR box 1893
Godshill	1897	Saxby & Farmer	4	Removed 1900
Whitwell	1897	Saxby & Farmer	10	
St Lawrence	1897	Saxby & Farmer	5	Removed 1900
Ventnor	1900	Railway Signal Co.	13	

In 1896 several cabins were renewed by the Railway Signal Co. retaining the old frames. One- and two-lever ground frames at other locations have not been listed.

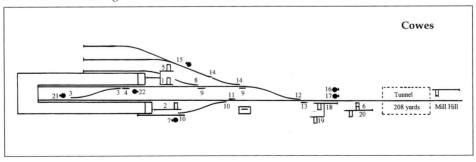

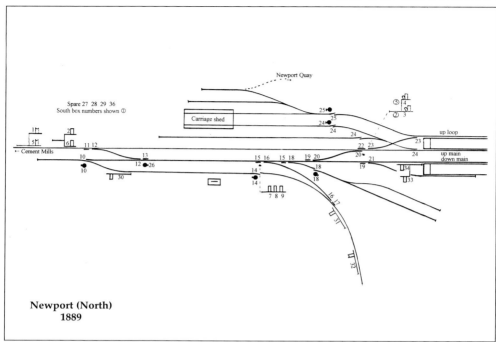

Newport Quay

Spare 27 28 29 36
South box numbers shown ①

Carriage shed

← Cement Mills

**Newport (North)
1889**

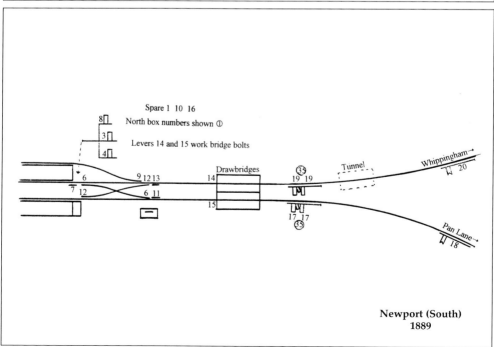

Spare 1 10 16

North box numbers shown ①

Levers 14 and 15 work bridge bolts

Drawbridges

Tunnel

Whippingham

Pan Lane

**Newport (South)
1889**

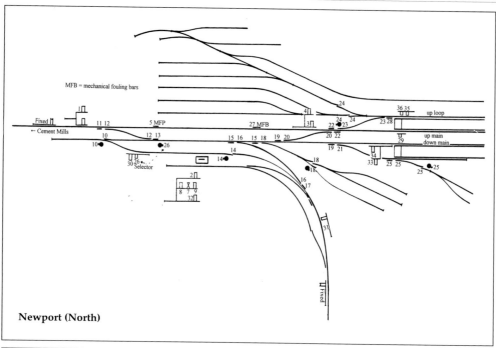

Newport (North)

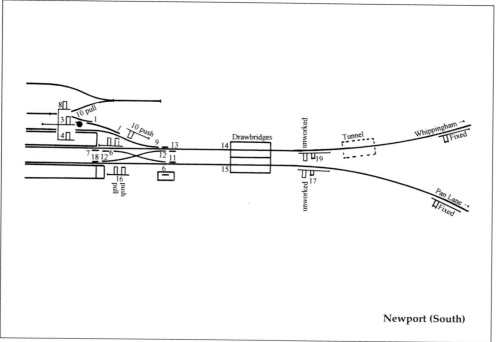

Newport (South)

Whippingham

Whippingham
a drawing dated 7 December 1911
Railway Signal Co.

11 lever frame relocked to give 6 signals, 2 points and 3 spare levers

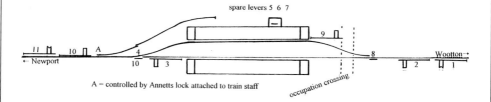

spare levers 5 6 7

A = controlled by Annetts lock attached to train staff

occupation crossing

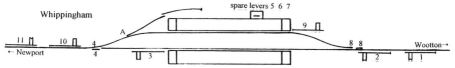

Whippingham

spare levers 5 6 7

A = controlled by Annetts lock attached to train staff

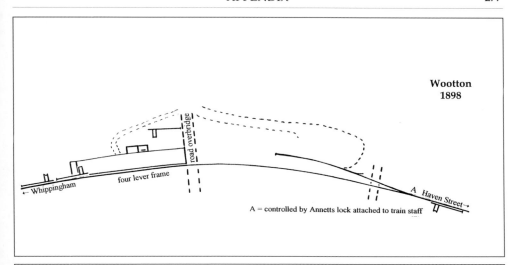

Wootton
1898

← Whippingham   four lever frame   road overbridge   A   Haven Street →

A = controlled by Annetts lock attached to train staff

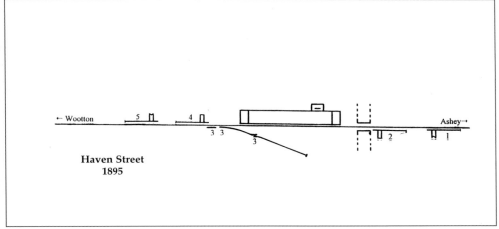

← Wootton   5   4   3 3   3   2   1   Ashey →

Haven Street
1895

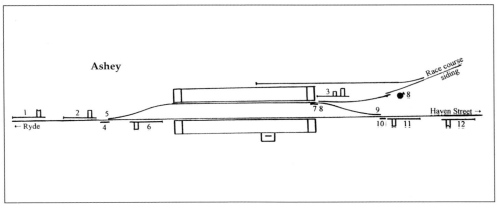

Ashey

Race course siding

1   2   5   3   8   7 8   9
← Ryde   4   6   10 11   12   Haven Street →

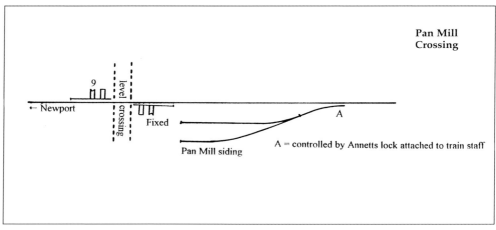

Pan Mill Crossing

A = controlled by Annetts lock attached to train staff

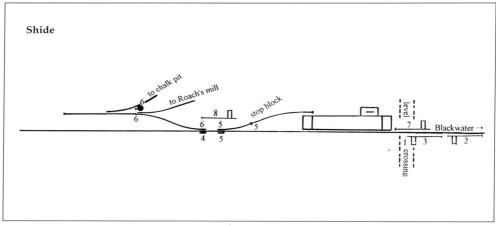

Shide

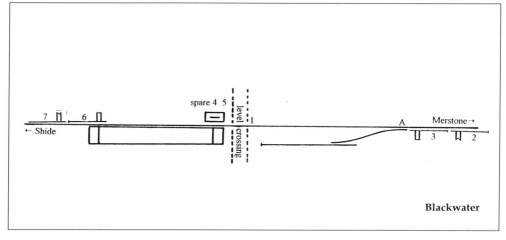

Blackwater

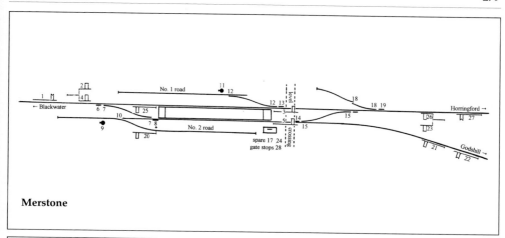

Merstone

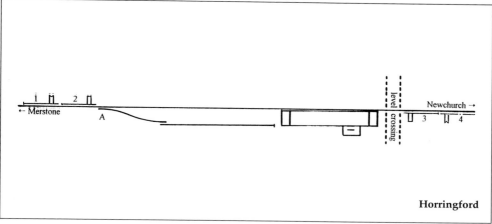

Horringford

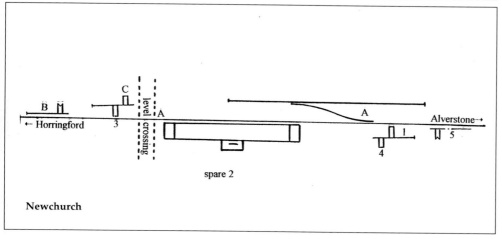

Newchurch

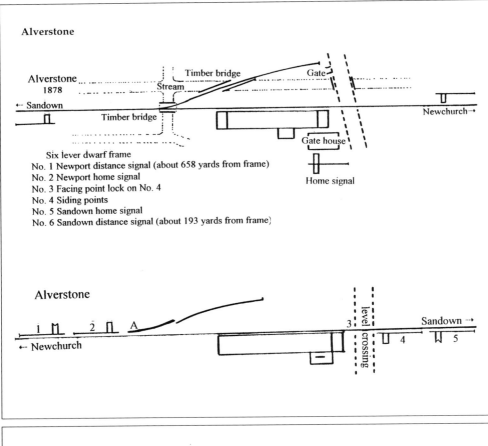

Alverstone

Alverstone 1878

← Sandown

Timber bridge

Stream

Timber bridge

Gate

Newchurch →

Gate house

Home signal

Six lever dwarf frame
No. 1 Newport distance signal (about 658 yards from frame)
No. 2 Newport home signal
No. 3 Facing point lock on No. 4
No. 4 Siding points
No. 5 Sandown home signal
No. 6 Sandown distance signal (about 193 yards from frame)

Alverstone

← Newchurch

1   2   A

3   level crossing   4   5

Sandown →

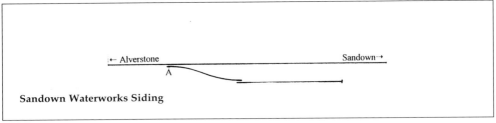

← Alverstone

A

Sandown →

Sandown Waterworks Siding

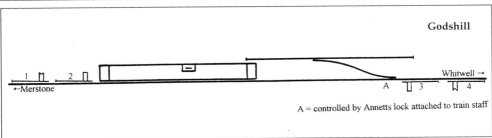

Godshill

←Merstone

1   2

A   3   4

Whitwell →

A = controlled by Annetts lock attached to train staff

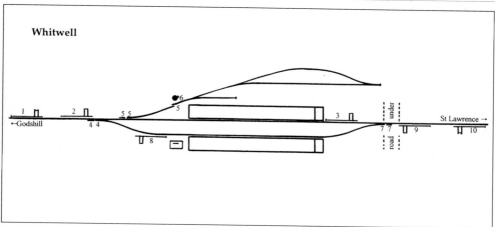

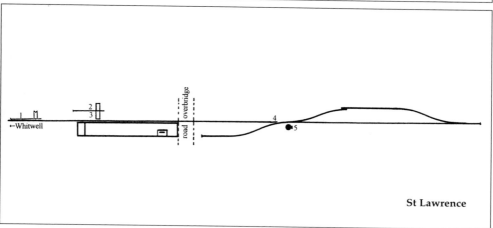

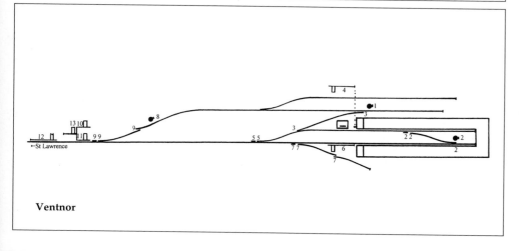

Appendix Five

Summary of Locomotives

Built	Maker	Type	Order No.	Date to IoW	Purchaser	Cost £	Name	IWC No.	Disposal
1861	Slaughter, Gruning & Co.	2-2-2T	453	1861	CNR	1,960	Pioneer	1	withdrawn 1901, broken up 1904
1861	Slaughter, Gruning & Co.	2-2-2T	454	1861	CNR	1,960	Precursor	2	withdrawn 1900, broken up 1904
1870	Black, Hawthorn & Co.	0-4-2T	116	1870	CNR	1,385	Mill Hill	3	sold 1918
1876	Beyer, Peacock & Co.	2-4-0T	1583	1876	RNR	1,765	Cowes	4	withdrawn 1925, broken up 7.25
1876	Beyer, Peacock & Co.	2-4-0T	1584	1876	RNR	1,765	Osborne	5	withdrawn 1926, broken up 8.26
1861	R.W. Hawthorn & Co.	2-2-2T	1128	1874	IWNJ	750	Newport	6	broken up 1895
1890	Black, Hawthorn & Co.	4-4-0T	999	1890	IWC	1,913		6	withdrawn 1925, broken up 3.26
1861	Slaughter, Gruning & Co. (a)	4-4-0T	443	1880	RNC	750		7	withdrawn and broken up 1906
1882	Beyer, Peacock & Co.	2-4-0T	2231	1906	IWC	695		7	withdrawn 1926, broken up 7.26
1898	Beyer, Peacock & Co. (b)	2-4-0T	3942	1898	IWC	1,961	Whippingham	8	withdrawn 28.12.29, broken up 1930
1871	LBSC class 'A1' (c)	0-6-0T		1899	IWC	800		9	See below
1874	LBSC class 'A1' (d)	0-6-0T		1900	IWC	700		10	See below
1878	LBSC class 'A1'	0-6-0T		1901	IWC	600		11	See below
1880	LBSC class 'A1'	0-6-0T		1903	IWC	725		12	See below
1906	Hawthorn, Leslie & Co.	0-4-0T	2669	1906	IWC	1,450		1	sold 1918
1895	Londonderry Railway (e)	0-4-4T		1909	IWC	750		2	sold 1917

LBSCR No.	LBSCR name	Rebuilt class A1x	SR No.	SR name	To Mainland	Withdrawn	Disposal
75	Blackwall	not	9	-	19.5.36	1926	broken up 5.27
69	Peckham	4.30	10	Cowes	22.2.47	12.36	broken up 2.4.49
40	Brighton	7.18	11	Newport	5.5.36	9.63	preserved
84	Crowborough	7.16	12	Ventnor		12.36	broken up 2.4.49

Notes:

(a) 2-2-2T No. 6 built for the Whitehaven & Furness Junction Railway as No. 10 *Queen Mab*. Became LNWR No. 1553, later 1580, 1262 and 1825. Sold to IWNJ in June 1874.

(b) 4-4-0T No. 7 built for the North London Railway as No. 35, later 106. Sold to Henry Martin 1880 and resold to the RNC Joint Committee.

(c) 2-4-0T No. 7 built for the Swindon, Marlborough & Andover Railway as No. 6, later the Midland & South Western Junction Railway. Sold to IWC 1906.

(d) 2-4-0T No. 8 was withdrawn before it could received the SR name *Bembridge*.

(e) 0-4-4T No. 2 built at Seaham as Londonderry Railway No. 21. Passed to North Eastern Railway in 1900. Sold to IWC 1909 .

Goods Stock

Type	IWC Nos.	SR Nos.	Withdrawn
6 ton open wagons	8, 37, 154, 156, 331, 332	27976-27981	1923-1927
8 ton open wagons	50 with various numbers	27982-28131	1923-1932
10 ton open wagons	95 with various numbers	28132-28226	1924-1934
8 ton covered vans	186-87, 126, 281, 295-296, 298-300 303, 305-306, 323, 326-328	46987-47002	1925-1929
10 ton covered vans	49-50, 88-89, 274-280, 282, 286-294 301-302, 304, 307-310, 324-325	47003-47031	1925-1930
8 ton cattle wagons	45, 47-48	53380-53382	1927-1930
10 ton cattle wagons	41-44, 46	53383-53387	1928-1934
4 ton timber & flat wagons	283, 335-336	59024-59026	1928
6 ton timber & flat wagons	353	59027	1928
10 ton timber & flat wagons	320-322, 333, 334	59028-59032	1926-1930
Open carriage trucks	162-167	4385-4390	12.24
Tar tank wagon	140	61383, later 443s*	1968
7 ton brake vans	2, 3	56035-56036	1928-1929
10 ton brake van	5	56037, later 445s*	3.54
Ballast wagons	30, 329, 330	62881-62883	1927, 1930 & 1970
Travelling crane	5	429s	1967
Match truck for above	28	429sm, later DS3139	1967
Water tank wagon	141	428s*	1968
Tool van	6	427s	1923

Notes: * The tank wagons were retained as weed killer tank wagons and the brake van an Engineering Dept. Signal section tool van. The travelling crane and match truck are preserved on the Isle of Wight Steam Railway. The Westinghouse brake was carried by cattle trucks and carriage trucks but only piped on covered vans. Goods brake vans were numbered in their own series; the travelling crane and tool van were in a fourth series that included the four Medina Wharf steam cranes.

In 1902 three goods brake vans were purchased from the LBSCR. No. 3 was rebuilt by the IWC with large sliding doors as a goods brake and transhipment van so that they could carry 'smalls' traffic. It is seen in SR days after entering departmental use.

R. Silsbury Collection

Bibliography

This book is one of a series of histories of the Isle of Wight railways:
The Isle of Wight Railway, R.J. Maycock and R. Silsbury, The Oakwood Press, 1999.

General

Rails in the Isle of Wight, P.C. Allen and A.B. MacLeod, George Allen & Unwin Ltd, 1967.
Once Upon a Line (4 volumes), A. Britton, Oxford Publishing Co., 1983, 1984, 1990 and 1994.
The Ventnor West Branch, P. Paye, Wild Swan Publications, 1992.
The Isle of Wight Railways. Cowes to Newport, O. Smith, Irwell Press, 1993.
The Signalling of the Isle of Wight Railways, Signalling Record Society 1993.
Wight Report and *Island Rail News*, magazines of the Isle of Wight Steam Railway.

Locomotives and rolling stock

A Locomotive History of Railways on the Isle of Wight, D.L. Bradley, Railway Correspondence & Travel Society, 1982.
The Island Terriers, M.J.E. Reed, Kingfisher Railway Publications, 1989.
Isle of Wight Steam Passenger Rolling Stock, R.J. Maycock & M.J.E. Reed, The Oakwood Press, 1997.
An Illustrated History of Southern Wagons (2 volumes). G. Bixley & others, Oxford Publishing Company, 1984 & 1985.

Locomotive No. 9 arrives at Newport North with a Cowes-Ryde train formed mainly of low roof LSWR stock. The fireman is surrendering the single line token to the signalman. The existence of the large inner home signal gantry dates the photograph as 1919 or later. *T. Cooper Collection*

Index

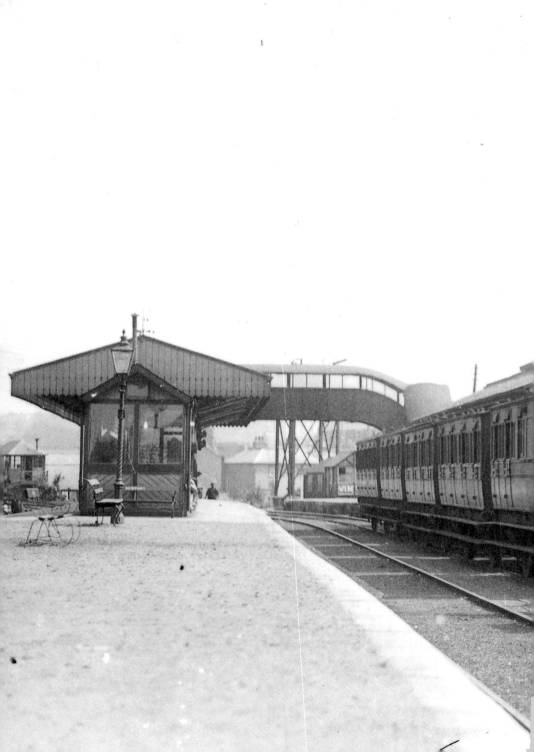